ISSUES IN INTERNATIONAL RELATIONS

Students come to study international relations at university driven by a variety of motives and active concern to study great contemporary issues, such as the causes and persistence of war, threats of nuclear proliferation and terrorism, the persistence of global poverty amid globalization's riches and longer-term threats to sustainable development.

Building on the success of the first edition, *Issues in International Relations*, second edition, provides students with a clear, but stimulating, introduction to the most significant issues within international relations in the twenty-first century. Written by experienced teachers in a jargon-free way, it assumes no prior knowledge of the subject, and allows students approaching international relations for the first time to gain confidence in what is an often complicated and confusing discipline.

Completely revised throughout with the addition of ten new chapters, this textbook:

- introduces key conceptual issues, including theories of international relations, power, sovereignty and globalization
- considers contemporary global problems such as: force and security, law and military intervention, terrorism, the environment and religion
- explains the relationship between global politics and economics, with chapters on international organizations, international political economy and development
- provides students with boxed 'revision-style' notes and case studies throughout the text and a guide to further reading and useful websites at the end of chapters.

This book is ideal reading for students on introductory international relations courses.

Trevor C. Salmon is Professor of International Relations at the University of Aberdeen and the Director of Teaching and Learning in the College of Arts and Social Sciences. He has been an academic since 1973, and has worked in Limerick University, the University of St Andrews and the College of Europe.

Mark F. Imber is a Senior Lecturer in International Relations at the University of St Andrews.

ISSUES IN INTERNATIONAL RELATIONS

Second Edition

Edited by Trevor C. Salmon and Mark F. Imber
With the assistance of Trudy Fraser

Routledge
Taylor & Francis Group

LONDON AND NEW YORK

First edition published 2000
Second edition, 2008
by Routledge
2 Park Square, Milton Park, Abingdon, Oxon OX14 4RN

Simultaneously published in the USA and Canada
by Routledge
711 Third Avenue, New York, NY 10017

Routledge is an imprint of the Taylor & Francis Group, an informa business

© 2000, 2008 Editorial selection and matter, Trevor C. Salmon and
Mark F. Imber; individual chapters the contributors

Typeset in Garamond by
RefineCatch Limited, Bungay, Suffolk
Printed and bound in Great Britain by
TJI Digital, Padstow, Cornwall

British Library Cataloguing in Publication Data
A catalogue record for this book is available from the British Library

Library of Congress Cataloging in Publication Data
A catalog record for this book as been requested

ISBN10: 0–415–43126–3 (hbk)
ISBN10: 0–415–43127–1 (pbk)
ISBN10: 0–203–92659–5 (ebk)

ISBN13: 978–0–415–43126–2 (hbk)
ISBN13: 978–0–415–43127–9 (pbk)
ISBN13: 978–0–203–92659–8 (ebk)

In gratitude and with love to June and Jenny Salmon, and to Susie Imber

CONTENTS

BOXES

CONTRIBUTORS

John Anderson is Professor of International Relations at the University of St Andrews. His research interests lie in the fields of religion and politics, and in post-Soviet politics. His most recent books are *Religious Liberty in Transitional Societies: The Politics of Religion* (Cambridge University Press, 2003) and *Religion, Democracy and Democratization*, (Routledge, 2005).

Antje Brown gained her Ph.D. in 1999 from the Department of Politics, University of Stirling, and has subsequently taught on EU, Environmental and International Politics courses at a number of Scottish Universities. She has published a book on EU environmental policy implementation in Scotland and Bavaria and is currently working on her latest project on the implementation of the Environmental Liability Directive in Scotland.

David Brown is a Senior Lecturer at the Department of Defence and International Affairs, Royal Military Academy, Sandhurst. His recent publications include *Unsteady Foundations: The European Union's Counter-terrorism Strategy 1991–2006*, (Manchester University Press, 2007) and with Alistair J.K. Shepherd (eds), *Wider Europe, Weaker Europe? Assessing Security in an Enlarged European Union*, (Manchester University Press, 2007).

Roger Carey has been the Director of the Isle of Man International Business School since its foundation in 1999. He has an academic background in the discipline of International Politics, which he has taught in various universities in the UK. His main research interests lie in the area of International Security where he has contributed both to the literature and to debate.

Trudy Fraser is a double graduate of the University of Aberdeen and a Ph.D. candidate in the School of International Relations at the University of St Andrews, where she is writing her thesis under the supervision of Dr Mark Imber. Her main area of research is United Nations Security Council reform.

David Galbreath is a Lecturer in International Relations in the Department of Politics and International Relations at the University of Aberdeen. His recent publications include *The Organization for Security and Cooperation in Europe* (Routledge, 2007) and with M. Malksoo and J. Lamoreaux, *Continuity and Change in the Baltic State Region* (Rodopi, 2008).

Steven Haines is Professor of Strategy and the Law of Military Operations at Royal Holloway College, University of London. For five years before he retired from the Royal Navy, in 2003, he was a staff officer in the Policy Area of the Ministry of Defence's Central Staff. The author of the United Kingdom's Strategic Doctrine (*British Defence Doctrine*, 2001), he also chaired the editorial board of the UK's official *Manual of the Law of Armed Conflict*, published in 2004.

Mark F. Imber is Senior Lecturer and Director of Teaching in the School of International Relations at the University of St Andrews. He is the author of numerous works on the role of international organizations in the protection of the global commons, including 'The Reform of the UN Security Council' (*International Relations*, 2006). His books include *Environment, Security and UN Reform* (Macmillan, 1994), and, with John Vogler (eds) *The Environment and International Relations* (Routledge, 1996).

Vivienne Jabri is Director of the Centre for International Relations and a Professor in International Relations, at King's College, London. She joined King's in 2003, having previously lectured at the University of St Andrews and Kent University. Her most recent book is *War and the Transformation of Global Politics* (Palgrave Macmillan, 2007). Professor Jabri holds research funding from the European Commission funded project, CHALLENGE: The Changing Landscape of European Liberty and Security, investigating the political implications of war and practices of exception and emergency in the post-9/11 context.

Gabriela Kütting is Associate Professor of Political Science and of Global Affairs at Rutgers University. She has published widely in the field of Global Environmental Politics and is the author of *Environment, Society and International Relations* (Routledge, 2000) and *Globalization and Environment, Greening Global Political Economy* (SUNY Press, 2004 and 2007).

Norrie MacQueen teaches International Relations at the University of Dundee. Previously he had taught and researched in universities in Australia and the South Pacific. He has worked in Mozambique, as well as in various universities and colleges in Britain. His most recent books are *Peacekeeping and the International System* (Routledge, 2006) and *Colonialism* (Longman, 2007).

Trevor C. Salmon is Professor of International Relations at the University of Aberdeen and Director of Learning and Teaching in the College of Arts and Social Sciences. He has previously worked at Limerick University, the University of St Andrews and the College of Europe in Bruges and Natolin. His recent publications include *Towards a European Army: Military Power in the Making?* (with Alistair Shepherd) (Lynne Rienner, 2003), *Understanding the European Union* (with Sir William Nicoll) (Longmans, 2001), and 'The European Union: Just an Alliance or a Military Alliance?' (*Journal of Strategic Studies*, 2006).

Archie Simpson holds an MA (Hons) in Political Studies, M. Ed. in Educational Studies, MA International Politics and M. Res. (Political Research) and a Ph.D. from the Department of Politics and International Relations at the University of Aberdeen. His doctoral research explored a theoretical explanation into the survival of the European micro-states. He has been an undergraduate tutor at the University of Aberdeen (2000–2005) and a Teaching Fellow at the University of St Andrews (2005–2007). He is also a founding member of the Centre for Small State Studies at the University of Iceland.

Gabriella Slomp is a Lecturer in History of Political Thought at the University of St Andrews. She is the author of *Thomas Hobbes and the Political Philosophy of Glory* (Macmillan, 2000) and of *Carl Schmitt and the Politics of Hostility, Violence and Terror* (Palgrave, forthcoming).

Andrea Teti is Lecturer in International Relations at the University of Aberdeen, having previously taught at the Universities of Exeter and Plymouth. Recent publications include 'Bridging the Gap: International Relations, Middle East Studies and the disciplinary politics of Area Studies controversy' (*European Journal of International Relations*) and 'Divide et Impera: International Relations, Middle East Studies, and the colonization of knowledge', in O. Begum *et al.* (eds), *Troubled Engagements: Commitment and Complicity in Cultural Theory and Practice* (University of Amsterdam Press, 2007).

Ben Thirkell-White is a Lecturer in the School of International Relations at the University of St Andrews, having previously taught at the universities of Bristol and Sheffield. He recently published *The IMF and the*

Politics of Financial Globalisation: From the Asian Crisis to a New International Financial Architecture (Palgrave, 2005) and is currently working on a ERSC project on the comparative political economy of pro-poor adjustment, in collaboration with researchers at the University of Sheffield.

Alison Watson is Head of the School of International Relations at the University of St Andrews. She is part of the editorial team for the *Review of International Studies* and recent publications include *The Child in International Political Economy* (Routledge, 2007) and *Children and War* (Polity Press, 2008).

James Wyllie is Reader in International Relations and Director of the M.Sc. Strategic Studies degree programme at the University of Aberdeen. His research interests are in strategic theory, Middle East security and European security. He has also taught and researched at the Universities of Durham, East Anglia and Calgary and has been a regular contributor to *Jane's Intelligence Review*.

ACKNOWLEDGEMENTS

The editors are very grateful to a number of individuals for their support in bringing this volume to press. We are most obviously indebted to our contributors who have produced their chapters within the required limits of time and length and with grace and efficiency. We are also indebted to Archie Simpson and Gillian Fleming for editorial assistance with certain readings from web-sources, and most especially to Trudy Fraser, a graduate of Aberdeen, and Ph.D. candidate at St Andrews for her exemplary work in bringing this manuscript to a final state to meet the exacting demands of our publisher. We would finally like to acknowledge the support and encouragement of Natalja Mortensen at Routledge for commissioning this expanded second edition and supporting its progress to publication, the work of our copy-editor, Graeme Leonard and production editor, Vicky Claringbull.

CHRONOLOGY, 1945–2005

1945 February: Yalta Conference – Churchill, Roosevelt, and Stalin plan postwar Europe.
May: War in Europe ends.
June: UN Charter signed in San Francisco.
July: Potsdam Conference – the last of the 'big three' conferences during the war.
August: Hiroshima and Nagasaki destroyed by atomic weapons. Pacific war ends.

1946 January: First meeting on UN General Assembly and Security Council (in London).
April: League of Nations dissolved.

1947 March: Truman doctrine of support for 'free peoples' and financial support for Greece and Turkey.
June: George Marshall's speech outlining plan for economic recovery of Europe.
August: Independence and partition of India, leading to independence for India and Pakistan.
October: Indian–Pakistan war over Kashmir.

1948 February: Communist coup d'etat in Czechoslovakia.
March: The Brussels Treaty of collective defence against the Soviets is signed by UK, France and the Benelux states.
April: The Organisation for European Economic Cooperation (OEEC) is formed by 16 European states (renamed Organisation for Economic Cooperation and Development in 1960 with the addition of US and Canada). Organization of American States formed.
May: State of Israel established; attacked by Arab forces. Organization of American States (OAS) established.
June: Berlin blockade; Western Allies supply city by airlift.

1949 January: Comecon launched.
April: North Atlantic Treaty (NAT) signed.
May: Establishment of Federal Republic of Germany. Statute of Council of Europe signed. Berlin blockade ends.
August: Soviet Union explodes its first atomic weapon.
October: People's Republic of China proclaimed in mainland China.

1950 May: Robert Schuman proposes that France, Germany and other European states should pool their coal and steel industries.
June: North Korea invades the South.

1951 April: European Coal and Steel Community Treaty signed.

1952 May: Proposed establishment of European Defence Community.
November: United States explodes the first hydrogen bomb.

1953 March: Stalin dies.

July: Final armistice declared in Korea.

August: first USSR hydrogen bomb test.

1954   May: Dien Bien Phu falls.

July: Vietnam divided into North and South.

August: French refuse to ratify European Defence Community Treaty.

September: Southeast Asia Treaty Organization (SEATO) formed.

October: A modified Brussels Treaty establishes the Western European Union; the Federal Republic of Germany admitted to NATO and permitted to rearm.

1955   April: Bandung conference of 29 African and Asian states to promote economic and cultural cooperation and to oppose colonialism.

May: The Federal Republic of Germany joins NATO. Warsaw Treaty Organization (Warsaw Pact) formed. Austria becomes independent.

1956   February: Twentieth Congress of Soviet Communist Party; de-Stalinization begins.

July: Nasser announces nationalization of Suez Canal.

October: Hungarian uprising crushed by Soviet invasion; Israel invades Sinai.

November: British and French troops land at Port Said on Suez Canal.

1957   March: The Treaty of Rome establishing the European Economic Community signed.

May: Britain explodes its first thermonuclear bomb.

October: Soviet Union launches Sputnik satellite.

1958   June: Charles de Gaulle takes over leadership of France (elected president in January 1959).

December: Fidel Castro overthrows President Fulgencio Batista in Cuba.

1959   March: Dalai Lama flees Tibet, Chinese take control.

1960   January: The Stockholm Convention establishing the European Free Trade Association is signed.

February: France explodes an atomic weapon.

June: Belgian Congo becomes an independent state and civil war begins.

December: Sharpeville massacre in South Africa when police open fire.

1961   April: Abortive US Bay of Pigs invasion of Cuba. First manned space flight by Soviet Union.

August: Berlin Wall built.

September: First meeting in Belgrade of the Non-Alignment Movement with the aspiration to be non-aligned between the USA and USSR.

December: India occupies Goa.

1962   March: Ceasefire to Algerian war signed at Évian by French.

October: Cuban missile crisis.

October–November: Sino-Indian war.

1963   May: Organization of African Unity created (OAU).

November: President John F. Kennedy assassinated in Dallas.

1964   October: Khrushchev deposed by Leonid Brezhnev and Aleksei Kosygin. China explodes its first nuclear device.

1965   February: US commits troops to Vietnam: bombing of North begins.

August: War between India and Pakistan over Kashmir begins.

November: The white administration of Rhodesia unilaterally declares independence from Britain.

1966   April: Mao-inspired Cultural Revolution begins in China.

June: France leaves integrated military structure of NATO.

October: NATO headquarters moves from Paris to Brussels. The UN takes Namibia from South Africa.

1967 May: The Nigerian civil war begins with Biafra wanting independence.

June: Six-Day War between Israel and Arabs. China explodes its first thermonuclear device.

1968 January: Tet Offensive in Vietnam.

May: student uprising in Paris nearly topples de Gaulle.

July: Non-Proliferation Treaty signed.

September: Soviet and Warsaw Pact troops invade Czechoslovakia which leads to the Brezhnev Doctrine – that Socialist states had a duty to suppress counter-revolution.

1969 March: Undeclared combat between Soviet and Chinese troops.

July: American astronaut Neil Armstrong is the first human being to walk on the moon.

August: Violence erupts in Northern Ireland. Nuclear Non-Proliferation Treaty signed.

1970 September: Marxist Salvador Allende elected president of Chile (killed during a coup to over-throw his government in September 1973).

1971 February: Treaty to denuclearize the seabed signed.

October: People's Republic of China admitted to United Nations.

December: Bangladesh established by breakaway of East Pakistan after civil war and India–Pakistan War.

1972 January: Britain, the Republic of Ireland and Denmark join European Economic Community.

February: US President Richard Nixon visits People's Republic of China.

May: United States and the Soviet Union sign Strategic Arms Limitation Treaty (SALT) 1.

June: United Nations Conference on the Human Environment (Stockholm).

December: East and West Germany recognize each other's sovereignty.

1973 January: Vietnam cease-fire agreement signed. Denmark, Ireland and UK join EEC.

October: Yom Kippur War between Israel and Egypt and Syria (ends in November). Vienna talks on mutual balanced-force reductions open.

November: Arab members of OPEC embargo oil to United States, Japan and Western Europe, quadrupling prices.

1974 April: Coup d'état in Portugal.

May: India explodes nuclear device.

July: Coup in Cyprus: Turkey invades.

August: Nixon resigns as president of United States.

1975 April: Fall of Saigon (South Vietnam) and Phnom Penh (Cambodia).

May: Pol Pot takes over in Cambodia.

June: Mozambique becomes independent from Portugal.

August: European Final Act signed in Helsinki, which launches Conference on Security and Cooperation in Europe (CSCE).

November: Angola becomes independent from Portugal after long guerrilla war.

1976 September: Mao Zedong dies.

1977 July: Deng Xiaoping, purged Chinese leader, restored to power.

November: Egyptian president Anwar Sadat makes dramatic trip to Israel.

1978 December: United States and People's Republic of China establish full diplomatic relations.

1979 January: Shah leaves Iran; Ayatollah Khomeini forms revolutionary government in February.

March: Egyptian–Israeli peace treaty signed at Camp David.

June: President Jimmy Carter and Brezhnev sign SALT II in Vienna.

July: Sandinista rebels take control in Nicaragua.

November: US embassy seized in Tehran, 63 hostages taken.

December: Soviet invasion of Afghanistan. Agreement reached on independence for Zimbabwe (Rhodesia) under majority government.

1980   March: Brandt Report on International Development published. Mugabe becomes prime minister of the newly independent Zimbabwe.

May: Tito dies in Yugoslavia.

September: Iraq attacks Iran in First Persian Gulf war, which lasts until 1988.

October: Strikes by Polish workers' union (Solidarity) force extensive concessions from government.

1981   January: Greece joins European Economic Community.

December: General Jaruzelski declares martial law in Poland and arrests Solidarity members.

1982   April: Argentina seizes Falkland Islands; British navy and air force retake them by June. Israeli forces enter Lebanon.

May: Spain becomes 16th member of NATO.

December: The Law of the Sea Convention signed.

1983   March: President Reagan announces Strategic Defence Initiative programme (Star Wars).

October: United States invades Grenada to overthrow Marxist government.

1984   October: Prime Minister Indira Gandhi assassinated.

1985   March: Mikhail Gorbachev becomes leader of USSR.

1986   January: Spain and Portugal join European Community.

May: Nuclear accident at Chernobyl power station in the Soviet Union.

1987   January: Gorbachev calls for glasnost and political reforms.

September: Treaty to protect the ozone layer is approved.

December: United States and the Soviet Union sign Intermediate Nuclear Forces Treaty to eliminate intermediate-range missiles.

1988   May: Soviet troops begin withdrawal from Afghanistan.

August: Iran and Iraq agree to cease-fire.

1989   June: Chinese massacre students in Tiananmen Square.

November: Berlin Wall falls.

1990   February: South African government legalizes the African National Congress and Nelson Mandela is freed from jail.

March: Communist party loses its monopoly in the Soviet Union. Namibia becomes independent.

August: Iraq invades Kuwait.

October: East and West Germany unite.

November: The UN authorizes the use of force against Iraq. CSCE summit meeting ends the Cold War and signing of Conventional Forces in Europe Treaty.

December: Slovenia referendum on independence leads to war with Yugoslavia.

1991   January: Comecon disbanded. UN coalition, led by the United States, launches air war against Iraq.

May: Croatia referendum on independence leads to war with Yugoslavia.

June: South Africa repeals land laws that are central to apartheid. Fighting erupts in Yugoslavia over Slovenian and Croatian secession. Boris Yeltsin elected president of the Russian Republic.

July: Warsaw Pact dissolved.

August: Attempted KGB/military coup to oust Gorbachev fails.

November: Macedonia secedes from Yugoslavia. Union of Soviet Socialist Republics dissolved.
December: Commonwealth of Independent States created.

1992   March: Referendum among South African whites endorses new Constitution and end to minority rule. Bosnia secedes from Yugoslavia and fighting erupts.

June: United Nations Conference on Environment and Development held in Rio de Janeiro, Brazil.

December: United States, Canada and Mexico sign North American Free Trade Agreement (NAFTA) treaty.

1993   January: United States and Russia sign Strategic Arms Reduction Talks (START) II nuclear arms agreement.

September: Israeli Prime Minister Rabin and PLO Chairman Arafat agree to framework for interim Palestinian self-rule.

November: European Union is created following Maastricht Treaty coming into effect.

1994   January: North American Free Trade Agreement launched.

March: Bosnian Muslims and Croats join forces against Serbs.

April: Over 800,000 Rwandans killed in civil war.

May: Nelson Mandela and ANC emerge victorious in South Africa's first universal suffrage elections; PLO assumes self-rule in Gaza and parts of the West Bank.

December: Russian army invades breakaway republic of Chechnya.

1995   January: The World Trade Organization (WTO) begins its work as successor to the General Agreement on Tariffs and Trades (GATT); Austria, Finland and Sweden officially enter the European Union, bringing EU membership to fifteen.

May: Representatives of over 170 countries approve the indefinite extension of the Nonproliferation Treaty; NATO launches air attacks against Bosnian Serb positions for ceasefire violations (more attacks would follow).

November: Dayton Accord ends fighting in Bosnia, and leads to NATO deployments to keep the peace.

1996   January: Yasir Arafat is elected president of the Palestinian Authority.

September: US launches air strikes against Iraq after Iraqi military seizes Kurdish town under UN protection.

1997   June: Russia joins the Group of Seven economic summit.

July: Britain returns Hong Kong to China. A currency crisis in Thailand provides the spark that would later ignite a wider Asian financial crisis.

1998   April: Britain and Ireland and non-government actors sign peace accord on Northern Ireland to end the 30-year conflict.

May: India and then Pakistan explode five underground nuclear devices.

July: UN General Assembly votes to create a permanent international Criminal Court to prosecute perpetrators of genocide and other crimes against humanity.

1999   January: Eleven EU currencies joined the Euro and the European Central Bank begins its work.

March: NATO begins prolonged air assault against Yugoslavia in response to continued attacks against ethnic Albanians in Kosovo. The EU's entire European Commission resigns following charges of mismanagement and corruption.

April: India and then Pakistan test-launch intermediate-range ballistic missiles.

May: Another India–Pakistan war over Kashmir.

June: Peace settlement provides for NATO and other peacekeeping forces in Kosovo, as well as substantial autonomy for the province.

December: Putin becomes Acting President of Russian Federation.

2000 The new millennium. January 1: Y2K passes without serious, widespread computer failures, as some had feared.

May: Putin sworn in as President of Russian Federation. Israel withdraws its forces from southern Lebanon after 22 years.

September: Yugoslav opposition claim victory after election. Danish voters reject Euro.

October: Milosevic leaves office after widespread demonstrations.

2001 January: Libyan convicted over bombing on Flight 103 over Lockerbie, Scotland.

March: Bush abandons Kyoto Protocol.

June: Syrian forces evacuate Beirut area after decades of occupation. Milosevic delivered to UN tribunal in The Hague.

September: Hijacked planes ram into twin towers of New York World Trade Center and the Pentagon, and more than 3,000 die as a result.

October: US and Britain bomb Afghanistan, where the Taliban government refuses to hand over Al Qaeda. The Provisional Irish Republican Army (PIRA) dismantle their weapons.

December: Enron forced into bankruptcy.

2002 January: Twelve European states adopt the Euro. Bush makes his 'axis of evil' speech, naming Iran, Iraq and North Korea.

February: Milosevic goes on trial.

October: The Bali bombings.

November: The UNSC says that Iraq must disarm or face 'serious consequences'.

2003 January: North Korea withdraws from Non-Proliferation Treaty.

March: The US and Britain lead a war against Iraq.

April: Baghdad falls.

August: NATO assumes control of peacekeeping in Afghanistan.

December: Saddam Hussein captured.

2004 February: US lifts 23-year travel ban against Libya. Haiti rebellion – Aristide resigns as President.

March: Madrid bombings, over 190 killed. Expansion of NATO from 19 to 26.

April: Referendum on Cyprus re-unification – Turkish Cypriots says yes, Greek Cypriots say no.

May: EU expands from 15 to 25.

June: US-led coalition occupying Iraq transfers sovereignty to an Iraqi interim government.

October: EU leaders sign European Constitution.

November: Ukraine presidential election declared fraudulent.

December: Tsunami hits Pacific and eleven Asian states are affected.

2005 January: Iraqis elect National Assembly.

May: France says no to European Union Constitution.

June: The Netherlands says no to Constitution and EU leaders decide on a period of reflection on Constitution.

July: London hit by Islamic terrorist bombings killing 52 and wounding over 700. The G8 meet at Gleneagles amid pressure to 'Make Poverty History'. PIRA announce they are ending violence.

August: Hurricane Katrina hits the Gulf coast on the US.

October: Merkel elected German Chancellor. Iraqis vote for a new constitution.

December: 70 per cent of Iraqis vote for a new parliament.

Source: Trevor C. Salmon

CHAPTER 1

Introduction

Trevor C. Salmon

International relations, or international politics, is not merely a field of study at university but is an integral aspect of our (increasingly international) everyday lives. We now live in a world where it is impossible to isolate our experiences and transactions from an international dimension. If a British student watches the sitcom *Friends* or the soap opera *Neighbours* they are both learning about and participating in a culture different from their own. If a student flies from Washington DC to London they are subject to international air space agreements and contributing to global warming. If a student chooses to buy a fair-trade coffee they are making a conscious decision about contributing to a state and a people's development. Should you work for an international company or international organization, or even if you work for a locally based company there will inevitably be an international dimension to the functioning of the company as it negotiates the myriad of EU laws, international trade laws, international employment laws and tax laws. The limits to how international relations will continue to impact your life is tremendous.

Studying international relations or politics enables students and professionals to better comprehend the information we receive daily from newspapers, television and radio. People not only live in villages and towns, but form part of the wider networks that constitute regions, nations and states. As members of this world community, people have to be equally aware of both their rights and their responsibilities – and should be capable of engaging in important debates concerning the major issues facing the modern international community. One crucial feature of the world in which we live is its interconnectedness – geographically, intellectually and socially – and thus we need to understand it.

BOX 1.1 INTERNATIONAL RELATIONS

- Individuals live in villages/towns but are also part of a wider community
- Individuals have rights as well as responsibilities
- The world is interconnected

Originally, the study of international relations (a term first used by Jeremy Bentham in 1798) or politics was seen largely as a branch of the study of law, philosophy or history. However, following the carnage of the First World War there emerged an academic undertaking to understand how the fear of war was now equal only to the fear of defeat that had preceded the First World War. Subsequently, the first university chair of international relations was founded at the University of Wales in 1919. Given such diverse origins, there is no one accepted way of defining or understanding international relations, and throughout the world many have established individual ways of understanding international relations. Any attempt to define a field of study is bound to be somewhat arbitrary and this is particularly true when one comes to international relations or politics.

The terms 'international relations' and 'international politics' are often used interchangeably in books, journals, websites and newspapers. In the last generation some have preferred to use 'world' or 'global' politics where the focus of activity is not the state but some notion of a global community or global civilization. For many laypersons there is no real difference between these words, but technically there is more than a semantic difference as terms can reflect a difference of focus and field of study.

BOX 1.2 FOCUS AND FIELDS OF STUDY

International relations ≠ International politics ≠ World politics ≠ Global politics

Similarly, there are legal, political and social differences between domestic and international politics. Domestic law is generally obeyed, and if not, the police and courts enforce sanctions. International law rests on competing legal systems, and there is no common enforcement. Domestically a government has a monopoly on the legitimate use of force. In international politics no one has a monopoly of force, and therefore international politics has often been interpreted as the realm of self-help. It is also accepted that some states are stronger than others. Domestic and international politics also differ in their underlying sense of community – in international politics, divided peoples do not share the same loyalties – people disagree about what seems just and legitimate; order and justice. It is not necessary to suggest that people engaged in political activity never agree or that open and flagrant disagreement is necessary before an issue becomes political: what is important is that it should be recognized that conflict or disagreement lies at the heart of politics. To be political the disagreement has to be about public issues. Recent experience has taught us that the matters that were once purely domestic and of no great relevance internationally can feature very prominently on the international political agenda. Outbreaks of bovine spongiform encephalopathy (BSE), severe acute respiratory syndrome (SARS) and avian flu all exemplify how domestic incidents can become international and can lead to foreign policy changes and commitments.

BOX 1.3 THE DOMESTIC AND THE INTERNATIONAL

Domestic	International
• Laws generally agreed and obeyed	• Competing legal systems
• Sanctions	• No common enforcement
• Monopoly of force	• No monopoly of force (each state judge and jury in own case)
• A sense of community	• Diverse communities

Today, international relations could be used to describe a range of interactions between people, groups, firms, associations, parties, nations or states or between these and (non)governmental international organizations. These interactions usually take place between entities that exist in different parts of the world – in different territories, nations or states. To the layperson interactions such as going on holiday abroad, sending international mail, or buying or selling goods abroad may seem personal and private, and of no particular international concern. Other interactions such as choosing an Olympics host or awarding a film Oscar are very public, but may appear to be lacking any significant international political agenda. However, any such activities could have direct or indirect implications for political relations between groups, states or international organizations. More obviously, events such as international conflict, international conferences on global warming and international crime play a fundamental part in the study of international relations. If our lives can be so profoundly influenced by such events, and the responses of states and people are so essential to international affairs, then it is incumbent on us to increase our understanding of such events. As John Donne said in 1624:

> No man is an island, entire of itself; every man is a piece of the continent, a part of the main. If a clod be washed away by the sea, Europe is the less, as well as if promontory were, as well as if a manor of thy friend's or of thine own were. Any man's death diminishes me, because I am involved in mankind; and therefore never send to know for whom the bell tolls; it tolls for thee.

As of 2007, the world population has reached six and half billion, and it is estimated to rise to seven billion by 2013. The largest population in the world is in China with 1,321,852,000 persons, followed by India with a population of 1,129,866,000, and third is the USA with 301,139,000. The European Union has 490,426,000. The smallest population, the Vatican, has 1,000 persons. All of the individuals in these populations share basic human needs for air, food, drink and shelter and have hopes to ultimately realize their personal growth and fulfil their potential. It is also clear that there is an infinite variety of languages, cultures, religions, philosophies, states and governments. Although diverse, people are also inescapably interdependent.

BOX 1.4 HUMAN NEEDS

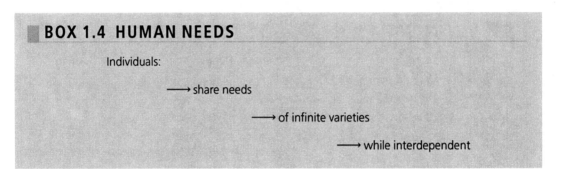

Individuals:

⟶ share needs

⟶ of infinite varieties

⟶ while interdependent

The immediacy of our globalized world can be exemplified by the immediacy and international diversity of the terrorist attacks of 9/11. Within minutes of the horrific events unfolding, international news media was feeding images of the attacks throughout the world. Of 2,617 deaths, 20 per cent were born outside the United States, 110 of whom were from the European Union.

In terms of conflict, one could argue that the new age began when Napoleon marched into Russia in 1812 with an army of 453,000 men. Or with the American Civil War (1861–1865) where 617,528 men were killed and 500,175 men were injured out of a total of 2,356,000 combatants from the combined Federal and Confederate forces. Others would cite the 8,500,000 dead and 21,000,000 wounded from the First World War. Others might look to the Second World War, just over 20 years later, during which 15,000,000 to 20,000,000 combatants and 9,000,000 to 10,000,000 civilians were killed, and the first nuclear weapons were used against the Japanese cities of Hiroshima and Nagasaki during August 1945. More recently, there have been 111 armed conflicts recorded in 74 locations around the world between 1989 and 2000 – seven were interstate and nine were intrastate wars with foreign intervention. There are no official figures recording how many people have been killed in Iraq since 2003 although one British medical journal has estimated that 2.5 per cent of the Iraqi population died as a result of the war between March 2003 and July 2006 – a hotly disputed figure. Similarly there are no official records of how many Iraqis were killed when Saddam Hussein was President of Iraq between July 1979 and April 2003.

The study of contemporary international relations encompasses much more than war and conflict, but preserving life, justice and sustainability remains a key ingredient. During April 1986 the world's worst nuclear power accident occurred at Chernobyl in the former USSR (now Ukraine). The Chernobyl accident killed more than 56 people immediately and exposed approximately 6,600,000 people to radiation, of whom as many as 9,000 have subsequently died from radiation-induced cancers. Twenty years later there are still areas of the Europe where farms face post-Chernobyl controls. Clearly the Chernobyl disaster exemplifies how global relationships and agendas remain crucial.

Participation in international relations or politics is inescapable. No individual, people, nation or state can exist in splendid isolation or be master of its own fate; but none, no matter how powerful in military, diplomatic or economic circles, even a giant superpower, can compel everyone to do its bidding. None can maintain or enhance their rate of social or economic progress or keep people alive without the contributions of foreigners or foreign states. Every people, nation or state is a minority in a world that is anarchic, that is, there is an absence of a common sovereign over them. There is politics among entities that have no ruler and in the absence of any ruler. That world is pluralistic and diverse. Each state is a minority among humankind. No matter how large or small, every state or nation in the world must take account of 'foreigners'.

BOX 1.5 THE COMPLEXITIES OF INTERNATIONAL RELATIONS

International relations

- War
- Economics
- Socio-economics
- Development
- Environment

International relations, therefore, is too important to be ignored but also too complex to be understood at a glance. Individuals can be the victim or victors of events but studying international relations helps each one of us to understand events and perhaps to make a difference. This, however, requires competence as well as compassion.

Some come to study international relations because of an interest in world events, but gradually they come to recognize that to understand their own state or region, to understand particular events and issues they have to move beyond a journalistic notion of current events. There is a need to analyse current events, to examine the why, where, what and when, but also to understand the factors that led to a particular outcome and the nature of the consequences. Studying international relations provides the necessary tools to analyse events, and to gain a deeper comprehension of some of problems that policy-makers confront and to understand the reasoning behind their actions.

Scholars and practitioners in international relations use concepts and theories to make their study more manageable. This book will introduce both, but that is only the first step. For instance, let us consider the United Nations which currently has 192 member states. If each member state consulted with every other member state regarding a particular issue, the scale of the political transactions and exhanges would be very difficult to define as a mere number. Rather, such transactions only become intelligable when they become organized and structured to fit with a specific arrangement or inter-pretation of facts. However, the very act of interpreting, organizing and structuring concepts suggests that they are inaccurate and incomplete. This is one example of how social scientists frequently find themselves in disagreement about the soundness of 'facts', concepts or theories.

Such disputes have historically led to major philosophical disputes about the fundamental nature of international relations: the Hobbesian versus the Lockeian state of nature in the seventeenth century, and the Realist versus Utopian debate of the first part of the twentieth century. Hobbes, writing in 1651, interpreted the state of society to be: 'continuall feare, and danger of violent death; And the life of man, solitary, poore, nasty, brutish, and short'. Hobbes also noted that:

> Yet in all times, Kings and Persons of Soveraigne authority, because of their Independency, are in continuall jealousies, and in the state and posture of Gladiators; having their weapons pointing, and their eyes fixed on one another; that is, their Forts, Garrisons, and Guns upon the Frontiers of their Kingdoms; and continuall Spyes upon their neighbours; which is a posture of War.

This is not, of course, an accurate reflection of contemporary international relations, but the concepts articulated by Hobbes still reverberate in many modern fundamental assumptions about the nature of the system and of human beings. Locke took a more optimistic view and suggested that sociability was the strongest bond between men – men were equal, sociable and free; but they were not licentious because they were governed by the laws of nature. He was clear that nature did not arm man against man, and that some degree of society was possible even in the state preceding government per se. Three and a half centuries later the differing perceptions and assumptions concerning human nature that influenced Hobbes and Locke are still able to divide approaches to the study of the nature of international relations.

■ BOX 1.6 ASSUMPTIONS AND APPROACHES

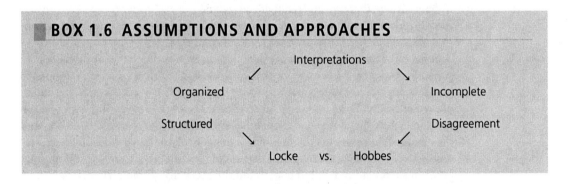

Other concepts are equally discussed and debated. For instance, in the 1970s it was common to distinguish between domestic politics and international politics on the basis of territory. In the United States, a continental power, or the United Kingdom, an island(s), for the most part, one could distinguish between home affairs and international affairs – international affairs involved people beyond the water's edge. For all states it involved people outside their own territory. What happened within a territorial boundary was the sole business of that territory's government and it has historically been accepted to mean that no state or organization – except in certain circumstances authorized by the United Nations Security Council – is subject to the demands or rules of another state. However, even if states are independent and equal units in terms of the law, it is a very different matter to consider individual state's capacity to exercise that independence or equality. For instance, as 'equal' members of the North Atlantic Treaty Organization it is absurd to think that Iceland, Luxembourg or Latvia have the same operational power as the United States, the United Kingdom or the Federal Republic of Germany.

International relations, even foreign relations, involve the study of the interactions that take place between seemingly disparate societies or entities, and the factors that affect those interactions. Whilst accounting for the pre-state and modern state system, such definition also accounts for the emergence of systems where the state is superseded by some new form of government such as the European Union, which is neither a state nor a nation, but acts on the international stage via treaties such as the Common Commercial Policy and Association Agreements, and the Common Foreign and Security Policy. Additionally, 12 members of the European Union now share a single currency and 27 members of the European Union have also accepted that in some areas covered by the European Union there is a now a supreme court – the European Court of Justice – which can impose fines on member states, in certain circumstances. Subsequent spill-over from some of these policies into non-treaty areas (for example the link between industrial policy and the arms industry) also contributes to a significant level of inter-national interconnectedness.

The prevalence of 'sub-national actors' (SNA) and 'non-central governments' (NCG) must also be acknowledged on the international stage. For instance, when Governor of California, Arnold Schwarzenegger, embarked on a campaign to produce an inter-national alliance to combat global warming, against the wishes of his fellow Republicans in the Senate and White House, he did so not as a representative of the United States but as a 'sub-national actor'. However, he was still able to effect significant impact on international relations by signing an agreement (not a treaty) in 2006 to share ideas and information to cut carbon emissions with British Prime Minister Tony Blair. Con-sequently, California and Britain have exchanged delegations and Britain has a seat on California's Market Advisory Committee and has sent representatives to the California Air Resources Board. In 2006–2007 California was engaged in similar 'sub-national' agreements with the Canadian province of Manitoba and with the Premier of the Australian state of Victoria. In the latter part of the twentieth century and the beginning of the twenty-first century 'sub-national actors' and 'non-central govern-ments' have played an increasingly dominant role on the international stage.

Similarly, multinational corporations (MNCs) – often with headquarters in one state and operational capability in a range of others – contribute significantly to international relations. Additionally there are other transgovernmental organizations where the rela-tions between players are not controlled by the central foreign policy of the state – such as the exchange rate of a state's currency being determined by the money markets. Clearly there has been a blurring of boundaries between domestic politics and inter-national politics. Indeed, some have talked about states being penetrated or permeated by outside agencies – as outsiders gain entry to gain influence, information, infiltrate a domestic society, or even partake in decisions in another society. Indeed, some Chief Executive Officers (CEOs) have phoned and negotiated with cabinet ministers, members of administrations, and even presidents and prime ministers.

Despite the obvious challenges posed to states in the modern world there also remains a strong culture in national individualism, wherein states and such persons who identify their nationality via the state, wish to proclaim and practise their separate cultures and different languages. In fact, rather than vanishing, nationalism and the demand for separate states have increased. However, despite all the challenges and many new theories of international politics/relations the state remains, for many, the primary actor in international politics.

These ideas and debates demonstrate that although the term 'international relations' has for centuries inferred a particular concern with relations between nations, it does not have to remain so confined. Thus, contrary to the narrow traditionalist realist view of international relations and foreign policy/relations, which focuses on the physical security and protection of the territory of the state and its people, one needs to look wider. The traditional view implicit in much international relations literature follows the assumption of Bodin that social and political order and legality are the highest values of a society and that in every given territory sovereignty must be united in one clear, secular authority to establish and maintain order. Following this, the Treaties of Westphalia established that sovereign rulers are the sole creators and executors of the law. Thus, only those holding authority on behalf of states could have political relations with each other. Increasingly, however, there is a diminishing salience of territorial issues and a 'domestication' of international politics coinciding with a growing awareness that people, nations and states are entering an era when foreign policy and national security will increasingly revolve around commercial interests and economic diplomacy. Increasingly, it is also apparent that the number of government departments (central, regional and local) conducting relatively low-level negotiations or exchanging technical information, with their opposite numbers in other states is virtually equivalent to the number of departments that actually exist at any given time. It has certainly become increasingly true that each major department of central government has its so-called foreign ministry.

But despite the political relocation of much of international relations it is important to remember that power, force, coercion, authority or influence remain central to international relations as a means to resolve disagreements about values. Such actions can involve physical acts of violence or attempts to influence the mind of an opponent. Terrorism as a strategic objective aims to weaken the will of the opposition, although obviously there can be a grey area where intellectual distinctions become suspect and to some extent artificial. Even a gathering of the most virtuous might well disagree as to which is the most efficient way to solve global warming. International peace is another good example: is it achieved by disarmament, by a balance of power, by deterrence, or by having one power or organization running the globe? Apart from the latter, reasonable people can reasonably disagree about the means even if they agree on the ends. Choice is necessary – choice between the values that society and state wish to pursue, choice between the resources required to fulfil the values and choice between different outcomes. The choice of priority for one area will have repercussions on another. For example, one could argue that the wars in Iraq and Afghanistan have taken resources from (1) other parts of the defence budget and/or (2) other parts of government expenditure such as hospitals or universities, and oftentimes leaders take decisions without knowing all the facts. Disagreement is not necessarily an indication that people or states or organizations are immoral or wicked or unintelligent. There can be disagreements as to what should be done, how it should be done, when it should be done, and for some crucially, who is going to pay. Many states and organizations say, as does the European Union that they believe in supporting the United Nations Charter, the preservation of peace and international cooperation, but as was seen in 2002–2003 in regard to Iraq, those organizations and the states comprising them can be split in trying to determine what these aspirations mean in terms of actual policy.

International politics is pre-eminently concerned with the art of achieving group ends against the opposition of other groups. But this is limited by the will and ability of other groups to impose their demands. International politics involves the delicate adjustment of power to power. If physical force were to be used to resolve every disagreement there would result an intolerable existence for the world's population. Society would not prosper and every human being would be suspicious of every other human. Sometimes this happens on the international stage, given that every state is judge and jury of its own interests and can decide for itself whether to use force – with the 2003 invasion of Iraq by a US coalition of the willing as a prime example. In order to resolve these disagreements it is necessary that states and international organizations can come up with a way of resolving differences. Although such ideals have been difficult to establish across the board it has become the case that there are non-violent options available to states. Politics is about maintaining order. But that order has to be maintained in an anarchical world.

The arena of international relations and politics seems to be continually expanding. To appreciate this, one needs to reflect on the multiplication of independent states. In 1800 there were no international organizations, but now there is one for almost every activity – both governmental and non-governmental. When the United Nations Charter was signed in October 1945, 51 states signed it. In the first decade of twenty-first century the UN grew between 189 and 192 member states. There has also been the continuing growth of governmental and international services. Of particular importance is that national and international decisions and choices cover a much broader range of subjects. Both are increasingly concerned with organized labour, citizens' welfare and human rights, living standards, literacy and health. Secondly, there is the increased complexity of society and the economy. There are now increased organizational demands in terms of meeting the ordinary everyday needs of citizens. Interdependence implies that people, businesses and organizations rely on each other (and their rivals) in different places for ideas, goods and services. International relations and politics is necessary for all states, but political power is not centralized and unequal. That is why power, coercion and bargaining still hold sway.

BOX 1.7 INTERNATIONAL RELATIONS AS AN EXPANDING FIELD

- Number of states
- Amount of services and choices
- Complexity of international system

CONCLUSION

Many people assume international relations or politics is easy – it is what they read in newspapers or see on television – but academic study of international relations or politics is much more complex. Students of international relations need to go beyond the 'alleged facts' or 'photo-opportunity' and instead use theoretical tools of analysis. Not all courses in international relations or politics will enable you to answer all questions; indeed, there is no international relations view and many departments have members who disagree about these fundamentals. Our understanding of international relations or politics is often about conflicting views and students need to comprehend the origins of such conflicting views and to consider their philosophical or theoretical basis. This is particularly true given that our world has entered a period of dramatic and confusing change that is unlikely to be resolved in the near future. A reasonable question for a student of international relations or politics is thus: how can we influence, if not completely change, that future?

CHAPTER 2

Reflections on the Study of International Relations

Vivienne Jabri

THE BOUNDARY PROBLEM

The politics of global interactions is more accessible now in the present age than it ever has been in the past. Whether it is conflict in the Middle East, the break-up of Yugoslavia, human rights violations or poverty in Sub-Saharan Africa, we are daily confronted by images of global interactions which in some way cross national boundaries, involve a variety of factors, and impact upon a widespread number of issues which may or may not affect our own lives, values and welfare. What is beyond dispute is that we, as individuals, may no longer claim immunity or distance from events which occur elsewhere, which affect others beyond our shores. Relationships which take place across state boundaries seem, therefore, to include interactions involving not only the diplomatic core or representatives of our individual states, but the business community, the media, charitable organizations and so on. Furthermore, within a multicultural society such as that of the United Kingdom or United States, it could be said that we are already involved in global interactions on a daily basis from the classroom to the local supermarket. Given the increasing complexity of such processes, the primary question becomes how we limit the remits or boundaries of a discipline named international relations.

International relations has a number of concerns and equally varied perspectives which seek to make sense of the world around us. From its formal establishment in 1919 to the present day, we see a discipline occupied by debates and contentions relating to the subject matter that should be within our remit and to the nature and legitimacy of our theories about this subject matter. Conceived in direct response to the devastations

BOX 2.1 NO IMMUNITY FROM GLOBAL INTERACTIONS

Global interactions:

- Cross national boundaries
- Involve a variety of actors
- Impact on a widespread number of issues
- Involve business, media, charities, etc.

Question: How to limit IR as a discipline?

witnessed in the First World War, the original aims of those involved in the creation of this discipline were underpinned by the assumption that a greater understanding of the nature of relations between states would lead to the prevention of war in the future. Statesmen, in other words, would be better equipped with the intellectual tools considered necessary to deal with international crisis situations so that these might reach resolution prior to the onset of all-out war. This early *normative* concern, that our theories contain within them the basis for action and change, has its parallels in contemporary thought in international relations.

BOX 2.2 THEORY

A way of making things more intelligible

+

Description

+

Set of limited propositions designed to connect, interpret and organize facts

+

Explaining

+

In some theories predicting, that is constructing 'if . . . then . . .' hypotheses

BOX 2.3 NORMATIVE THEORY

- Deals with how things *ought* to be
- The choices policy-makers *should* make
- Contains explanation and/or predictions
- Based on *ethical* concerns

As will be seen later, the discipline's trajectory has now returned to these early ethical concerns and, after a long period dominated by the view that the discipline was somehow separate from the realm of practice, those involved in the discipline increasingly recognize the responsibilities which emerge from the intimate relationship between theory and practice.

The aim of this chapter is to provide an introductory overview of the discipline and its theoretical perspectives. The chapter highlights the defining features of these perspectives by concentrating on how they view the subject matter, their core conceptual frameworks and underpinning assumptions. Each perspective comes to constitute a frame or a lens through which global interactions or world politics are viewed. The review will seek to highlight the relationship between the academic study of international relations and the practice of world politics, arguing that this is both a complex and mutually formative relationship. In being so intimately related the discipline and its theoretical perspectives have come under increasing scrutiny by contemporary thinkers in international relations.

THE 'REALITIES' AND 'THEORIES' OF INTERNATIONAL RELATIONS

As a number of writers have indicated, the terms 'international relations' is in itself problematic as it immediately points to an ambiguity around the subject matter with which we are concerned (Brown, 1997: 3). As we saw in the opening paragraph of this chapter, global interactions are highly complex and now involve a number of different actors and issues, and may occur at our doorstep and in distant lands. How we provide a coherent image or set of images which reflects this complexity has been the defining problem in the discipline since its inception.

It could initially be stated that the study of international relations may refer to relations between states, between nations or peoples, between cultures, or international institutions such as the European Union or the United Nations. Reminded of business or charitable connections, we may wish to include firms and humanitarian organizations among our growing list of those we see as being involved in global interactions. What we see as the *actors* or *units* of our investigations greatly informs and differentiates the different perspectives that dominate the discipline.

BOX 2.4 THE ACTORS

- 'What we see as the *actors or units* . . . greatly informs and differentiates the different perspectives that dominate the discipline'
- Relations between states?
- Diversity: business, international institutions, Amnesty International, etc.?

If investigations are confined to relations between states we would, by definition, negate the influence of non-state actors such as Amnesty International and ignore the impact of supranational institutions such as the European Union. We could conclude, as many in the discipline and in the media have done, that Amnesty may well be involved in issues relating to human rights, or that the European Commission may well pronounce on matters relating to EU budgets, but what matters ultimately are decisions made by sovereign states, for these are the actors with most influence, with the greatest capacity to make a difference.

Considered in relation to the primacy of the state, international politics come to be defined in terms of interactions between states in an international system of states where these are 'sovereign' entities, territorially bound, and independent ultimately of any external authority. The 'international' is hence structurally differentiated from the 'domestic' in that where the former, according to this 'realist' perspective, is defined as 'anarchical', the latter is hierarchical. State sovereignty comes to be the defining element in the study of international relations, even where other perspectives challenge the primacy of the state.

If it is recognized that lived experience is influenced by global firms, international institutions, or non-governmental organizations, we would seek to expand the remit of our investigations in order to account for the diversity of actors and forms of interactions which take place in global politics. In doing so, however, we come face to face with one of the most challenging and contentious issues in the history of the discipline, namely the question of power, its definition, and how it translates to influence in the global arena. Theorizing the international is hence not only concerned with the definition of the actors implicated, but with underlying assumptions relating to the primacy of the state as opposed to and in comparison with other entities.

Considered in terms of the dynamics of change and how we provide explanations of change, the question begins to shift attention back to an earlier problematic, namely the capacity to make a difference. When thought of in terms of 'capacity', the 'agency' of states is as much as that of the UN or Amnesty International, for each acts within a wider whole, whether this is conceived in terms of the international political economy or the international legal order, or indeed the anarchical international system (Giddens, 1984). This wider whole is 'structural' in that it has an existence that exceeds the sum of its constituent parts, it might hence be identified separately from these parts, and has effects that both confer identity to these parts (the agents) while having both constraining and enabling effects. Schools of thought in international relations hence differ not just in terms of the agents identified as primary, but crucially also in terms of how the *structure* of the international system is conceived. Any explanation of change must therefore account for agents as well as structures, for the capacity to make a difference (agency) is always subject to the enabling and constraining influence of institutional continuities of international life (structure).

BOX 2.5 AGENCY AND STRUCTURE

- *Agency*: the actor or units who have the capacity to make a difference or to influence outcomes
- *Structure*: but these operate within a wider whole: the international system, international political economy, international legal order, or anarchy etc., which can constrain or enable the agents
- For the capacity to make a difference (*agency*) is always subject to the enabling and constraining influence of institutional continuities of international life (*structure*)

The agency–structure problem emerges every time we begin to think about the boundaries of the discipline of international relations or the location of what we deem to constitute 'international' politics. We may place primacy with the state and concentrate on relations between states, but are such relations determined primarily by the distribution of power or are they in some way governed by rule-bound codes of conduct which render some modes of behaviour possible, or even legitimate and others not? Is there a form of international society that might reflect the features of a domestic society, including a form of contract, but one that lacks an all-encompassing global government? Furthermore, are relations between states governed by mutual cooperation and interdependence or are they best conceived as conflictual and subject to the imperatives of a self-help system based on survival in an anarchical system? How these questions are answered depends on assumptions made in relation to the elements (agents, structures) conferred primacy, how we acquire knowledge about these, and the arguments we present in justifying our claims to knowledge. Much controversy in the discipline of international relations relates to these assumptions and how they impact on explaining and understanding global politics and phenomena such as war, identity and affiliation, the workings of the international political economy, the causes of inequality and poverty, the potentials for regulating behaviour in relation to climate change, and so on.

BOX 2.6 DIFFERENT PERSPECTIVES

The identity of actors

The nature of interactions:

- based on power?
- bound by rules?
- is there a society?
- fundamentally cooperative or conflictual?

The nature of the subject matter

How we view the discipline will in itself reflect value positions which feed into the research questions asked. The relationship between the researcher's own value system and the theoretical and empirical interests she/he expresses is one among a number of philosophical questions which have occupied the discipline for a number of years and which currently form one of its most controversial areas. One of the controversies relates to how our theories reflect or mirror the world of practice and how near to the 'real' our descriptions of global politics are. Much of the discipline's historical trajectory has been dominated by the assumption that our theories of international relations are separate and independent from the world of practice. This outlook, as we see below, distinguishes between matters of 'fact' and matters of 'value' and aspires towards the replication of methods conventionally associated with the natural sciences. If we are to be as near to the 'real' as we could possibly be then our theories, according to this perspective, must seek to 'mirror' the world rather than change it. The methods by which this could be assured include clarity in conceptual use, precision in generalizing statements, and predictive modelling. Above all else, a theory which aspires to the 'real' must preclude any concern with the achievement of change or the incorporation of values in such issues as poverty, war, human rights or environmental protection. The task is set and it has its rules. The discipline's function is to provide descriptions of the world of practice, to explain as far as possible recurring phenomena such as conflict, and to locate particular historical events in wider theoretical explanations.

We may, however, reject the separation assumed above between theory and practice, between fact and value. The suggestion here is that rather than viewing theory as a reflection of the world, it is recognized as being deeply implicated in its *construction*. This *constructivist* perspective challenges the view that language (for example, the language of our theories) merely describes the world. It suggests, rather, that language also has a performative function: descriptions of global politics, or representations in discourse of how global politics work, are at the same time constructions. The representation of reality has a role in the constitution of reality. Understood in this way, the 'anarchy' of the international system loses its taken-for-granted, essential character assumed in the tradition of realism in international relations, but comes to be seen as constituted through the discourses and practices of states (Wendt, 1999). If, furthermore, we stress the importance of power as a determinant of relations between states, are we not implicated in the perpetuation of coercive relations as the norm of conduct on the international state? If we prioritize the imperatives of balances of power over and above international law, are we not denying the possibility of there existing norms and rules of conduct which may constitute a 'global civil society'? (Frost 1996). Posing these questions provides an immediate challenge to the view that we may so neatly separate the realm of theory from that of practice, or that we may so unproblematically refer to the 'real', as if 'the world' may be conceived separately from the words we use and the concepts we habitually draw upon in order to make sense of all that which goes on around us. What of those aspects of international relations which remain hidden from view? If our theories of the international take the state as given, for example, and state sovereignty as the mainstay of relations between states in an anarchic system, then we must preclude from our investigations any considerations which might challenge the primacy of the state, such as identity politics, race relations, gender and the place of women in the realm of the international. That which remains silent and hidden from view provides, as will be seen below, an invaluable insight into the relationship between power and knowledge and, therefore, between the world and the word.

International relations has, since its inception after the Great War, been structured around the issues highlighted above. Contentions relating to subject matter centre on the actors and issues most significant in global politics, but touch on fundamental questions relating to what constitutes politics, whether we may legitimately assume a separation of the domestic from the international, and whether we may indeed rely on concepts such as power and sovereignty to delimit the boundaries of our enterprise. The debate is often framed by dualisms which oppose the public realm to the private, the domestic to the international. These are dualisms that have foundations deep in Western political thought and it is not altogether surprising that their impact is strongly felt in a discipline such as international relations. Contentions about subject matter must be juxtaposed with the underpinning assumptions about what constitutes the international and what types of relations constitute global politics. Such assumptions powerfully inform empirical concerns in the discipline and these have spanned a wide range since

BOX 2.7 PHILOSOPHICAL BASIS

1

- Is theory separate from practice?
- 'Value-free' mirror of world?
- Clear concepts + precision + prediction
- Descriptive orientation

or

2

- Value and fact linked?
- Theory has a relationship with world?

the establishment of the discipline, from the study of war to global environmental politics. Contentions about subject matter must in turn be juxtaposed against philosophical issues that place theory itself under scrutiny, the criteria used for its justification, and its place in the construction of the world. These are questions that any student of international relations must be aware of and we will see them highlighted as we move through the trajectory of the discipline's history and its so-called 'great debates'.

THEORETICAL CONTENTIONS IN INTERNATIONAL RELATIONS

International relations as a formal discipline is a relatively young discipline compared to the other social sciences and humanities to which it is closely related. It has sought to establish clear boundaries that confer on it a distinct identity. While boundaries change and identities shift with time, what is clear is that the discipline is, by and large, constituted by the discourses or theoretical frameworks, that dominate at any stage during its evolution. It is these frameworks that provide the terms of reference for the discipline and it is these that function as gatekeepers for what is considered as its legitimate subject matter. Boundaries can by no means be taken for granted, however, and are always subject to contention and dispute within the discipline itself. How we construct such boundaries will, as stated earlier, have an impact on the delimitations of our subject matter and the theories we build to develop our understanding of such salient issues as peace and war, order and justice, the effectiveness or otherwise of international law and institutions and so on.

Whether we agree that international relations is a distinct discipline or prefer to see it as emerging from a long tradition of reflections on these issues, we may confer an all-encompassing identity to the discipline by stating that it deals with and seeks to develop understandings of international social, political and economic life, where each of these terms in turn, the international, the social, the political and the economic, are in themselves subject to contention and contestation. While some may view such debate with dismay, seeking a uniform approach to the subject, others celebrate such diversity as promoting a rich tapestry for how we may not only understand the complexities of the realm we label the international but seek to transform the practices which enable the continuation of violence and inequality in the global sphere.

The concerns which have preoccupied international relations have been the subject of speculation and reflection in writings that take us back to ancient Greece and the Romans, to Renaissance Italy and well into the birth of the Enlightenment and the eighteenth century. Whether we can consider international relations as a separate realm of knowledge is itself highly problematic and requires justification. What is beyond dispute is that the discipline has a classical tradition which, in its various forms and interpretations has contributed, as we will see below, to providing foundations for the perspectives associated with the field today. Foundations are often drawn upon in the setting of boundaries and the settling of identities. They are used as a method of justification, as if to state that today's theories are built upon and derive from discourses which preceded our time, our context. It must, however, be recognized that foundations in the social sciences are set in turbulent terrain and are thus often shaky and questionable, strong in parts and weaker in others. The classical tradition is, therefore, open to a number of different usages and interpretations, and how we use the tradition, how we read the texts, will say more about our contemporary thought processes, our present modes of disciplinary legitimation, than the assumptions held by the authors of those distant texts.

What we may state with certainty before this chapter moves to the contemporary debates is that much of the subject matter that delimits the discipline was already the focus of reflection among historians, philosophers and legal scholars much before the creation of the formal discipline we variously label international relations, international politics or international studies. Writers within the contemporary field have looked to this 'classical tradition' not only as an exercise in the history of thought, but, more crucially, as a means of justifying the theories put forward. Using the classical tradition as a method of justification suggests that assumptions contained within this tradition may be thought of as 'foundational' and therefore taken as the givens upon which all other premises may be built. The crucial idea in foundationalism as a method of justification is that beliefs are built upon and require the support of other beliefs which are in themselves secure and beyond question. Such beliefs may, for example, point to a view of human nature as the basis upon which we may build theories relating to human organization, the state and interstate relations. Clearly, a scrutiny of foundations, their subjection to different, often conflicting interpretations, endangers the edifice itself, the discipline's conceptual schema, and its intellectual content. It therefore becomes necessary to look to the foundations, not so much to uncover the details of the classical tradition, but to illustrate that thought on matters 'international' existed prior to the establishment of the discipline of international relations and that such thought has had a formative influence on the discipline's trajectory.

Theories of international relations have always been concerned with questions relating to the regulation of interstate relations and the maintenance of order in the international system. How we regulate such relations and what form of order we seek to establish are, however, matters for contention and debate. In the early years, from 1919 to the 1930s, the discipline was dominated by what is conventionally referred to as *liberal internationalism*. The primary concern of this approach was that conditions which had led to the outbreak of the First World War and the devastation which followed should not be allowed to occur in the future. The driving force was therefore normative in orientation and the underlying assumption was that the academic study of international relations had the potential to contribute to the prevention of war and the establishment of peace. With foundations in the Enlightenment and the eighteenth century, liberal internationalism, as Scott Burchill points out, suggested that 'the prospects for the elimination of war lay with a preference for democracy over aristocracy, free trade over autarky, and collective security over the balance of power system' (Burchill, 1996: 31).

The first of these, the view that democracy within states contributes to the establishment of peace between states, is a powerful idea whose primary exponent is Immanuel Kant in his pamphlet *Perpetual Peace*. Here in this eighteenth-century text on international relations, and one which some would view as having resonances in our own age, we see expressed the view that the internal governmental structures of a state have profound effects on how it conducts its relations with other states. The establishment of a 'perpetual peace' is dependent on a number of prerequisites which must be met if the conditions which have given rise to perpetual war are to be eliminated. Kant suggests that while war may benefit rulers, it cannot be in the interest of free citizens living within a republic for they would have 'great hesitation in embarking on so dangerous an enterprise'. Just as reason is the basis of a 'perfect civil constitution' which ensures freedom, so too reason, 'as the highest legislative moral power, absolutely condemns war as a test of rights and sets up peace as an immediate duty' (Reiss ed. 1991; 193–30). A democratic order within a state provides a free citizenry with the capacity to condemn war conducted in the interest of rulers and establishes public opinion as a primary constraint on the conduct of relations with other states. For peace to be secure, however, a 'pacific federation' would have to be created which would secure the rights and duties of the contracting parties and which would govern peaceful relations between states.

The two interrelated ideas that emerge from Kant's reflections on a perpetual peace and which formed the basic foundations for the liberal internationalism that dominated the discipline of international relations in its early days centred on democratic governance and institutionalized law-governed relations of cooperation between states. These were in themselves underpinned by the twin formative ideas of the Enlightenment, namely human rationality and a cosmopolitan moral order (that is, free from national limitation or interpretation) which saw humanity as a whole as the realm of a system of rights and obligations.

▌BOX 2.8 LIBERAL INTERNATIONALISM

- Normative: idealism
- Democracy + free trade + collective security
- Kant
- Democratic governance + cooperation based on law
- Human rationality + cosmopolitan moral order
- International institutions

The two formative pillars of liberal internationalism, democracy and free trade, required the establishment of international relations which would promote collectivist aspirations in place of the conflictual relations which formed the basis of balance-of-power thinking. For it was just such thinking, based as it was on the premise that relations between states are determined solely by the pursuit of power, which led to violations of international law and ultimately to the outbreak of war in 1914. A system of 'collective security' was advocated to replace antagonistic alliance systems with an international order based on the rule of law and collective responsibility. The domestic analogy of a social contract was deemed to be transferable for the international level. The creation of the League of Nations after the end of the First World War was the culmination of the liberal ideal for international relations. The League would function as the guarantor of international order and would be the organ through which states could settle their differences through arbitration. Any deviance from international law would be dealt with collectively in the name of a commonly held interest in the maintenance of peace and security.

Though liberal internationalist ideals are now recognized for their significant contribution in the development of normative approaches to the subject, they seemed, at the outset of the 1930s and ultimately the outbreak of the Second World War, futile and utopian. Thus it was that the subject matter of international relations, dominated as it had been by international law and diplomatic history, was transformed to an intellectual agenda which placed power and self-interest at the forefront of concern. The 'idealism' of the interwar period was henceforth to be replaced by *realism*, and it is this school of thought which, in its various articulations, remains dominant in the discipline. E.H. Carr's *Twenty Years' Crisis*, published in 1939, was the text which positioned what he called utopianism in opposition to realism.

Carr called for a 'science' of international relations, one which would move away from what he saw as the wishful thinking of liberal internationalism. By presenting the fact–value distinction, that which separates the 'what is' from the 'what ought to be', in dichotomous or oppositional terms, Carr's text called for a move away from utopian doctrine which, he suggested, was based on an unrealistic negation of power and its impact on international politics. In a statement that has manifest resonance for contemporary concerns in international relations, Carr states:

> The outstanding achievement of modern realism has been to reveal, not merely the determinist aspects of the historical process, but the relative and pragmatic character of thought itself. In the last fifty years, thanks mainly though not wholly to the influence of Marx, the principles of the historical school have been applied to the analysis of thought; and the foundations of a new science have been laid, principally by German thinkers, under the name of the 'sociology of knowledge'. The realist has thus been enabled to demonstrate that the intellectual theories and ethical standards of utopianism, far from being the expression of absolute and *a priori* principles, are historically conditioned, being both products of circumstances and interests and weapons framed by the furtherance of interests.
>
> (Carr, 1964: 67–8)

This statement points to the view that values are context bound, that morality is determined by interest, and that the conditions of the present are determined by historical processes. Where idealism sought a universally applicable doctrine, Carr's call is for a historical analysis of the contingent frameworks which determine politics. Though Carr himself recognized the ambiguities involved in the 'antitheses' that frame his text, others writing subsequently have, by and large, neglected the nuances surrounding Carr's critique of utopianism, preferring instead to concentrate on an unmuddied borderline between realism and idealism. This oppositional representation had a lasting impact on the discipline and indeed has been seen as its first stage of theoretical contention.

The formative assumptions of realism as a school of thought centre on the view that the international system is 'anarchic', in the sense that it is devoid of an all-encompassing authority. Where domestic society is ruled by a single system of government, the international system of states lacks such a basis and renders international law non-binding and ultimately ineffectual in the regulation of relations between states. Conflict is hence an inevitable and continual feature of international relations. Just as liberal internationalism sought foundations in the Enlightenment and the birth of reason, so realism locates its roots further back, citing Thucydides, Machiavelli and Hobbes as its founding voices. Thucydides and his account of the Peloponnesian War is read as the formative paradigmatic text in that it covers themes such as power, intrigue, conquest, alliance-building and the intricacies of bargaining. Here we see portrayed a system of city states, the units or members of which are self-reliant and independent, with war breaking out in 431 BC. This text, selected from an age which produced Herodotus, Sophocles and Euripides, not to mention Socrates and Plato, is deemed foundational and is used by more contemporary realists as a basis of justification for claims made. Classically, we see in this narrative a powerful state, Athens, expanding in influence and threatening the political and economic well-being of the Peloponnesian states, led by Sparta. What is of interest is not so much how the themes covered by Thucydides reflect those of the dominant paradigm in the discipline, but more what is left out of this selective reading, namely the race and class struggles that were apparent at the time and which interest Thucydides himself, or the effects of war on the lived experience of those involved.

Hans Morgenthau, whose *Politics among Nations* (1948) leads the realist perspective, points to a clear line of descent from Thucydides when he asserts that 'realism assumes that its key concept of interest defined as power is an objective category which is universally valid, but it does not endow that concept with a meaning that is fixed once and for all'. Morgenthau's text starts with the assumption that there are objective laws which have universal applicability:

> Political realism believes that politics, like society in general, is governed by objective laws that have their roots in human nature . . . Realism, believing as it does in the objectivity of the laws of politics, must also believe in the possibility of developing a rational theory that reflects, however imperfectly and one-sidedly, these objective laws. It believes also in the possibility of distinguishing in politics between truth and opinion – between what is true objectively and rationally, supported by evidence and

illuminated by reason, and what is only a subjective judgement, divorced from the facts as they are and informed by prejudice and wishful thinking.

(Morgenthau, 1978: 4–29)

BOX 2.9 REALISM

- What is
- Values are context-bound
- Morality and state behaviour determined by interest
- No all-encompassing authority
- Conflict inevitable
- Morgenthau: 'interest defined as power'
  - objective laws rooted in human nature
  - distinction 'between truth and opinion'; separation of fact and value
  - 'international politics, like all politics, is a struggle for power'
  - scientific and explanatory
  - state + power + Cold War concern

Ultimately, for Morgenthau and other realists, 'international politics, like all politics, is a struggle for power'. Where liberal internationalism had been openly normative and prescriptive in orientation, the realism expressed by Morgenthau purports to be scientific and explanatory. Theories of international relations must, according to Morgenthau, be consistent with the facts and it is these which must be the ultimate test of the validity of theoretical statements. Morgenthau, like other realists, hence assumes a clear separation of fact and value, of theory and practice. What we see on closer inspection, however, is a theory that is replete with politics and prescriptive content, one that is steeped in the Cold War international politics of its day, and one, finally, which seeks the legitimation of its claims and its status by recourse, first, to foundational ideas on human nature derived from Hobbes, and, second, to science as the ultimate guarantor of the truth of theory. This text, above any other in the discipline, has had profound influence, not only in setting the substantive agenda, but in placing positivism at the heart of the methodological and epistemological approaches to the subject.

BOX 2.10 POSITIVISM

- The truth of theory must lie in empirical observation
- Facts are distinct and independent of values and ideological orientations
- The methods of the nature sciences may be applied to the study of society, or the social sciences

By the late 1950s and into the 1960s we see a discipline dominated by realist conceptions of international relations, based as these were on the state as the primary unit of analysis, on interactions between states governed by the relentless pursuit of power, and on a substantive empirical agenda defined by Cold War concerns. Morgenthau's call for a 'science' of international relations was actualized in the so-called *behavioural revolution*, a methodological turn in international relations and the rest of the social sciences which sought to apply the rigorous testing methods of the natural sciences to social science research. The emphasis was on quantitative research, and any theory which could not be so subjected to 'operationalization' was deemed to be based on impression and ideology. Far from challenging realism presuppositions, behaviourism merely reinforced the realist orthodoxy. It was, however, its claims to methodological supremacy which invited the most vigorous criticism from those opposed to the idea that the methods of the natural sciences could easily be transposed to international relations. Prominent among such critics was Hedley Bull, who argued, along with other *traditionalists* that the greatest insights in International Relations derived from classical thought, from philosophy and history.

BOX 2.11 THE BEHAVIOURAL REVOLUTION

- New methodological approach: methods of natural science
- Rigorous testing
- Quantitive emphasis + operalization
- Reinforced realist orthodoxy
- Challenged by Hedley Bull: English School

Bull's concern was to argue that relations between states could not be reduced to measurable attributes of power or models of decision-making. If features of 'society' characterized relations between states and if, indeed, we could locate codes of conduct which formed such a society, we could legitimately look to history and philosophy to conceptualize the complexity of international politics. Bull's *The Anarchical Society*, first published in 1977, came to represent what subsequently has been referred to as the 'English School', demarcated from the United States-dominated realist and scientific perspective mainly through its normative approach to the subject (Bull, 1977).

It was during the 1960s, however, that other perspectives came to constitute alternative modes of conceptualizing international politics. With decolonization, the US withdrawal from Vietnam and the rise of a Third World alliance which made itself felt primarily at the United Nations, global relations came to encompass matters which seemed far removed from the Cold War rhetoric which underpinned relations between East and West. Economic and financial relations, development, social issues and regional integration seemed to challenge the primacy of the state as sole unit of analysis and power as the ultimate determinant of relations between states. One of the foremost challengers to the orthodoxy was John Burton, whose work came to be pivotal in the *pluralist* attempt to rewrite the discipline (Burton, 1968 and 1972). Central to Burton's corpus was the view that global relations were multiform in content and involved a number of different types of actor, from individuals to states, to non-state organizations. Others within this wide-ranging challenge to realism included Keohane and Nye's work on 'transnational relations' and on 'complex interdependence'. Where the former was an empirical description of Burton's position that states were not the sole actors in the international system, the latter, articulated in *Power and Interdependence*, saw global politics as multiple channelled, as being based on a variety of relationships rather than on force, and as ultimately centring on issues which were not hierarchically organized around the strategic interests of the most powerful (Keohane and Nye, 1971 and 1977). Taking these assumptions as baseline, the main research problematic came to focus on agenda-setting in global politics and it was this which led to the more recent emergence of 'regime theory', which acknowledges the place of power in the politics surrounding an issue area but which recognizes other dynamics, including legitimacy and rules of conduct, that may not so easily be reduced.

BOX 2.12 PLURALISM

- Global relations multiform in content
- Number of different actors
- Burton
- Keohane and Nye: 'transnational relations' + 'complex interdependence'
- Complex interdependence: multi-channels + force not only basis of relations + no single hierarchy
- Regime theory + issue areas + international organizations » neoliberal institutionalism

Pluralism did not so much challenge the realist orthodoxy as provide a wider perspective on global interactions. While Burton's trajectory came to focus on conflict, its resolution and the place of the individual therein (Burton, 1979), those involved in the interdependence school concentrated on the workings of international organizations, issue areas and the establishment of regimes. Despite such variation in outlook and research agenda, descriptions of the discipline have often far too easily placed these within one perspective. If pluralism's identity was based on its opposition to the realist orthodoxy, then it must be acknowledged that the theoretical underpinnings of realism, its derivation from classical thought and its foundational dependence on the essential rationality and sovereignty of the state as actor were not challenged. The contemporary derivation of pluralism, neoliberal institutionalism, based primarily in the United States, shares with realism a number of its founding assumptions.

A third perspective or paradigm which emerged as a critique of both realism and pluralism concentrated on the inequalities that exist within the international system, inequalities of wealth between the rich 'North', or the 'First World', and the poor 'South', or the 'Third World'. Inspired by the writings of Marx and Lenin, scholars within what came to be known as the *structuralist* paradigm focused on dependency, exploitation and the international division of labour which relegated the vast majority of the global population to the extremes of poverty, often with the complicities of elite groups within these societies. As Banks points out, exponents of this approach,

argued that most states were not free. Instead they were subjugated by the political, ideological and social consequences of economic forces. Imperialism generated by the vigour of free enterprise capitalism in the West and by state capitalism in the socialist bloc imposed unequal exchange of every kind upon the Third World.

(Banks, 1984: 17)

The basis of such manifest inequality was the capitalist structure of the international system which accrued benefits to some while causing, through unequal exchange relations, the impoverishment of the vast majority of others. The class system that predominated internally within capitalist societies had its parallel globally, producing centre–periphery relations that permeated every aspect of international social, economic and political life. Thus, where pluralism and its liberal associations had viewed networks of economic interdependence as a basis of increasing international cooperation founded on trade and financial interactions, neo-Marxist structuralism viewed these processes as the basis of inequality, the debt burden, violence and instability.

BOX 2.13 STRUCTURALISM

- Focus on inequalities
- Marx and Lenin inspiration
- Dependency + exploitation + division of labour
- Subjugation of states by consequences of economic forces
- Capitalism-class
- Frank, Amin and Wallerstein

Major writers in the structuralist perspective emerged from Latin America, Africa and the Middle East, primary among which were Andre Gunter Frank and Samir Amin, both of whom concentrated on dependency theory. Immanuel Wallerstein's world systems analysis provided a historicist account of the spread of capitalism from the sixteenth century to the present, providing a definitive statement on the impact of this structure on interstate, class and other social relations (Amin, 1989; Frank, 1971; Wallerstein, 1974, 1980, 1989).

Despite pluralist and structuralist attempts to move the discipline beyond the realist perspective, Kenneth Waltz's *Man, the State and War* (1959) and his later *Theory of International Politics* (1979) define a neo-realist agenda and absolutely dominated the discipline and some would argue do so to the present day. The substantive agenda that had already been set in place by theorists such as Morgenthau informed strategic studies and the Cold War struggle for power between East and West. It was this struggle which provided a reinforcing context that came to legitimize realism as a dominant approach in international relations and that located its institutional and intellectual base firmly in the United States. It was, therefore, within this context that Kenneth Waltz came to establish his dominance in the discipline. Where Morgenthau's realism concentrates on the attributes and behaviour of states within the international system, Waltz focuses on the international system itself and seeks to provide a structuralist account of its dynamics and the constraints it imposes on state behaviour. The international system is, for Waltz, anarchical and hence perpetually threatening and conflictual.

■ BOX 2.14 NEO-REALISM

- Waltz
- Focus on international system and its constraints on state behaviour
- Structural
- Importance of distribution of capabilities

What is of interest to Waltz is not the set of motives which may determine state behaviour, but the imperatives of the international system and the distribution of capabilities within it. This is hence a structural account, but it is an account that markedly differs in approach and substantive content from the neo-Marxist structuralism outlined above. It has much akin to realism and must therefore be placed within that perspective.

The three schools of thought highlighted, namely realism, pluralism and structuralism, came to be described by Banks and others as constituting the 'inter-paradigm debate' in international relations, a debate based on different images of the international system, its constitutive parts and relations between them.

■ BOX 2.15 INTER-PARADIGM DEBATE

- Banks
- Paradigm: a general pattern or world view providing the parameters of actors, events and facts for theory
- Realism/pluralism/structuralism = distinct agendas + concepts + language
- No real debate

Each 'paradigm' formed a perspective on global politics which was seen as so distinct in its research agenda, concepts and language as to be incommensurable in relation to its counterparts. Each was, in turn, represented as a general theory of international relations.

As the above survey indicates, the discipline has moved through a number of so-called debates, starting with the idealist–realist debate, moving through the methodological controversies which pitched the behaviouralists against the so-called traditionalists, and culminating by the early 1980s in the inter-paradigm debate. This phased development of the discipline has structured the teaching of theories of international relations and has formed the basic framework for the vast majority of textbooks on the subject. However, as Steve Smith has pointed out,

> the notion of an inter-paradigm debate is really misleading, since it implies that the three paradigms can confront one another over how to explain international relations. The problem is that there has been very little at all in the way of a debate between the rival positions. Rather, each has had its supporters, and these have referenced one another, been on one another's conference panels, and built incrementally on one another's work.

(Smith, 1995: 19)

Despite the construction of the discipline in terms of the inter-paradigm debate, there is agreement that realism and its neo-realist close cousin dominate the field, that other perspectives merely answer to realism and perpetuate its dominance in establishing the intellectual agenda, and that such dominance has negated the place of marginal voices, those critical of the orthodoxies which underpin international relations and discipline its discourses.

CRITICAL INTERNATIONAL RELATIONS AND THE REINSTATEMENT OF ETHICS

International relations has, as indicated in the previous section, sought to establish a distinct identity as a discipline with a remit that is distinguishable from political theory. Martin Wight's much-quoted question, 'Why is there no international theory?', (Wight, 1995) pointed to a widely held assumption that domestic political life was essentially different from international life and it was precisely this difference which called for a new language to reflect the realm of the international. The mainstay of theory in international relations, and in particular realism as a dominant school of thought, came to be framed by a Westphalian legacy which placed sovereignty, the state and the anarchical interstate system at the core of the discipline. While the pluralist challenge succeeded in widening the scope of research concerns and contributed to the development of specialized areas such as International Political Economy, Conflict Studies and Foreign Policy Analysis, it manifestly failed in questioning the theoretical underpinnings of realism and specifically its unquestioning reliance on constructs such as sovereignty, the state and even anarchy. The Marxist influence in the structuralist school did raise questions relating to the state and its relationship to the global capitalist system, analysed class relations which transcended state boundaries and determined relations of exchange at the global level, and brought into international relations a historicist, sociologically informed account of the global spread of capitalism, militarism and the state as predominant forms of human organization. The state as a unit of analysis could no longer be taken for granted, nor could relations between states. These were recognized to be historically contingent practices, situated in specific time and space relations, and steeped in relations of power.

Structuralism's Marxist underpinnings clearly impeded its development as a major school of thought in a US-dominated discipline. The questions it raised were, however, of central importance to the development of *critical perspectives* in International Relations, perspectives which concentrated on the relationship between knowledge and power, theory and practice, as well as language and the subject of our investigations. Theories of international relations and their role in the constitution of the world came under increasing scrutiny and the discipline could not longer assume an unproblematic distinction between the world and the word, between facts and the narratives we construct as 'expert' accounts of global politics. What was excluded from hegemonic accounts came to be as crucial as that which was included. Themes which were manifestly excluded, and which are to this day marginalized, included the inequalities which beset global relations, the vast riches accruing to the western countries while the rest and their populations remain trapped within a system which has historically enabled some while constraining the vast majority of others. Another theme, and one related to the above, is culture and the diversity of lifeworlds which constitute the global population. International Relations is predominantly a western discourse which draws upon western political thought, and largely assumes western institutions as legitimate and beyond question. Providing a powerful critique of the western liberal tradition, the postcolonial literature points to the material and representational legacies of the colonial era and its implications for the non-western world in the present (Grovogui, 2007). Crucially, the postcolonial literature highlights the differential experience of the postcolonial world in relation to the predominant institutions of modernity, namely the state and the international capitalist order. There is, as Stephen Chan has pointed out, an effective exclusion of other voices, other philosophies and a multiform series of other rationalities and ways of knowing the world we inhabit (Chan, 1993).

■ BOX 2.16 CRITICAL PERSPECTIVES (I)

- Relationship between knowledge and power
- Relationship between theory and practice
- Use of language
- The subject of investigation
- Taking account of previously excluded discourses = development of feminist account and re-examination of violence and war, international political economy and human rights, etc.
- Rejection of 'positivism' with its focus on:
  - testing hypotheses, especially quantatively
  - measuring and quantifying
  - recognizing only positive facts and observable phenomena

Just as cultural difference constitutes a crucial exclusion in hegemonic discourses in international relations, so too gender and sexual difference are deemed to belong to a private realm separate from the public sphere of global politics, diplomacy and war. As Jill Steans points out,

> Gender has been denied salience as an issue in International Relations because the discipline has been seen as constituted by a system of states which relate to one another in a context of anarchy . . . With respect of gender, International Relations theory grounded in realist assumptions has either been seen as neutral or assumptions about the position and status of women have not been made explicit.
>
> (Steans, 1998; 46)

Revealing such exclusion, Steans, as well as a number of other feminist scholars, has not only succeeded in deconstructing major discipline-defining texts, but has contributed to the development of a specifically feminist account of global politics, one which is rewriting subjects such as violence and war, the international political economy and the international division of labour, nationalism and identity, human rights and international law.

What distinguishes the 'critical turn' in international relations is a rejection of the positivist tenets which have dominated the discipline, as well as the assumption that international theory is somehow distinct from political and social thought.

A number of perspectives constitute this turn, and these have conventionally been labelled, if only for simplicities, in representation, as critical theory, poststructuralism or postmodernism and feminism. Each of these in turn represents a number of different perspectives primarily on issues relating to epistemology or the nature of justified belief, and ontology or modes of being in the world and the basis of subjectivity. Where critical theory owes a debt to modernity and the Enlightenment, and specifically the writings of Immanuel Kant, it also looks to Marxist social theory as well as to the Frankfurt School of the 1920s and 1930s, not only to provide a critique of positivism, but to develop a social theory based on emancipatory politics and human freedom.

Poststructuralism, on the other hand, looks to philosophers such as Nietzsche and Heidegger and more recent French philosophers such as Foucault and Derrida to provide a critique of Enlightenment thought and its reifications of instrumental reason and universalist accounts of truth. Both critical theory and poststructuralism have variously influenced feminist thought. Above providing a post-positivist critique of international relations and its dominant discourses, these three approaches scrutinize the discipline itself, the relations of power which determine its exclusions, and the ways in which theories are deeply implicated in the construction of naturalized concepts such as sovereignty, anarchy or security. Rather than considering these as given and beyond question, critical and poststructuralist approaches view all three as discursively constructed sociopolitical practices which have their own contingency in time and place. Where neorealist orthodoxy views anarchy, for example, as a given condition of the international system, a critical account views anarchy as constructed and situated within specific historical conditions (Wendt, 1992).

BOX 2.17 CRITICAL PERSPECTIVES (II)

- Critical theory
- Poststructuralism or postmodernism
- Feminism
- Postcolonialism

Issues as to:

- Nature of discipline
- Relations of power
- Role of theory in formulation of concepts
- Constitutive role of language

The postpositivist critique of the discipline has, paradoxically, brought the agenda of international relations back to reflections on ethics, on questions of rights, and on the nature of political community and the international public sphere. Normative international relations is conventionally framed by the 'cosmopolitan–communitarian' divide which, respectively, argues for a conception of rights and obligations situated in our common humanity as opposed to being constituted by the individual's membership of a specific cultural community. Where the first perspective, cosmopolitanism, argues for a single moral order linking humanity across the boundaries of culture and state, the second, communitarianism, confers moral standing to the state and the cultural community of which the individual is part.

BOX 2.18 COSMOPOLITAN–COMMUNITARIAN DIVIDE

- *Cosmopolitan*: conception of human rights and obligations situated in common humanity
- *Communitarian*: conception of rights and obligations constituted by membership of a *specific* community

There are significant substantive differences between contemporary interests in ethics and international relations and the original concerns which established the discipline. What links them is a recognition that international relations cannot be considered as separate and distinct from its subject matter, that the world and the words we construct of the world are intimately related, and this mutual constitution must, ultimately, confer a certain responsibility and demand a certain reflexivity on how we use the word and concept 'international'.

CONCLUSION

The discipline of international relations has, as has been discussed above, moved through a number of defining theoretical perspectives as successive scholars have sought to make sense of the apparently simple word 'international'. The diversity of approaches has been not so much a reflection of changes in the substance of global politics, as a series of contentions relating to more philosophical questions on how we know what we know, whether ethical issues have a role in theories of international relations, and how theory relates to the realm of practice. The 'international' as such comes to encompass our conceptions of the limits of political thought and practice, limits that have historically been identified with the sovereign state, but now in a globalised world, have shifted beyond the state, so that the concept of sovereignty itself might be conceived to apply to a location somehow beyond the state (Walker, 1993; Hardt and Negri, 2000). Such issues, concerned as they are with knowledge and being, challenge the orthodoxy in international relations and the dominance of the positivistic underpinning of neorealism, neoliberalism, and their adjuncts.

Such questions did not emerge with the discipline, but are the concern of a deeply rooted classical tradition which has informed our ideas on the nature of politics, democratic practice, the ethics of interstate relations and the spatial and temporal domain of what constitutes international politics. The realm of knowledge is deeply implicated in the construction of the political subject and the subject of politics. It is precisely this recognition which renders the discipline of international relations itself a contested site, only certain with its own categorizing practices, its own reductions of the complexity of human interactions and the societies which contain them.

REFERENCES

Amin, S., *Eurocentrism* (London, Zed Books, 1989)

Banks, M., ed., *Conflict in World Society* (Brighton, Wheatsheaf, 1984)

Brown, Chris, *Understanding International Relations* (London, Macmillan, 1977)

Bull, Hedley, *The Anarchical Society* (Basingstoke, Macmillan, 1977)

Burchill, Scott, 'Introduction', in Burchill, Scott and Linklater, Andrew *et al.*, *Theories of International Relations* (London, Macmillan, 1996)

Burton, John, *Systems, States, Diplomacy and Rules* (Cambridge, Cambridge University Press, 1968)

—— , *World Society* (Cambridge, Cambridge University Press, 1972)

—— , 'The Role of Authorities in World Society', *Millennium*, March, vol. 8 (1979), 73–9

Carr, E.H., *Twenty Years' Crisis*, (New York, Harper and Row, 1964 [1939])

Chan, S., 'Cultural and Linguistic Reductionism and a New Historical Sociology of International Relations', *Millennium*, vol. 22, no. 3 (1993)

Frank, A.G., *Capitalism and Under Development in Latin America*, (Harmondsworth, Penguin, 1971)

Frost, Mervyn, *Ethics in International Relations* (Cambridge, Cambridge University Press, 1996)

Giddens, Anthony, *The Constitution of Society* (Cambridge, Polity Press, 1984)

Grovogui, S.N. 'Postcolonialism', in Dunne, T., Kurki, M. and Smith, S., eds, *International Relations Theories*, (Oxford, Oxford University Press, 2007)

Hardt, M., and Negri, A., *Empire*, (Cambridge, MA, Harvard University Press, 2000)

Keohane, Robert and Nye, Joseph, eds, *Transnational Relations and World Politics* (Cambridge, MA, Harvard University Press, 1971)

—— , *Power and Interdependence* (Boston, Little, Brown and Co., 1977)

Morgenthau, Hans, *Politics among Nations: The Struggle for Power and Peace* (New York, Alfred A. Knopf, 5th edn, 1978 [1948])

Reiss, Hans, ed., *Kant: Political Writings*, (Cambridge, Cambridge University Press, 1991)

Smith, S., 'The Self-images of a Discipline: A Genealogy of International Relations Theory', in Smith, S. and Booth, K., eds, *International Relations Theory Today* (Cambridge, Polity Press, 1995)

Steans, Jill, *Gender and International Relations* (Cambridge, Polity Press, 1998)

Walker, R.B.J., *Inside/Outside: International Relations as Political Theory*, (Cambridge, Cambridge University Press, 1993)

Wallerstein, I., *The Modern World System*, vols 1–3 (New York, Academic Press, 1974, 1980, 1989)

Waltz, K., *Man, the State and War: A Theoretical Analysis*, (New York, Columbia University Press, 1959)

——, *Theory of International Politics* (Reading, MA, Addison-Wesley, 1979)

Wendt, Alexander, *Social Theory of International Politics* (Cambridge, Cambridge University Press, 1999)

——, 'Anarchy Is What States Make of it: Social Construction of Power Politics', *International Organisation*, vol. 46, no. 2 (1992)

Wight, M., 'Why Is There No International Theory', in Der Derian, J., ed., *International Theory: Critical Investigations* (Basingstoke, Macmillan, 1995)

▌FURTHER READING

Booth, K. and Smith, S. (eds), *International Relations Theory Today* (Cambridge: Polity Press, 1994) stretches students but has an excellent introductory chapter and a comprehensive review of the main theories.

Brown, Chris *Understanding International Relations* (London: Macmillan, 1997) provides a clear and accessible overview, and relates theory to events.

Carlsnaes, Walter, Risse, Thomas and Simmons, Beth (eds), *Handbook of International Relations* (London: Sage, 2002).

Dunne, Tim, Kurki, Milja and Smith, Steve (eds), *International Theories: Discipline and Diversity* (Oxford: Oxford University Press, 2007).

Knutsen, Torbjorn L. *A History of International Relations Theory* (Manchester, Manchester University Press, 1992)

Tickner, Arlene and Waever, Ole (eds), *The World of International Relations Scholarship: Geocultural Epistemologies* (London: Routledge, 2007).

CHAPTER 3

On Sovereignty

Gabriella Slomp

There is widespread agreement that sovereignty is a so-called master noun of international relations. However, there remains disagreement concerning the meaning, role and significance of sovereignty in the twenty-first century.

State sovereignty can be invoked to defend a people's right to establish an identity and to protect autonomy and self-determination against external interference. On the other hand, state sovereignty can equally be responsible for enabling bad governments to commit domestic atrocities, and even genocide, with impunity.

Phenomena such as liberation movements, nationalism and humanitarian intervention are also related to issues of sovereignty and indirectly paint a picture of modern sovereignty. For example, interventions in Iraq (1991) and Somalia (1993) reveal a general mistrust that state sovereignty does enough to protect state citizens; international failure to later intervene in conflicts in Rwanda and Bosnia in the mid-1990s suggests a revival of the idea of inviolable state sovereignty (perhaps as a consequence of the lack of success of previous interventions); international commitments in Kosovo and East Timor in 1999 expose another crisis of the sovereignty idea, probably following guilt feelings for not intervening in Rwanda, and so forth. The contemporary relevance of sovereignty cannot be underestimated, and consequently to understand the meaning of sovereignty enhances any understanding of international affairs. This chapter will provide an explanation of sovereignty, and will analyse the implications of state sovereignty on international relations. First, the works of Jean Bodin and Thomas Hobbes will be used to explain the definition and purpose of sovereignty. Second, there will be a consideration of eighteenth-, nineteenth- and twentieth-century responses to classical theories of sovereignty, paying particular attention to the views of Immanuel Kant.

Third, sovereignty will be considered in terms of three adjective-pairs – external and internal, legal and political, hard and porous.

TOWARDS A DEFINITION

According to Aristotle, the definition of any object – be it a knife, a flute, or the state – requires a consideration of the object's function or purpose. A blade with a handle may look like a knife, but cannot be defined as such if it is made of sugar and water because it would not be able to fulfil any of the basic functions of being a knife. Bearing in mind Aristotle's advice, any definition of sovereignty must first establish when and for what purpose sovereignty entered the world of politics and penetrated the political discourse. The philosophical issue of what came first, the egg (the concept of sovereignty) or the chicken (the reality of the sovereign state) is second to understanding if there was ever a time when there was no egg and no sign of a chicken.

On the origins of sovereignty there are, as with almost everything in International Relations, different schools of thought. Primordialists believe that the concept of sovereignty always existed with precursors in ancient writers such as Aristotle, Polybius and Dionysius of Halicarnassus. Dionysius is noted by Jean Bodin for having 'touched on all the principal points of sovereignty' (Bodin [1576] 1992: 47). The concept of sovereignty, though not the word itself, is also found in the writings of Ulpian, Augustine, Dante, Ockham, Marsilius and Machiavelli. Modernists, however, believe that sovereignty is a modern phenomenon linked to the birth and growth of the nation state in the seventeenth century and was first theorized by Jean Bodin and Thomas Hobbes.

Taking either a primordialist or modernist perspective, there can be no argument that the formulation of state sovereignty offered by Bodin and Hobbes formed the foundations of the theory and practice of sovereignty that was endorsed during the Westphalian period. Why did Jean Bodin devote four chapters of *Six livres de la Republique* to the definition and discussion of sovereignty? Why did Thomas Hobbes provide detailed explanations of the need for state sovereignty throughout his political writings? A brief look at the historical circumstances in which Bodin and Hobbes were writing can help to explain their concern with this issue and shed light on the notion of sovereignty that they developed.

PURPOSE AND MEANING OF STATE SOVEREIGNTY ACCORDING TO JEAN BODIN

Jean Bodin (1530–1596) witnessed the bloody religious wars that affected Europe in the sixteenth century and observed how the authority of monarchs was constantly challenged on internal and external fronts. In particular, being a Frenchman, Bodin was concerned with the predicament of France that had suffered a four decades long civil war as a consequence of the Reformation. Bodin published *Six livres de la Republique* in 1576, four years after the massacre of Huguenots, with the intention of providing a theoretical explanation as to why the power of the king was the only way to promote the peace and unity of the state. Bodin was intellectually close to a group of political thinkers known as Politiques who were similarly concerned by the implications of religious intolerance and eager to defend French identity regardless of religious disagreement. Historians such as George Sabine see the Politiques as among the first in the sixteenth century to envisage the possibility of tolerating several religions within a single state. Sabine remarks that the Politiques, although mostly Catholic themselves, were above all nationalists and advocated holding together French nationality even though unity of religion had been lost. Bodin shared the concerns of the Politiques and pointed out that regardless of differences in religion and in customs, the unity of a political community is guaranteed by the acknowledgement of a common sovereign. State sovereignty was seen by Bodin as a vehicle for internal cohesion, order and peace and such qualities, in turn, were needed for a so-called just commonwealth.

From George Sabine to Preston King, and from M.J. Tooley to Julian Franklin, generations of interpreters have argued that Bodin's theory of sovereignty contains many ambiguities and even contradictions. However, it is worth considering Bodin's definitions that: 'Sovereignty is the absolute and perpetual power of a commonwealth' (Bodin [1576] 1992: 1). Bodin goes on to distinguish between the attributes and the characteristics of the sovereign power. The primary attribute of Bodinian sovereignty is the power to give laws 'without the consent of any other, whether greater, equal, or below him' (Bodin [1576] 1992: 56). Bodin explains that the other attributes of sovereignty – the power to declare war and to make peace, the power to appoint magistrates and officers, the power to levy taxes and so on – are all consequences of the position of the sovereign as legal head of state (Bodin [1576] 1992: 48).

Additionally, in order to enable the sovereign power to perform all the above tasks, Bodin ascribes to the sovereign power a long list of characteristics. First, the sovereign power is described as absolute in the Latin sense of the word, *ab legibus solutus* (or unbound by the law). Bodin explains that sovereignty cannot be restricted by law because the sovereign is the source of the law:

> [A] king cannot be subject to the laws . . . Thus at the end of edicts and ordinances we see the words, 'for such is our pleasure' which serve to make it understood that the laws of a sovereign prince, even if founded on good and strong reasons, depend solely on his own free will.
>
> (Bodin [1576] 1992: 12–13)

Second, sovereignty is unconditional: 'sovereignty given to a prince subject to obligations and conditions is properly not sovereignty or absolute power' (Bodin [1576] 1992: 8). Third, sovereignty is unaccountable just as the king is not accountable to his subjects. However, Bodin does point out that God and natural law impose limits on the power of the sovereign, and hence sovereign power is not arbitrary. Accountability to God prevents rulers from forgetting about their mission to promote the well-being of the commonwealth. Fourth, sovereignty is indivisible. Although Bodin preferred monarchy to other forms of government, he believed that sovereignty can lie in a person or an assembly. For Bodin, the important point is that sovereignty cannot be divided between different agencies but must reside in one single place, whether it be king, assembly, or populace. Finally, Bodinian sovereignty is humanly unlimited and irrevocable or perpetual: 'Sovereignty is not limited either in power, or in function, or in length of time', (Bodin [1576] 1992: 3) and 'the law is nothing but the command of a sovereign making use of his power' (Bodin [1576] 1992: 38). Hence any limits imposed on the power to command cannot be but extra-legal. Bodin concludes that 'he is absolutely sovereign who recognizes nothing, after God, that is greater than himself' (Bodin [1576] 1992: 4).

BOX 3.1 BODINIAN SOVEREIGNTY

- Absolute
- Unconditional
- Indivisible
- Unlimited
- Unaccountable
- Irrevocable

Bodin defined sovereignty as the absolute, unconditional, indivisible, unlimited, unaccountable and irrevocable power to make, interpret and execute the law. Bodin argued that all the sovereign's other powers (to make peace, to wage war, to tax, to make coins and so on) were derived from this single law-making power. He believed that only such a formidable and supreme power would be able to protect the commonwealth from internal and external enemies and to provide order and peace. By formulating the first theory of state sovereignty of the modern age, Bodin revealed a great historical sensitivity to the growing importance of the nation state.

PURPOSE AND MEANING OF STATE SOVEREIGNTY ACCORDING TO THOMAS HOBBES

Just as Bodin had first-hand experience of the civil war in France, so Thomas Hobbes (1588–1679) witnessed the English civil war. Distraught by what he saw and at times fearing for his own life, Hobbes realized that without order or peace there is little much else that can function in a society. Hobbes understood that in a civil war as much as in a state of nature, there is:

[N]o place for Industry; because the fruit thereof is uncertain: and consequently no Culture of the Earth; no Navigation . . . no commodious Building . . . no account of Time; no Arts; no letters; no Society; and which is worst of all, continuall feare, and danger of violent death; and the life of man, solitary, poore, nasty, brutish, and short.
(Hobbes [1651] 1991: 89)

Bodin had observed that 'wrong opinion leads subjects to revolt from the obedience they owe their sovereign prince' (Bodin [1576] 1992: 19) and similarly Hobbes blames ignorance about the function of the sovereign power as the main cause of civil disobedience and civil strife. In *Behemoth*, Hobbes explains that the English Civil War occurred because people had false beliefs and wrong opinions about their political obligations. Hobbes claims that bad teachers, bad priests and bad parliamentarians had taken advantage of the people's lack of understanding of the purpose of the sovereign state. In *Leviathan*, Hobbes writes: 'The End of the institution of Sovereignty [is] the peace of the subjects within themselves, and their defence against a common Enemy' (Hobbes [1651] 1991: 150). Hobbes explains that sovereign power can be acquired by force, or created by institution but that the rights and consequences and ends of sovereignty are the same in both cases. Hobbes echoes Bodin and argues in favour of absolute, unlimited, irrevocable, humanly unaccountable, inalienable and indivisible sovereignty. For the sake of security and peace, Hobbes recommends that the 'Sovereign Power . . . is as great, as possibly men can be imagined to make it' (Hobbes [1651] 1991: 144). Hobbes concedes that such a power could be dangerous but never tires to highlight its advantages in terms of security and protection:

> And though of so unlimited a Power, men may fancy many evill consequences, yet the consequences of the want of it, which is perpetuall warre of every man against his neighbour, are much worse
>
> (Hobbes [1651] 1991: 144–5)

As Bodin condemned resistance and claimed that 'it is not licit for a subject to contravene his prince's laws on the pretext of honesty and justice' (Bodin [1571] 1992: 33), so Hobbes argues that a citizen only has the right to resist if the sovereign endangers his life (Hobbes [1651] 1991: 151). But whereas Bodin is happy to list the various characteristics of the sovereign power without offering a supporting argument, Hobbes tries to justify in some detail each and every one of those characteristics. For example, Hobbes attempts to offer a rational explanation for ascribing unlimited power to the sovereign. He points out that, by nature, we have the right to use all available means for self-defence. In spite of this right, in a state of nature or during a civil war, our life is in constant danger. We enter the political state with a view to entrusting the sovereign with our defence and security. As the end of the sovereign power is the protection of our life and the preservation of peace, it would be irrational to impose restrictions on the sovereign as this would limit its ability to protect our survival. Hence, sovereign power must be unrestricted and from a Hobbesian perspective, there is no escape from unlimited sovereign power: 'And whosover thinking Soverign Power too great, will seek to make it lesse; must subject himselfe, to the Power, that can limit it; that is to say, to a greater' (Hobbes [1651] 1991: 145).

In summation, Hobbes ascribes to sovereign power all the attributes and characteristics listed by Bodin. Moreover, using a more forceful and unambiguous argument than Bodin, Hobbes spells out that the sovereign provides protection in exchange of obedience and that therefore absolute protection requires absolute obedience to an absolute sovereign power.

SOVEREIGNTY AND THE PROTECTION/OBEDIENCE FUNCTION

Hobbes and Bodin both agree that the purpose or function of state sovereignty is to provide protection for citizens or subjects in exchange for obedience. For the sake of protection from internal and external enemies, both Bodin and Hobbes ascribe absolute, indivisible, unlimited, inalienable, unaccountable, irrevocable power to the sovereign, be it located in a man (monarchy), in an assembly (aristocracy) or in the populace (democracy). The protection/obedience principle forms the foundation of the Bodinian and Hobbesian concept of the sovereign state. Indeed, for Hobbes, a state that cannot provide protection cannot command obedience and hence is not a state at all. Furthermore, regardless of any differences in size, wealth or power, all sovereign states rely on the protection/obedience principle as the formative identifier of statehood.

From Hobbes to the modern era, the protection/obedience principle has remained the main function of the sovereign state by political thinkers and philosophers from many different ideological backgrounds. Realist writer Hans Morgenthau, as well as philosophers linked with liberalism and cosmopolitanism such as Immanuel Kant have all embraced the protection/obedience principle of state sovereignty. Marxists such as Antonio Gramsci and Nationalists such as Carl Schmitt have also endorsed the Hobbesian principle. Indeed, Carl Schmitt famously stated in *The Concept of the Political* that: 'The "*protego ergo obligo*" is the "*cogito ergo sum*" of the state' (Schmitt [1927] 1996: 52). In other words, Schmitt claims that as much as the Cartesian dictum 'I think, therefore I am', captures the identity of the individual, so the motto 'I protect, hence I oblige' captures the essence of the sovereign state.

▮ BOX 3.2 PROTECTION AND OBEDIENCE

Hobbes and Bodin both argue that the state's protection requires the citizen's obedience.

- Sovereignty provides the basis of the modern legal view that all states have equal rights in international relations, or 'sovereign equality'
- The duty of the state to protect its citizens is shared by a wide range of contemporary political ideologies of left and right

▮ IMMANUEL KANT ON SOVEREIGNTY

From the seventeenth century onwards there exist two main debates related to the Bodinian–Hobbesian concept of sovereignty. Philosophers and political theorists such as Benedict Spinoza, John Locke and J.S. Mill engaged with the problem of what the state ought to provide domestically in exchange of obedience, while lawyers and jurists such as Grotius, the Salamanca School, Christian Wolff and Emeric de Vattel addressed the issue of whether and how an international system of sovereign states could enable each state to protect its own citizens (Brown 2002: 30–3).

An outstanding contributor to both debates was Immanuel Kant (1724–1804). If Hobbes were placed at one end of the ideological spectrum, Kant would occupy the other, and hence Kant's take on sovereignty is particularly relevant. Indeed, while

Hobbes is associated with absolutism and realism, Kant is regarded as one of the founding fathers of liberalism and of cosmopolitanism.

First, as argued by Richard Tuck and Howard Williams, Kant attempted to combine the Hobbesian notion of sovereignty with a theory of limited constitutional government. In an essay entitled *On the Common Saying: 'This May be True in Theory, but it does not Apply in Practice'* Kant challenges Hobbes's view that the state can protect only the life of its citizens. Disagreeing with Hobbes, Kant contends that a sovereign state ought to protect basic human rights such as freedom, equality and independence of the individual (Kant 1991: 74). Additionally, Kant also challenges the Hobbesian claim that a state operating in an international system characterized by anarchy (derived from the Greek, lack of *arche*, or rule) can adequately protect its citizens.

For Hobbes, domestic politics and international politics are independent spheres. Hobbes saw his own political theory as a solution to civil war and to the problem of domestic political disorder. He did not, however, believe that there was a solution to potential international anarchy. Indeed, in *Leviathan*, Hobbes promises eternal peace domestically but does not envisage the end of inter-state wars. Against Hobbes, Kant insists that the international and domestic political orders are, in fact, closely linked. It follows that the stability and justice of one is dependent on the stability and justice of the other. In his 1784 essay *Idea for Universal History with a Cosmopolitan Purpose* Kant states that 'the problem of establishing a perfect civil constitution is subordinate to the problem of a law-governed external relationship with other states, and cannot be solved unless the other is also solved' (Kant 1991: 52).

While Kant accepts the Hobbesian principle that the function of the sovereign state is to provide protection in exchange for obedience, he expands the list of rights that the state is supposed to protect and argues that only a federation of republican states, and not a system of totally independent states, can offer true protection, security and perpetual peace. Of course, doubts have been raised about Kant's view that Hobbesian sovereignty is compatible with liberal principles and international institutions. Indeed many scholars have maintained that the doctrine of state sovereignty is inimical to the very notion of international law. In the realist camp, Hans Morgenthau has argued that 'sovereignty is consistent only with a weak, non-interventionalist international legal order' (Morgenthau 1950: 246). At the other end of the spectrum, David Held has pointed out that the greatest obstacle to the development of international democracy is the idea that states are sovereign and that international institutions may limit their sovereignty.

BOX 3.3 IMMANUEL KANT

- Kant's writing greatly enlarges the range of citizen's rights that the sovereign state should protect
- Kant creates a strong connection between order and stability as practised internally and order and stability at the international level
- For some modern authors sovereignty remains the basis of international order, for others it is an obstacle to international order

THE LOCATION OF SOVEREIGNTY

The notion of sovereignty developed by Bodin and Hobbes is often associated with the absolutist monarchies that dominated Europe in the seventeenth and eighteenth centuries, but during this time questions were also raised regarding whether or not sovereignty must lie in a single body, as Hobbes and Bodin claimed, or whether it could be divided. During the eighteenth and nineteenth centuries, the disagreement developed into a discussion of whether sovereignty was best located in a king, an assembly or the whole people. By the twentieth century, however, the debate shifted towards the question of whether it was possible or desirable for one such body to exist at all. Many writers pointed out that the belief that sovereignty lies in a single place or body was being increasingly undermined by the experience of pluralist societies. Simultaneously, a growing number of thinkers from different ideological perspectives claimed that the diffusion and fragmentation of power in pluralistic societies is superficial and that systems of checks and balances only hide the concentration of power within liberal democracies.

From Carl Schmitt to Giorgio Agamben, it has been argued that in an emergency or the case of exceptional danger – from either inside or outside the state in the form of terrorism or any other lethal threat – the location of supreme sovereign power becomes unambiguous. These writers believe that in any state – liberal or totalitarian – we can find the true location of sovereign power by looking at the will responsible for the final decision-making. The opening sentence of Carl Schmitt's study of the concept of sovereignty is very well-known: 'Sovereign is he who decides on the exception' (Schmitt [1922] 1985: 5)

INTERNAL AND EXTERNAL SOVEREIGNTY

It is often said that one of the characteristics of modernity was the creation of great dichotomies such as nature vs. artifice, private vs. public, reason vs. passion and so on. It is therefore not surprising that sovereignty – regarded by many as a quintessentially modern concept – is predicated on a dichotomous inside/outside principle.

Internal sovereignty is the supreme power that the state has over its own citizens within its own borders or the supreme decision-making and enforcement authority in a specific territory and towards a population. Conversely, external sovereignty embodies the principle of self-determination and implies that in international relations each state is in a position of independence vis-à-vis all other states. External sovereignty refers to and assumes the absence of a supreme international authority. In a nutshell, 'the doctrine of sovereignty implies a double claim; autonomy in foreign policy and exclusive competence in internal affairs' (Evans and Newnham 1998: 504).

Internal and external sovereignty may not be mentioned specifically in classical international relations texts, but the concepts exist nonetheless. Both Bodin and Hobbes suggest that domestic and external sovereignty, although distinct, stand and fall together – a view that can also be found in earlier writers such as Machiavelli. Bodin explains that internal disorder fosters external attacks. Hobbes too stresses that a state afflicted by internal discord is vulnerable to attacks from external enemies;

similarly, when the external sovereignty of a state is in crisis, its domestic sovereignty could also be challenged because the citizens may want to submit to a stronger state that is more capable of protecting them from external enemies.

Internal sovereignty is said to go hand in hand with domestic hierarchy and vertical order, whereas external sovereignty implies equality and the possibility of horizontal disorder. Hobbes explains that equality among agents (be they 'natural men' or 'artificial men', i.e. states) brings about confrontation, conflict and ultimately war because every agent tries to dominate every other agent. In the political state the sovereign power introduces inequality between the rulers and the ruled and the resulting hierarchy ensures order and peace (Hobbes [1651] 1991: 238). Hobbes illustrates this inequality with the following image:

> As in the presence of the Master, the Servants are Equall, and without any honour at all, so are the Subjects, in the presence of the Soveraign. And though they shine some more, some less, when they are out of his sight; yet in his presence, they shine no more than the Starres in presence of the Sun.
>
> (Hobbes [1651] 1991: 128)

In international relations, however, all agents remain in a state of equality and the result is a situation of potential horizontal disorder or anarchy. Hobbes famously describes international relations thus:

> But though there had never been any time, wherein particular men were in a condition of warre one against another; yet in all times, Kings, and Persons of Soveraigne authority, because of their Independency, are in continuall jealousies, and in the state and posture of Gladiators; having their weapons pointing, and their eyes fixed on one another; that is, their Forts, Garrisons, and Guns upon the Frontiers of their Kingdomes; and continuall Spyes upon their neighbours; which is a posture of War.
>
> (Hobbes [1651] 1991: 90)

In previous centuries attention was predominantly focused on internal sovereignty, but during the twentieth century external sovereignty has occupied central stage. Indeed, in contemporary times, issues related to the external sovereignty of states raise not just very heated debates among scholars but also deep disagreements within the international community. The external sovereignty of states is fiercely defended as the right of peoples to define their own identity and to shape their own future free from external interference. External sovereignty, however, can be criticized on the grounds that it can be seriously abused. For example, events in Kosovo and Rwanda raised serious questions concerning whether or not there exists a moral duty to question the external sovereignty of states when atrocities are committed within their borders.

The distinction between external and internal sovereignty aims at attracting attention to the issues of self-determination and to the independence of states. The concept of external sovereignty raises high feelings both from the supporters of nationalism and from the supporters of universal human rights and of humanitarian intervention.

■ BOX 3.4 THE LOCATION OF SOVEREIGNTY

- Sovereignty may be vested in a monarchy, in an elected government or the whole people (popular sovereignty)
- Sovereignty has both internal and external dimensions

■ LEGAL AND POLITICAL SOVEREIGNTY

In addition to the internal/external dichotomy, there exists another distinction between legal and political sovereignty. Originally articulated by the nineteenth-century thinker A.V. Dicey there remains much disagreement concerning the meaning of legal and political sovereignty and their relationship.

Legal or *de jure* sovereignty is said to differ from political or *de facto* sovereignty as much as the concept of authority differs from the concept of power. Legal sovereignty is based on the *right* to command, political sovereignty instead is based on the *power* to ensure compliance. The former has much to do with the law; the latter has to do with force. In textbooks, legal sovereignty is sometimes exemplified (Heywood 1994: 90) with reference to Bodin. In particular, interpreters draw attention to the fact that Bodin was very keen to offer an account of sovereignty in terms of legal authority and to oppose the Machiavellian argument that princes are not bound by promises in their international dealings. Conversely, political sovereignty is sometime elucidated (Heywood 1994: 91) by reference to Hobbes and his view that the sovereign has the monopoly of coercive power. Hobbes's remark that 'there is scarce a common-wealth in the world, whose beginnings can in conscience be justified' (Hobbes [1651] 1991: 486) is often cited to support the claim that he believed that sovereignty is about force.

No careful reader of Hobbes or Bodin, however, could deny that both their writings reference both legal and political sovereignty and that the difference between the two writers is mainly one of emphasis. Indeed Hobbes, like Bodin, believed that sovereignty is not just about power and force but also about authority, legality, and legitimacy. However Bodin, like Hobbes, pointed out that the origin and foundations of commonwealths lie in force and violence. Most thinkers agree that neither political nor legal sovereignty constitute a viable form of sovereignty on their own. As observed by Antonio Gramsci, political sovereignty based entirely on the monopoly of coercive power is not sufficient ground for a regime to last. This is why, for example, both Hitler and Mussolini were keen to claim the legality and legitimacy of their regimes. Conversely, legal sovereignty without the ability to enforce a command 'will carry only moral weight, as the peoples of the Baltic States – Latvia, Estonia and Lithuania – recognized between their invasion by the Soviet Union in 1940 and their eventual achievement of independence in 1991' (Heywood 1994: 92). Indeed, the political/legal distinction does not describe two different types of sovereignty but two facets of the same phenomenon, and as such the value of the political/legal distinction is mainly heuristic and analytical in that it highlights the multi-layered nature of the concept of sovereignty.

HARD SOVEREIGNTY VERSUS POROUS SOVEREIGNTY

There is also a distinction to be made between porous and hard sovereignty, with the twenty-first century experiencing a very different type of sovereignty to that described by Bodin and Hobbes. Globalization theory suggests that the boundaries of states are permeable, and that the line of demarcation between the internal and external spheres of a state's existence has also become blurred. Consequently, there exists the argument that the notion of sovereignty will eventually be abandoned as a result of integrative developments such as the EU. For many scholars, the idea of state sovereignty is already anachronistic as a result of developments in human rights regimes, in international norms and in international law. Twenty-first-century economic interdependence and the power of multinationals also feed into the discussion that state sovereignty is becoming a nostalgic memory. All such claims to the erosion of sovereignty are to some extent well grounded. What is less convincing is the view that there once existed a time when sovereignty was truly impenetrable. Consider, as an example, the following remark by Bodin:

> For if we say that to have absolute power is not to be subject to any law at all, no prince of this world will be sovereign, since every earthly prince is subject to the laws of God and of nature and *to various human laws that are common to all peoples [lex omnium gentium communis]*
>
> (Bodin [1576] 1992: 10, emphasis added)

Bodin repeatedly supports the idea that human laws common to all peoples (*jus gentium*) served to limit and restrain sovereigns in international affairs. Moreover, the contention that the twenty-first century is experiencing the demise of sovereignty is exaggerated:

> The continued relevance of the idea of sovereignty in international affairs is testified by the fact that at the political level it remains the primary organizing principle of world politics. Since sovereignty implies constitutional independence from other states, a decentralized international system will always have recourse to some such ideas.
>
> (Evans and Newnham 1998: 505)

BOX 3.5 SOVEREIGNTY IN REVIEW

- Sovereignty has both political and legal dimensions
- The worst dictatorships will seek a legal justification
- Claims that sovereignty is being eroded or penetrated are associated with globalization and interdependence
- Claims to statehood, and the emergence of over twenty new members of the United Nations since 1990 suggest that sovereign statehood remains a powerful goal for those who do not already possess it

CONCLUSION

Bodin and Hobbes first developed the principle of state sovereignty as a result of their experiences of war and their desire to protect states from religious interference, as well as interference from the emperor and from other potential external and internal enemies. A superficial reading of Bodin and Hobbes suggests that a state system predicated on their notion of unlimited, indivisible, and absolute sovereignty would imply that sovereign states are the ultimate judges in their own cases, have an absolute right to go to war as they please and can treat their own citizens as they want. In this respect historians and International Relations scholars such as Krasner (1999) and Brown (2002) have pointed out that states were never able to act in such a way. A more careful reading of Bodin and Hobbes suggests that their notion of state sovereignty is much subtler than is generally acknowledged. Neither Bodin nor Hobbes identified sovereign power with arbitrary power – for both Bodin and Hobbes the function of state sovereignty (and its justification) was the protection of the well-being of the commonwealth. This important insight needs to be revisited not only for a fairer assessment of Bodin and Hobbes but, more importantly, because it can enrich current debates on sovereignty and humanitarian intervention.

In contemporary times there seems to be widespread consensus among scholars that a commitment to human rights conflicts with the principles of state sovereignty. Indeed it is often pointed out that in order to protect human rights one has sometimes to violate state sovereignty; and vice versa, that the respect of the state for sovereignty may sometimes imply the impossibility of preventing domestic injustice. However, the founding fathers of the concept of sovereignty maintained a very different approach. Although the notion of human rights (as we currently understand it) was foreign to Bodin and Hobbes, they both maintained that state sovereignty had one specific function: the protection of citizens. In other words, both Hobbes and Bodin defended state sovereignty not for its own sake but as a vehicle to protect the life of people, and a state that commits atrocities against its own citizens, arguably, does not deserve its own sovereignty.

REFERENCES

Agamben, Giorgio (2005) *State of Exception*, Chicago, IL: University of Chicago Press.
Bodin, J. (1992) *On Sovereignty*, edited and translated by J. Franklin, Cambridge: Cambridge University Press.
Brace, L. and Hoffman, J. (1997) *Reclaiming Sovereignty*, London: Pinter.
Brown, C. (2002) *Sovereignty, Rights and Justice: International Political Theory Today*, Cambridge: Polity.
Dicey, A. V. (1885) Introduction to the Study of the Law of the Constitution.
Evans, G. and Newnham, J. (1998) *The Penguin Dictionary of International Relations*, London: Penguin Books.
Held, David (1995) *Democracy and the Global Order*, Cambridge: Polity Press.

Heywood, A. (1994) *Political Ideas and Concepts: An Introduction*, Houndmills: Macmillan.

Hobbes, T. (1991) *Leviathan*, Cambridge: Cambridge University Press.

Kant, I. (1991) *Kant's Political Writings*, edited by H. Reiss, Cambridge: Cambridge University Press.

Krasner, S.D. (1999) *Sovereignty: Organised Hypocrisy*, Princeton: Princeton University Press.

Morgenthau, H.J. (1950) *Politics among Nations: The Struggle for Power and Peace*, 2nd edn, New York: Alfred A. Knopf.

Schmitt, C. (1996) *The Concept of the Political*, Chicago: University of Chicago Press.

Schmitt, C. (1985) *Political Theology: Four Chapters on the Concept of Sovereignty*, Cambridge: MIT Press.

Weber, C. (1995) *Simulating Sovereignty: Intervention, the State and Symbolic Exchange*, Cambridge: Cambridge University Press.

Walker, N. (ed.) (2003) *Sovereignty in Transition*, Oxford: Hart.

Walker, R.B.J. (1993) *Inside/Outside: International Relations as Political Theory*, Cambridge: Cambridge University Press.

USEFUL WEBSITES

For Bodin see: http://www.arts.yorku.ca/politics/comninel/courses/3020pdf/six_books. pdf

For Hobbes' *Leviathan* see: http://www.uoregon.edu/~rbear/hobbes/leviathan.html

CHAPTER 4

Nations and States

Archie Simpson

The issue of nationality and citizenship is a complex topic. A seemingly simple question about nationality might lead to a number of different perspectives and ideas on the issue. If you come from the British Isles it might be easy to assume that you are British, but many people would consider themselves English, Scottish, Irish or Welsh before being British. Other British citizens might classify themselves as being a Londoner, a Glaswegian or coming from Yorkshire or Cornwall. Similarly, an American might consider themselves as coming from a particular Federal state like Texas, California or Pennsylvania, or describe themselves as an African-American or Irish-American. Defining nationality relates to the idea of political identity, and to the idea of belonging to a particular nation and to a particular state.

In this chapter, the concepts of 'nation' and 'state' are outlined alongside a number of associated concepts such as self-determination, nationalism, sovereignty and nation-states. These are core concepts in international relations partly because they establish the main units of study in the discipline but also because they are usually central to many of the theories, issues and themes that are being studied. Disputes about nationality, self-determination and statehood have caused many wars throughout history including two world wars in the twentieth century. In the post-Cold War period there have been wars and violent conflicts in the Balkans, in Chechnya, in East Timor and in parts of Africa like Ethiopia and Eritrea in which questions of statehood and nationalism have been central causes. This means that knowledge of nationhood, states and sovereignty is vital for any student of international relations.

NATIONS

For nationalists, a nation is a collective group of people who share a number of common social, cultural and ethnic characteristics. It is a social collective involving various criteria and characteristics that are unique to each nation. These characteristics can include language, tradition, ethnicity, religion, myths, beliefs, symbols and blood ties. The combination of such features alongside other factors such as economics and sharing a homeland become so strong and pervasive that a collective consciousness emerges to bond this group of people together. Moreover, there is no fixed template of what constitutes nationhood as each nation is unique. This collective consciousness, or group identity, can be reinforced by shared experiences like war, famine or persecution indicating that the nation is an enduring community of people with a sense of a shared past and a shared future. The idea of the nation is largely subjective and is self-selective in the sense that each nation defines what it is to be part of that nation. The nation, in this sense, is a social phenomenon that differentiates different peoples in the world. There are, however, other ways of defining the nation. In Iceland it has been demonstrated by scientific research that the vast majority of people are highly homogenous in ethnic terms. Advances in DNA testing mean that many in Iceland can trace their ancestry back to the original settlers of the island suggesting that a strong historical lineage exists that bonds the Icelandic people together as a nation.

Benedict Anderson suggests the idea of nation as being an imagined community wherein the nation is a social construct rather than a naturally occurring social phenomenon. Anderson argues that as an imagined community, the nation is limited (or finite), sovereign and is a community (as it involves comradeship). The argument here is that the idea of the nation is born out of modernity and was created by a number of interrelated factors such as the evolution of the printing press, industrialization and urbanization, and through historical developments such as the Reformation, revolution (in France, the USA and elsewhere) and the increasing role of the state. The development of the national consciousness of nations across Europe was complex, took some time and was substantially helped by the development of mass communications like newspapers and books. Such developments meant there was a need for a common language, an education system and therefore the involvement of the state. Collectively such processes created the idea of nation according to Anderson. In effect, the state builds the nation rather than the nation creating the state. He writes that nations, nationhood and nationalism are, 'cultural artefacts of a particular kind' (Anderson 1991: 4) that were created at the end of the eighteenth century and throughout the nineteenth century by these various processes. In the age of nationalism, the idea of the nation and nationhood became increasingly important and led to the unification of Italy by 1861 and Germany by 1871. The cultural, linguistic and ethnic homogeneity of Italians saw Italy emerge as a single nation-state whereas before 1861 it was a collection of smaller Italian and Papal states. In 1801, there were 125 German states occupying the territory we now know and call Germany until, under the Prussian leadership of Bismarck, the German nation was unified. These two examples seem to follow the idea of the nation as an imagined community. In each case, political mechanisms like war and revolution based upon the ideas of national unity brought together the German people and Italian people to create the German state and Italian state.

The idea of the nation is potent and involves community, identity and a shared historic and future trajectory. Nations exist, for good or ill, but how they exist and what constitutes each separate nation is an open question. For example, the American nation bases itself upon the ideals of the US Constitution and the ideas of liberty, freedom, democracy and tolerance while the Jewish nation is based upon a shared religious identity and practice. Nationhood is about belonging to a particular group and not being the Other. A strong sense of Them and Us lies beneath the idea of the nation and this is often metamorphosed into the political realm. The idea of the nation as a political unit is the essence of nationalism.

NATIONALISM

At the heart of nationalism is the idea that nations are distinct entities and that this being so, each nation should have self-determination. Self-determination is the principle that nations should be able to form their own states. That is, each nation has the right to form its own political, legal and administrative order located within a territorial area or homeland. Nationalism therefore extends the idea of nationhood into the political. According to Ernest Geller, nationalism can be defined as: '[P]rimarily a political principle, which holds that the political and national unit should be congruent' (Geller 1983). Michael Ignatieff expanded on this definition by noting that:

> As a political doctrine, nationalism is the belief that the world's peoples are divided into nations, and that each of these nations has the right to self-determination, either as governing units within nations or as nation states of their own. As a cultural ideal, nationalism is the claim that while men and women have many identities, it is the nation that provides them with their primary form of belonging. As a moral ideal, nationalism is an ethic of heroic sacrifice, justifying the use of violence in the defence of one's nation against enemies, internal or external.
>
> (Ignatieff 1994)

Joseph Nye further elucidates the concept of nationalism by noting that 'nationalism is not merely a descriptive term, it is also prescriptive', and as such is a 'political word[s] used in struggles for power' (Nye 1993).

At the Versailles conference following the First World War, US President Woodrow Wilson called for self-determination as a means of promoting peace, collective security and international order. Wilson opposed the idea of Empire and believed that nations should govern themselves. Many of Wilson's famed fourteen points related to the principle of self-determination such as the establishment of an independent state in Poland and the dissolution of the Austro-Hungarian Empire into its many constitutive parts. Self-determination has consequently become an important guiding principle in international politics. However, fuelled by nationalism, this principle also represents the idea of state creation at the expense of existing states.

The emergence of India in 1948 was seen as model for colonies to gain their sovereign independence and in 1960 British Prime Minister Harold MacMillan spoke of a 'wind of change' in reference to the idea that Empire was no longer acceptable. Self-determination was occurring, partly encouraged by the United Nations but also because of the changing economic status of many of the imperial powers such as Britain and France. Throughout much of the 1960s, many colonies in Africa, Asia and elsewhere became sovereign states, including the decolonization of Cyprus in 1960 and Malta in 1964. In 1974 a revolution in Portugal saw many of its colonies gain independence including Mozambique, Angola and Guinea-Bissau. Many of these newly established sovereign states joined the United Nations to affirm their newly acquired status and to establish new diplomatic relations with others around the world.

At the end of the Cold War, a wave of nationalism occurred in parts of East Central Europe leading to the dissolution of Czechoslovakia, the Soviet Union and Yugoslavia. The demise of communism as an underlying legitimate source of domestic authority was replaced by nationalism. The creation of new states such as the Czech Republic, Slovakia, Estonia, Lithuania, Latvia and many others followed the principle of self-determination and the logic of nationalism. The Soviet Union broke up into fifteen new states including Russia, Ukraine, Azerbaijan, Belarus and others. In the case of Yugoslavia, the break-up of this federal state into its ethnic constituent parts was brutally violent involving policies of ethnic cleansing, rape, genocide and forced repatriation. Tragically, Yugoslavia was an artificial state created by the Treaty of Versailles in 1919; the creation of Yugoslavia did not fully adhere to the principle of self-determination and it was not until the end of the Cold War that nationalistic tensions broke into large-scale violence. From 1945 until the end of the Cold War, Yugoslavia was a communist state in which national, social and religious differences were suppressed by the government. With the end of communist rule across East Central Europe, leaders such as Slobodan Milosevic from Serbia and Franjo Tudjman of Croatia used nationalism as a means of legitimizing their authority, and decades of tensions and rivalries turned into violence. Fighting between Serbs, Croats, Bosnian Muslims, Kosovan Albanians and other ethnic groups occurred throughout much of the 1990s. The republic of Bosnia–Hercegovina was, and still is, composed of many different ethnic groups including Serbs, Croats, Muslims and Albanians. This led to intense violence as each group sought control over the territory at the expense of their ethnic neighbours. The promotion and protection of nationalism was taken to its most extreme as each national group tried to eliminate rivals. Such behaviour echoed the extremist nationalism of Nazi Germany under Adolf Hitler in the 1930s and 1940s. It was not until the NATO intervention in 1999 that some level of peace and order were established. In 2006 Montenegro became an independent state after splitting away from Serbia and joined the United Nations to become its 192nd member state. Kosovo also finally declared its independence in March 2008 and has received limited recognition mostly from western powers.

Nationalism is a major force behind the break-up of states and empires and the creation of new states and provides a source of loyalty to states. Consequently nationalism is often cited as a source of wars, ethnic conflict, persecution of minorities and belligerence. While the nationalism of the nineteenth century was perhaps viewed as a positive phenomenon that brought people together, as in the case of Germany, the experiences of the twentieth century discredited the idea of nationalism. The policies of fascist governments in the 1930s and 1940s took nationalism to a violent extreme with war and genocide being justified through the rhetoric of nationalism. In the post-Cold War period, nationalism led to wars in Yugoslavia but also devolution in Britain suggesting that it is possible to identify different types of nationalism. These include civic nationalism which is based upon citizenship, ethnic nationalism based on ethnicity, and liberal nationalism which involves equality and individual rights.

In Scotland, the main nationalist party, the Scottish National Party (SNP), espouses civic nationalism. The *raison d'être* of the SNP is to establish Scotland as an independent sovereign nation-state but its definition of Scottishness encompasses ethnic Scots and those people who have chosen to live, work and stay in Scotland. This civic nationalism is based upon citizenship, democracy and inclusiveness. The SNP are seeking independence for Scotland from the rest of the United Kingdom through democratic means and in 2007, the SNP were able to form a minority Scottish government (called the Scottish Executive) following elections that year. Scottish First Minister Alex Salmond, who is also leader of the SNP, has suggested that he wishes to hold a referendum on Scottish independence by 2010.

BOX 4.1 MAIN TYPES OF NATIONALISM

- *Civic nationalism*: A 'social contract' between citizens and the state
- *Ethnic nationalism*: Often involving a strong hereditary principle
- *Cultural nationalism*: The nation is bonded together through a sense of shared culture.
- *Liberal nationalism*: Nationalism based upon the principles of equality, freedom, tolerance, individual rights and identity
- *Pan-nationalism*: Form of ethnic and cultural nationalism in which various groups in different states shares similar features or characteristics
- *Diaspora nationalism*: National grouping of ex-patriots who live outside their homeland or home state

STATES

The term International Relations is perhaps synonymous with Inter-state Relations because the study of international relations, while inter-disciplinary in many ways, pays particular attention to states and to state-based actors in the international system. Throughout history states have existed in many forms, from the city states of ancient Greece to the feudal states of the medieval period to the modern system of states in place today. It is claimed by many scholars, such as Hans J. Morgenthau and Henry Kissinger, that the modern system of states originates from the Peace of Westphalia in 1648. A number of important principles emerged from the Westphalian settlement such as territoriality, secularism and reciprocal recognition. The Peace of Westphalia also codified an important feature of statehood, namely sovereignty. Sovereignty will be explored in more detail in the next chapter but there are a number of points that should be made here.

The Westphalian peace established the dynamics of internal sovereignty and external sovereignty which are central to any discussion involving states. Internal sovereignty, also known as domestic sovereignty, involves a number of important features. First, that within the state resides a final or single source of power and authority. Hinsley writes, 'the term sovereignty . . . expressed the idea that there is a final and absolute authority in the political community and no final and absolute authority exists elsewhere' (Hinsley 1966: 21). Sovereignty is therefore a special kind of authority within a territory that exceeds other forms of authority. Second, the principle of non-intervention was established, meaning that the internal politics of each state should be respected by other states. Following from the Thirty Years War (1618–1648), which was essentially a religious war between Catholics and Protestants in Europe, many states sought to ensure that the Pope could not interfere in their internal politics and consequently the principle of non-intervention was established. This principle has been enshrined in the United Nations Charter as Article 2(4). Article 2(4) reads, 'All members shall refrain in their international relations from the threat or use of force against the territorial integrity or political independence of any state, or in any other manner inconsistent with the purposes of the United Nations.' Third, states have their own political institutions which are responsible for governing the state, making laws, providing public goods and ensuring the security of the citizens. Political institutions such as the executive, judiciary or legislature are the executors of sovereignty within the state. Recognition of the political institutions by the citizens legitimizes the internal sovereignty of the state and is inextricably related to issues of nationalism, self-determination and popular sovereignty that reside within the boundaries of the state. (Popular sovereignty is where the political authority of the state emanates from the citizens of the state.)

External sovereignty relates to two factors. The first is that of recognition. States formally recognize each other through diplomatic means and by international treaties. Recognition is an acknowledgement of the existence of states in international politics by other states. For Oyvind Österud (1997), recognition of statehood is like joining a rather exclusive club; the club of sovereign states. Österud writes that while the criteria of recognition have changed over the centuries, entry to this club is monitored by existing states in the international system (1997). There exists, however, confusion regarding the issue of the number of states that are required to recognize a new state. Northern Cyprus, or the Turkish Republic of Northern Cyprus, is currently only formally recognized by one state, Turkey, and is not recognized by Britain or the other four permanent members of the United Nations Security Council. Therefore, Northern Cyprus is not regarded as a sovereign state by the international community at large and cannot become a member of the United Nations. As a general rule, recognition by the five permanent members of the United Nations Security Council has become vital for the legitimization of any new states.

The second factor relating to external sovereignty is that of legal equality. Whilst states differ economically, militarily, politically and in territorial and population terms, states are legally equal. In essence this means that states have equal rights under international law. Such equality reflects the importance of being sovereign and ensures that states can sign treaties, join international organizations and retain their domestic sovereignty. The equality of states is derivative in the sense that it stems from being recognized as a state, is a sign that states have certain capacities, and that states are members of the international community.

The 1933 Montevideo Convention on the Rights and Duties of States sets out the four main criteria of statehood. These are: population; territory; government; and the capacity to enter into relations with other states. The scholar Alan James (1986) argues that a fifth unwritten criterion exists, that of 'constitutional independence'. James argues that a key aspect of being sovereign is being constitutionally separate from other sovereign states in a constitutional way. So places like Gibraltar and the Falkland Islands or Northern Cyprus cannot be recognized as states as they are legally bound to others in international politics. This means that Greenland and the Faeroe Islands are not sovereign states as they are under Danish rule. And the Isle of Man or the Channel Islands are not states as they have constitutional links to Britain.

BOX 4.2 CRITERIA OF STATEHOOD: 1933 MONTEVIDEO CONVENTION

A permanent population:

- Implies a birth-rate
- The only exception is the Vatican City whose population is decided on a professional basis

A defined territory:

- Cannot be based upon artificial human-made structures
- Suggested that the territory should be above sea-level. There are a few exceptions and geographical anomalies to this rule

Government:

- Does not specify *type* of government (e.g. democratic; totalitarian; theocracy; monarchy) but shows that some effective governmental and administrative structures are required

Capacity to enter into relations with other states:

- States will recognize other states and diplomatic relations can begin

The four criteria established by the 1933 Convention are perhaps rather obvious but remain the only set criteria in international law. The first criterion of having a permanent population implicitly implies that there should be a birth rate. The only exception to this rule is the Vatican City State where the population is decided on a professional basis; that is to say that those with Vatican citizenship are appointed based upon their profession. However, this criterion does not specify any maximum or, more importantly, minimum population thresholds. The smallest state in the world, in population terms, is the Vatican with between 500–1,000 citizens. There are, however, a further 3,000 people who live in Rome but work in the Vatican and so its population might be said to be around 4,000. There are a number of other very small states in the world such as Tuvalu in the South Pacific with a population of just over 10,000, San Marino in Europe with a population of around 29,000, and Dominica in the Caribbean with a population of just over 70,000. In 2006, there were 43 micro-states in the world; a micro-state being a sovereign state with a population of 1 million people or less.

The second criterion relates to a defined territory or, in simple terms, landmass. Territoriality is a central aspect of statehood and represents the physical underpinning of the state. In terms of detail this criterion suggests that human-made structures cannot be regarded as legitimate territory. This means that offshore oil platforms or similar structures are not deemed as territory under international law. In addition, there is a general rule that territorial landmass should be above sea level. This is to discount coral as a territorial basis rather than land reclaimed from the seas. Coral is a living material but there has been at least one claim, in the 1960s, off the Great Barrier Reef in Australia to establish a new state. The Netherlands has, over the decades, reclaimed much land from the North Sea and has a series of barriers in place to maintain its integrity. Other states such as Finland, Belgium, Monaco, South Korea and Singapore have also been involved in land reclamation projects to either extend their territorial base or protect their existing territory. Furthermore, states can extend their sovereignty and have jurisdiction over seas and waterways in accordance with international law. In 1982 the United Nations Law of the Sea conference set in place various criteria and limits involving the oceans. In general terms, coastal states can exercise sovereignty over their territorial sea of up to 12 miles and allow innocent passage through these waters for peaceful navigation. In addition to this, a 200-mile Exclusive Economic Zone can be claimed by coastal states subject to whether they border other states. See the later chapter (12) on global commons for more on international law relating to the oceans.

The third criterion is that of government. International law does not specify what type of government. Government is made of important political institutions designed to make decisions for the populace as a whole and administer policy processes. Government involves the higher echelons of decision-making within the state and is one of the key executors of sovereignty domestically. There are many types of government from democratic models (presidential or parliamentary), theocratic models (such as in the Vatican City), monarchical (such as in Saudi Arabia or Thailand), authoritarian rule (through military dictatorships or one-party states), or totalitarian rule (in which the government seeks to penetrate and totally change society). The government of each state differs as each state has a different history, territorial size and location. The point here is that government must exist – in whatever form – in order for the state to exist.

The fourth criterion somewhat follows from the existence of government but also reflects the question of recognition. Having the capacity to enter into relations with other states means both being recognized as a state and having the administrative capacity to engage with others. In order to recognize other states and form diplomatic relations there has to be some form of government. There are a number of polities in the world today that have territory, population and government and may have the capacity to enter into relations with other states but, for political reasons, are not widely recognized. The lack of recognition means they cannot be deemed as being sovereign states and consequently that they lack the capacity to enter into relations with others. Examples of these include the aforementioned Northern Cyprus as well as other highly contested places such as Taiwan and the Palestinian Authority. Their existence and status is contested, especially in the case of the Palestinians. The Palestinian Authority is recognized by a number of states, but not by any permanent members of the United Nations Security Council.

The state is central to politics, international relations and social theory. In many ways states form the apex of political authority and power at both the domestic and international levels. Many stateless nationals like the Palestinians, Québécois and Chechens – as well as a large amount of other nationalist groups, secessionist movements and minority groups – seek statehood in order to gain a certain international status and protection. Thomas Hobbes (1651) set forth an influential rationale for the existence of states with the argument that human nature dictates that individuals are self-interested entities who naturally and instinctively regard others as enemies, resulting in a permanent state of conflict and anarchy. In order to prevent a state of nature from existing a *Leviathan* or common power is created to restrain the natural instincts of mankind. The *Leviathan* creates order, security and has sovereign power. The *Leviathan* is simply another name for the state. A compact between the citizens and the state exists in which laws, punishments and public goods are provided by the state to prevail over anarchy. The state as a security mechanism is one of the key reasons that Jews sought a homeland in Israel following the Holocaust. Jewish nationalism or Zionism is based on the notion that in order to prevent another Holocaust in which millions of Jews were killed by the Nazis a Jewish state was necessary and today Jews from anywhere in the world can become Israeli citizens through the 1950 Law of Return. However, the Israeli state was created out of Palestinian territory and there has consequently been a long-term conflict between Israelis, Palestinians and their regional Arab neighbours concerning territorial ownership. The example of Israel highlights that state creation often involves violence, long-standing fears and tensions, and regional instability.

In addition to Thomas Hobbes, a number of other scholars have also made important contributions to the analysis of the state. The works of German sociologist Max Weber, writing at the beginning of the twentieth century, provide an important explanation as to what constitutes a state. Weber argues that the state has a number of important features including a monopoly over the legitimate use of physical force, or violence, within a given territory. Weber studied the state sociologically and found that this monopoly distinguished the state from other forms of political organization. In essence, the state can employ armed forces, declare war and implement capital punishment, and agents acting on behalf of the state can use violence. An example of this might be police using force to break up a riot or fighting. For Weber, the state is a differentiated and impersonal institution which has the authority to make laws and is able to maintain organizational and policy-making powers.

In addition, political power is centralized through the state and recognition of the powers of the state from its citizens exists. Such analysis of the state provides important insights and emphasizes that the centrality of the state stems from its many functional abilities. In terms of the study of international relations, the legitimate monopoly of coercion means that states can make war. Weber also sets out some key features of the bureaucracy of the state. While it is the government that decides policy and initiates new laws, bureaucracy carries out policies and implements decisions. Bureaucracy is the administration of government and is central to the organization of the state. Weber saw bureaucracy as a structured hierarchy in which salaried officials reached rational decisions by applying rules to the facts before them. Bureaucracy in this sense is a rational-legal part of the state that carries out the day-to-day tasks of administration.

States are charged with a number of functions such as internal order, defence, and the provision of infrastructure such as roads and ports, and economic redistribution.

BOX 4.3 TIMELINE OF THE ISRAELI–PALESTINIAN CONFLICT

November 1917:   Balfour Declaration advocates a Jewish homeland in Palestine

1922:   Britain given a mandate over Palestine by the League of Nations

1947:   Britain asks the United Nations to resolve the problems of Palestine

May 1948:   Israel declares statehood, and war immediately breaks out between Israel and the Arab League

1949:   Israel joins United Nations

1956:   Suez crisis

1964:   Formation of the Palestinian Liberation Organization (PLO)

1967:   Six-day war. Thereafter Israel occupies the Sinai dessert, Gaza Strip, West Bank and Golan Heights

1973:   Yom Kippur war: Egypt and Syria launch surprise attack on Israel.

1975–8: Egypt regains Sinai desert from Israel and becomes first Arab state to recognize the existence of Israel.

1981:   Egyptian President Sadat assassinated

1982:   Israel invades Lebanon

1987:   First *intifada* or uprising against Israel in the occupied territories

1994:   Oslo accords (secret year-long talks between Israel and PLO in Norway)

1995:   Israeli Prime Minister Yitzhak Rabin assassinated by opponents of Oslo Accords

2000:   Second *intifada* occurs

2006:   Prime Minister Ariel Sharon is replaced by Ehud Olmert and following elections for the Palestinian Authority, Hamas enters government

July 2006:   Israel invades Lebanon following the kidnapping of two Israeli soldiers by Hizballah

BOX 4.4 MAX WEBER'S FIVE FEATURES OF BUREAUCRACY

1 Bureaucracy involves a carefully defined division of tasks

2 Authority is *impersonal*, meaning that decisions are based upon rules and evidence and not upon personal motives

3 Civil servants (or bureaucrats, or administrators) are recruited based upon their proven or potential competency

4 Officials have secure jobs and salaries. The nature of bureaucracy means that officials may need to be in place for long periods of time; partly because of their specialization, partly to ensure continuity to aid efficiency

5 The bureaucracy is a *disciplined hierarchy* in which officials are subject to authority from superiors

Such functions are organized and run by governments with the help of the bureaucracy. Michael Mann writes that the state can be defined in terms of what it looks like, as an institution, or what it does in terms of functionality (Mann 1984: 187). From a functional account of the state it is possible to offer a six-fold matrix of state functions. Such a matrix conveys what states actually do and further shows why states are central to political life at both the domestic and international levels. The function of defence involves armed forces, border security and aspects of foreign policy. It is possible to break down state functions into more specific tasks. Moreover, states have a legal personality and are embodied with jurisdictional powers within its borders. Such powers, along with the political, economic, administrative and military capabilities of states, mean that states are central to the study of politics and international relations.

BOX 4.5 STATE FUNCTIONS

State functions:	What the functions involve:
Internal order	Law-making; law enforcement; police; prisons; emergency services
Defence	Armed forces; foreign policy; security of borders; defence procurement
Infrastructure-communications	Transport; utilities; communications; and public works
Economic redistribution	Currency; taxation; trade; welfare state; education
Membership of international community	Diplomacy; membership of international organizations; ability to negotiate international treaties
Nation-building/nation-sustaining	Symbols; anthems; culture; education; citizenship procedures

NATION-STATES

The term nation is often used wrongly as a synonym for the term state but each term has a different and distinct meaning. The term nation-state is also often cited to mean sovereign state but there are currently very few genuine nation-states in the international system. In 1972 scholar Walker Connor calculated that out of 132 states, only 12 could be said to be genuinely homogeneous with a further 25 states having a population in which around 90 percent were from one ethnic grouping (Connor 1972: 320). Whilst these figures are somewhat outdated, the result of a similar study at the start of the twenty-first century, if repeated in a world of 194 states, would probably have a similar outcome. The concept of the nation-state encompasses the nationalist idea of a marriage between the nation and the state.

If each separate national and ethnic group, however defined, were to obtain self-determination there would literally be thousands of nation-states in the international system. Srebrnik writes, 'There are as many as 3,500 groups around the world who describe themselves in ethnic or national terms, so most of the world's sovereign states are multinational patchwork units of different – often hostile – ethnic communities'

(Srebrnik 2001: 2). A world composed of thousands of states based upon ethnicity or nationality would mean a world of small states and micro-states and such a scenario is highly unlikely.

A number of nation-states can be easily identified, such as Japan, Iceland, France, Germany or Italy. Yet there are a number of other cases where there may be some doubt or confusion. The first question in this chapter asked about nationality in Britain. There are many people in Britain who will say that they are British. Equally there are many in Britain who would call themselves Scottish, English, Irish or Welsh. And since the 1999 creation of a Scottish Parliament in Edinburgh, an Assembly in Northern Ireland at Stormont, Belfast, and a Welsh Assembly in Cardiff due to the process of devolution, the question of identity in Britain has been at the heart of many constitutional changes in Britain. Older generations such as those who lived through the Second World War may consequently consider themselves to be British as a result of this shared historical experience. However, younger generations have not experienced the effects of such a total war and consequently may identify themselves with their core national identities. Devolution in Scotland, Northern Ireland and Wales has provoked debates about Englishness within England and some calls for an English assembly. Additionally many immigrants to the United Kingdom with relatives across different parts of the British isles may often describe themselves as British. Prime Minister Gordon Brown, who is Scottish, has called for Britishness to be at the centre of political life in the United Kingdom. Britain can perhaps be described as being a multinational state as it is a composite of different nations. Other recent examples of multinational states include the Soviet Union and Yugoslavia.

The processes of interdependence, globalization and the enlargement of the European Union have prompted mass levels of migration across the globe and there is currently an important debate in Western Europe regarding multiculturalism. Multiculturalism considers the treatment and inclusion of minority groups within society at large. Minorities often have different cultures, languages, religions and traditions, and questions of tolerance, assimilation, education and representation of minorities has become an important political issue. In some states, including Britain, France and the Netherlands, there has been a consequential xenophobic reaction to such trends as seen during the French Presidential elections in 2002 when the leader of the French National Front Jean-Marie le Pen progressed to the final runoff election.

Multiculturalism is an especially important debate in the United States which was historically populated by immigrants who travelled to the New World in search of a more prosperous future. For many, the American poet Emma Lazarus epitomized the American immigrant experience in her poem *The New Colossus* (1883): 'bring me your tired, your poor, your huddled masses yearning to breathe free'. The United States has consequently become a melting pot of peoples founded upon the ideals of democracy, tolerance and liberty and based upon civic rather than ethnic nationalism. However, issues of race still dominate American politics and inform a significant aspect of the American experience and there remain some very serious issues concerning the mistreatment of the indigenous Americans under the policies of the immigrant Americans.

At the end of the twentieth century the modern sovereign, or Westphalian state, was the dominant form of political organization in the world. States have a range of functions, rights and prerogatives embodied with their sovereign status. The territorial division of the world into states, including nation-states, coincides with the near universal membership of the United Nations which currently has 192 member states, with the Vatican City and Palestinian Authority participating as observer members.

ISSUES

Questions involving nationalism, statehood and self-determination remain central to many debates and conflicts in international relations – as demonstrated by the number of ongoing disputes and conflicts pertaining to states and nationalisms, including the case for Palestinian statehood, the unity of Cyprus, and the future of Kosovo. Additionally, there remains a range of border disputes concerning control over territory existing between India and Pakistan over Kashmir, as well as an ongoing dispute over Western Sahara and border tensions between Ethiopia and Eritrea. Britain itself has been embroiled in a number of territorial disputes over the years including the 1982 Falklands crisis that saw armed conflict break out between the UK and Argentina over the islands in the South Atlantic. Japan and Russia also have a long-running dispute over the Kuril Islands in the North Pacific. Such disputes highlight the importance of territory to states. However, these issues are but the tip of the iceberg concerning the nature of statehood at the start of the twenty-first century.

Since the end of the Cold War in 1989 a number of failed states have emerged in the international system. Failed states, sometimes called failing states, are those that can no longer carry out the basic functions of statehood. Robert Rotberg defines failed states as, 'tense, deeply conflicted, dangerous, and bitterly contested by warring factions' (Rotberg 2002: 85). While Hans-Henrik Holm adds, 'when basic state functions are no longer carried out, and when people have no security, humanitarian crises erupt' (Holm 2002: 457). Examples of failed states since the end of the Cold War include Somalia, Rwanda, Haiti, Afghanistan and Liberia. Many would argue that Iraq has become a failed state following the 2003 US-led intervention. In each of these cases, central government has broken down and ethnic differences have led to internal violence and humanitarian disaster. Often the international community intervenes in order to re-establish order and limit the international effects of failed states such as regional instability, refugees and to enforce international human rights laws. A range of other problems are associated with failed states including organized international crime, the spread of disease like AIDS, cholera and TB, and the fear that terrorists may move to gain control over a state in order to fill the political vacuum left by state collapse. Consequently, the preservation of the state system has become an important factor in international relations since the end of the Cold War.

Alongside the phenomenon of failed states there exists the issue of quasi-states. In 1990 Robert Jackson wrote the book *Quasi-states: Sovereignty, International Relations and the Third World* wherein it is argued that a number of post-colonial states, particularly in Africa, are institutionally weak at the domestic level. While such states have juridical statehood and are internationally recognized, they lack certain other important qualities. Consequently quasi-states, 'do not enjoy many of the advantages traditionally associated with independent statehood' (Jackson 1990: 21). Essentially quasi-states lack domestic sovereignty whilst maintaining the status of Westphalian sovereignty –

essentially, quasi-states are recognized by the international system as being sovereign, but they lack the corresponding domestic sovereignty usually inherent in being recognized as a sovereign state. Quasi-states come to rely on other members of the international community for aid and development funds. Such states are close to state failure or collapse and ethnic divisions usually exist within their borders. Jackson also argues that quasi-states, 'lack established institutions capable of constraining and outlasting the individuals who occupy their offices' (Jackson 1990: 22). This suggests that many state institutions such as the police or army are loyal to the leader and not necessarily to the state. Contemporary examples in Africa would include Sudan and the Côte d'Ivoire.

Another issue involving states at the start of the twenty-first century involves globalization. Globalization is an elusive concept in many respects but broadly relates to a series of interacting processes involving economics, technology, politics, communications, culture and other interactions. Globalization is an expansion and intensification of cross-border activities, trans-national actions and global exchanges that are changing many aspects of international relations. For some scholars like Susan Strange, Peter Van Ham and Graeme Gill globalization is transforming the state in many ways. The argument is that the structural changes of globalization are fundamentally changing the nature of the sovereign state. The de-territorialization of many activities, including economic exchanges like the transfer of money, may be undermining the authority of the state. For example, multinational corporations can avoid paying taxes, move their factories from state to state and give governments demands before they invest. Susan Strange suggested that instead of states controlling market forces, market forces were now controlling states. In addition, as processes like privatization occurred in many Western states, private firms were – and are – taking over important state functions suggesting that states are giving up many of their powers. Such developments mean that many new actors are involved in international relations and that it is not just states that are involved in global politics. Arguably, technological innovations such as the development of the Internet have also undermined aspects of the state because it allows people to spread information and news, offer dissenting voices to a global audience, sell and buy goods, and transfer money instantly with little control by the state. A few states like North Korea, China and Iran are resisting such developments by imposing controls over internet usage and imposing censorship over websites. However, the development of new technologies is indisputably allowing individuals and groups to have greater autonomy that may be contrary to the interests of the state. State transformation may mean that the state increases its surveillance function through the introduction of biometric passports and identity cards, use of lists to identify or target specific groups in society, and to increase its monitoring of people moving from one state into another. If a state transformation is occurring then this suggests that the state is able to adapt, change and respond to the changing global environment.

REFERENCES

Anderson, B. (1991) *Imagined Communities*, London and New York: Verso, revised edition.

Connor, W. (1972) 'Nation Building or Nation Destroying?', *World Politics*, 24 (4): 319–55.

Gellner, E. (1983) *Nations and Nationalism*, Oxford: Blackwell.

Hinsley, F.H. (1966) *Sovereignty*, London: C.A. Watts and Co.

Hobbes, T. (1991) *Leviathan*, Cambridge: Cambridge University Press.

Holm, H.H. (2002) 'Failing Failed States: Who Forgets the Forgotten?', *Security Dialogue*, 33 (4): 457–71.

Ignatieff, M. (1994) *Blood and Belonging*, London: Vintage.

Jackson, R. (1990) *Quasi-states: Sovereignty, International Relations and the Third World*, Cambridge: Cambridge University Press.

James, A. (1986) *Sovereign Statehood*, London: Allen and Unwin.

Mann, M. (1984) 'The Autonomous Power of the State: Its Origins, Mechanisms and Results', *European Journal of Sociology*, 25 (2): 185–213.

Nye, J. (1993) *Understanding International Conflicts*, New York: Harper Collins College Publishers.

Österud, O. (1997) 'The Narrow Gate: Entry to the Club of Sovereign States', *Review of International Studies*, 23 (2): 167–84.

Rotberg, R. (2002) 'The New Nature of Nation-state Failure', *Washington Quarterly*, 25(3): 85–96.

Srebrnik, H. (2001) 'Mini-nationalism, Self-determination and Micro-states in a Globalized World', *Canadian Review of Studies in Nationalism*, 28(1–2): 1–8.

Strange, S. (1988) *States and Markets*, London: Pinter.

Strange, S. (1996) *The Retreat of the State*, Cambridge: Cambridge University Press.

van Ham, P. (2000) *European Integration and the Postmodern Condition*, London: Routledge.

Weber, M. (1967) *From Max Weber: Essays in Sociology* (edited and translated by H. H. Gerth and C. Wright Mills), London: Routledge and Kegan Paul.

Weber, M. (1978) *Economy and Society* (edited by Guenther Roth and Claus Wittich), Berkeley and Los Angeles and London: University of California Press.

FURTHER READING

Gill, G. (2003) *The Nature and Development of the Modern State*, London: Palgrave.

Sørenson, G. (2004) *The Transformation of the State*, London: Palgrave.

USEFUL WEBSITES

Governments of the world http://www.gksoft.com/govt/en/

United Nations http://www.un.org

CHAPTER 5

Power
Roger Carey

Any examination of power should begin with a close examination of the context within which power is used. Threatening a nuclear attack on a small state in order to win a vote at the United Nations is hardly likely to work; indeed it is likely to be counter-productive. Military and political power is less liquid than commodities such as economic resources; military and political power cannot easily be translated into other forms of power.

Size and power are contextual and relational. For example, the Ukraine seems large with a population of 46 million (making it one of the top 30 most populated states) and having over four times the population of neighbouring Belarus. However, both Ukraine and Belarus are dwarfed by their other neighbour, the Russian Federation, that has a population of over 140 million. Furthermore, powerful states such as the USA and former USSR could lose conflicts with much smaller states such as Vietnam and Afghanistan because of a mistaken belief that power resources useful in one context would be equally useful in a different one.

Power in international relations can be defined as the ability of one state to exert influence or control over the actions of other states. This influence can be exerted overtly – via war or sanctions – or by the recognition by other states of a potential for action – and this may be done consciously or unconsciously. Power has a purpose. The leaders of states make an assumption that power will enable them to defend or extend the national interest – however it is defined – and will allow them to defend and project the goals and aims of the state. Power will, therefore, have many abstract elements in its composition. It may be better, therefore, to attempt to measure power on some sort of political scale – such as ability to achieve goals – rather than on any sort of military head count, whether in manpower or missiles, market shares or megabytes.

Power is multifaceted but can be defined in two distinct forms – hard power and soft power. Hard power is the ability to physically hurt and damage and is usually associated with military force and physical persuasion. Soft power is the ability to exert pressure and influence without using physical threat. Since the 1950s, soft power in the international system has grown to the extent that there are those who argue that soft power is now of greater significance than hard power. Additionally, there are aspects of power that do not neatly fit into this simple typology, such as terrorism, resource control, and IT; but however power is defined it is designed to generate influence and influence comes from an ability to project power.

The perceptual element is crucial, since state action is not the result of some deterministic logic or unseen hand or plan. It requires decision-makers to decide and individuals to act. These individuals act on their beliefs or perceptions of what the world is like. They cannot know what the other side is thinking. Until power is used, it is merely what people think it is, and as such remains a very difficult concept to quantify.

BOX 5.1 POWER

- Contextual and relational
- Subjective and perceptual
- Scope: types of behaviour and situations
- Domain: over whom?

MILITARY POWER

Classical writers such as Thucydides and Pericles associated power with military capability. Likewise, Sun Tsu equated power with military capability, and Mao Tse Tung once famously noted that power rolls out of the mouth of a gun. Scholars of international relations in the twentieth century such as E.H. Carr, Hans Morgenthau and Kenneth Waltz have similarly associated state power with military power.

Traditionally, military power was used to impose the will of one sovereign upon another, or to resist the forces of another sovereign. As a consequence of the 1648 Peace of Westphalia state citizens began to identify with the state and nationalism and international politics emerged. Since then, a key function of the state has been to provide external protection and security to the citizens of the state, and to participate on their behalf in the international system. Power is the popularly defined mechanism by which the state fulfils this function. Power is gained, or lost, in a struggle to acquire resources.

Military power lends itself to simple conceptualizations, the most common of which is the balance of power wherein equilibrium is perceived to exist, either from alliance or from unilateral effort, relative to potential opponents. Early twentieth-century Europe experienced an extremely unstable multi-polar balance of power between the Triple Alliance and the Triple Entente. By contrast, the bi-polar balance of power experienced by the USA and USSR during the Cold War was much more stable. Hegemony is when there exists a single dominant power, such as the USA following the collapse of the USSR.

BOX 5.2 THE BALANCE OF POWER

- *Balance of power*: Equilibrium is perceived to exist relative to potential opponents (such as the extremely unstable multi-polarity of power is the early twentieth century between Triple Alliance and Triple Entente
- *Bi-polar*: A stable balance of power dominated by the USA and USSR during the Cold War
- *Hegemony*: A single dominant power, such as the USA following collapse of the USSR

These conceptualizations imply that power can be measured with some accuracy, but military power is very complex. The number of tanks, battleships, battalions, submarines, aircraft and other measurable devices is relatively simple to calculate – each year the International Institute for Strategic Studies publishes the authoritative *Military Balance* listing who has how many of what. However, two states with identical amounts of military equipment will not yield an identical amount of power. At a very base level, equipment manned by professionally trained forces will yield much greater power than similar equipment manned by poorly motivated and trained conscripts. For example, throughout the Cold War period the USSR deployed a greater number of forces than the USA, but there was no doubt as to the greater ability of US forces to use their equipment more effectively. The United States has suffered from the reverse of this same asymmetry in Iraq. The US coalition to overthrow Saddam Hussein's regime did so very quickly and with very few military obstacles. However, the US's high-technology resources have not been very beneficial in their subsequent mission to establish a new and stable regime in Iraq and the lesson so far seems to be that military power is not the key component in controlling an essentially Third World country of about 30,000,000 people.

Variables in the measurement of power are almost infinite. The problem for decision-makers is the weight that they should attach to each of these many variables, both in their calculation of their own power and that of their rivals. Any calculation of power will be made at a single point in time, but will need to take into account the potential of all parties to engage in protracted conflict. Geopolitical assessments of factors such as infrastructure, population size, industrial capability, levels of education and raw material supplies can be used to evaluate how potential power can be translated into effective and directed power. It is worth noting that many wars have come to an end because of the sheer exhaustion of the parties concerned, such as the 1945 defeat of the German Third Reich because ultimately it did not have the ability to sustain the conflict.

Physical measurements of power take no account of the skill with which these forces are used – such as the quality of the bargaining and negotiating that can take place; the quality of the information that is available to decision-makers; the willingness of statesmen to involve the state in strategies that carry with them various degrees of risk.

Military power has always been tempered by the abilities of military leaders and politicians. History is full of battles won by militarily weaker powers through the use of skilled troop deployments, cunning, and sometimes luck. Power is the combination of capability and the ability to use and display that capability in such a way as to achieve a given goal. The ability to use a capability means that power is not an absolute – it cannot be measured by totting up battalions and fleets and squadrons – but can only be measured by the uses to which it is put and the perception of total capability held by other states and statesmen. Since the 1980s, the UK, for example, is perceived to have 'punched above its weight'. Such a perception stems not from the absolute size of the British armed forces but because of a willingness to commit those forces to the resolution of conflicts around the world. Under Prime Minister Tony Blair, British troops were deployed to the Balkans, Sierra Leone, Afghanistan and Iraq. Such willingness to deploy troops, combined with a skilled diplomatic corps, has contributed to the UK retaining great power status when, by all objective criteria, this label is no longer appropriate.

Perceptions of power are often as important as the reality of power. At the founding of the United Nations, the Security Council was granted five Permanent Members representing the so-called great powers of post-Second World War international society – the USA, the USSR, China, France and the UK. It is, perhaps, no coincidence that the permanent five are now all nuclear weapon states, driven in that direction by their own perception of themselves as great powers as much as by military necessity.

Alliance

Perceptions of military strength or weakness have long led states to enter into alliances, not always for the purposes of aggrandisement. Faced with a particular threat a state may determine that it has inadequate power to resist the threat or to preserve its values and will choose to augment its power by entering into an alliance – either with another state facing the same or similar threat, or by linking with another state enjoying a similar value system. Alliances are, therefore, a matter of expediency rather than choice. In a perfect society it is unlikely that states enter into alliances, and oftentimes states perceive that the rewards of alliance are not equal to states' contribution (such has been a constant theme within NATO).

Alliances result from kaleidoscopic groupings of states in the international political system wherein the nature of the system remains unchanged but the groupings within it shift and vary. States encounter three possible options for dealing with the everchanging international system. First, a state can increase its power relative to any potential opponent by its own efforts. Second, a state can increase its power by augmenting it with that of an ally. Third, a state can indirectly strengthen its own power position by allying with a third party in order to prevent that state allying with a potential opponent.

Alliances require some coincidence of interest. Obviously if there is no coincidence of interest, or geographical proximity, an alliance is either impossible to forge or impossible to execute and consequently a basic common interest and an ability to operate together are essential components to any successful alliance. Alliances must also address the interests that provoked the alliance. Additionally, alliances that are formed in response to a threat must share a common perception of the threat.

Historical alliances provide the first indications that states recognized their inabilities to maintain self-sufficiency in the international system. For example, in 1870 Bismarck knew that the fledgeling German state would not be able to survive a two-front war against France and either Russia or Austria-Hungary, and consequently allied Germany with both Austria-Hungary and Russia to form the Dreikaiserbund in order to isolate France. Early versions of the Dreikaiserbund treaty had no military clauses – a weakness that was remedied in later versions. Later nineteenth- and early twentieth-century alliances were little more than agreements to fight together against a common enemy, with no integrated planning. Members of early alliances were also notably fickle in their interpretation of alliance obligations. For example, despite being a signatory to the Pact of Steel with Germany and Japan, Mussolini declined to take Italy to war in support of his allies in 1939.

BOX 5.3 THE DEFINITION OF ALLIANCE

- *Alliance*: Association (formal or informal) between states, often but not always with a security dimension

The twentieth century saw the beginning of bloc developments wherein states grouped together around a common fear or a common ideology. For example, NATO was founded in 1948 as a formal military alliance to counter the perceived Soviet threat. In essence, NATO was cloaked in an ideological coat but was a classical military alliance of states facing a common perceived military threat, and designed to balance the power of the perceived opponent. NATO, however, may be the last great classical military alliance and even at NATO's formation there was a recognition that other forms of power were beginning to become significant, most notably economic forces.

It turns out that ideology had the perverse effect of making the international political system less flexible. In the multi-polar world of the late nineteenth and early twentieth centuries most significant states were monarchies and states were constrained only by geography in choosing allies. In the ideological, bi-polar world of the last half of the twentieth century ideology became the guiding principle in choosing allies. For example, following the Second World War the UK chose to ally itself with the USA over the USSR on ideological grounds. The freedom of the state to exercise its power to make choices was already being eroded.

Nuclear power and deterrence

The rapid development of military technology and nuclear weapons following the Second World War meant that military power virtually outgrew its own usefulness. Thermo-nuclear war between the great powers was considered an impossible option (Herman Khan asked: 'Will the survivors envy the dead?' and Albert Einstein similarly observed that the war after a nuclear war would be fought only with sticks and stones) and consequently military power became a purely political asset. The concept of deterrence is not new, or confined to the field of international politics. The military adage of 'making a show of force in order not to have to use it' has existed as long as peoples have been in conflict and the notion of punishing offenders to deter others is a simple example of deterrence in civil society. Despite the perversity of the idea of thermo-nuclear deterrence – acquiring vast power in order not to use it – the ability of the two major powers to inflict mutually assured destruction formed the foundation of a lengthy period of remarkable stability in international relations. Two major power blocs emerged that encompassed most states in the international political system meaning that even minor conflicts were carefully controlled for fear of escalation. In the case of the Cold War, power on an immense scale brought security and stability. The number of conflicts since suggests that similar tactics in the post-Cold War era have not been so successful.

BOX 5.4 THE DEFINITION OF DETERRENCE

- *Deterrence*: Measures taken by a state or alliance to prevent hostile action by another state, usually by convincing the potential attacker that the benefits of action will be outweighed by the costs incurred

Power, risk and negotiation

The resolve to incur risks and potential costs forms the foundations of a strong bargaining position. However, resolve is difficult to signal – not only requiring measurable capability for action, but also a much more subjective willingness to take risks and communicate that subjective element. Such difficulties are compounded by an inevitable lack of precise information concerning the will of an opponent – is the threat real or is the opponent bluffing? Being reliant on functioning technology can also factor into a state's commitment to act. Posing a threat and forming alliances constitutes a complex interaction between the parties concerned.

Perceptions of threats, or likely action or inaction, are significantly influenced by behaviour in previous crises. After Prime Minister Neville Chamberlain was characterized as weak for his capitulation to Hitler at Munich in 1938, and then again in the subsequent invasion of the remainder of Czechoslovakia in 1939, it is very likely that Hitler maintained an expectation that his demands in relation to Poland would be similarly met. For Chamberlain, however, the perception of weakness had to be reversed and he chose to signal to Hitler that any incursion into Poland would be met with resistance. US President John F. Kennedy faced a similar dilemma following the Bay of Pigs invasion of Cuba. When USSR President Khrushchev attempted to turn Kennedy's perceived weakness to his own advantage Kennedy responded with a military and political resolve that Khrushchev might not have expected and consequently Khrushchev chose not to test the resolve of the USA. In essence this process is identical to that of buying any expensive article in domestic society – the purchaser has the ultimate sanction of walking away from the deal but the outcome is a concession by both parties. The Cuban missile crisis also illustrates a further complication in the assessment of power –

the ease of deployment. By factors of geography, it was relatively simple for the USA to place a naval blockade around Cuba and infinitely more difficult for the USSR to challenge the blockade or to deploy force so far away from its bases. In the Cuban missile crisis factors of geography gave the USA greater leverage.

The existence of military forces can be as potent in their influence as the deployment of military forces. For instance, a militarily weak state will not seek to declare war, or have a negative influence on a militarily powerful state because of the potential for resultant asymmetrical conflict. Only if the weaker state has a completely fallacious view of its own capability, and miscalculates that it will win a conflict, or that it will benefit from losing a conflict in a provocative manner, will it precipitate a crisis or conflict. International history is littered with the consequences of such miscalculations. However, the classical security dilemma concerns how to use military power to send out an defensive, not offensive, message, as characterized by the late nineteenth-century *Dreadnought* naval race between the UK and Germany that led to British public demonstrations proclaiming: 'We want eight and we won't wait'. The irony of arms races however is that although they may result in an increase in power as measured by the number of guns on a warship, or deliverable tons of TNT equivalent on nuclear warheads, they do not necessarily give an increase in security, and when the UK built HMS *Dreadnought* it increased British military power by making all German warships obsolete, but it also made every other warship in the British navy obsolete. A new arms race – a new power race – then began with the winner being determined not by the fleet in being, but by the industrial capacity, the financial capacity, and the political will to build warships faster than the potential opponent. This produced more power, but did not necessarily give a concomitant increase in security.

BOX 5.5 THE SECURITY DILEMMA

- *Security dilemma*: As each state acts to accrue weapons as a means of security, another state interprets the action as threatening and builds their own arms in response, thus decreasing both states' security and potentially leading to an arms race

ECONOMIC POWER

Trade between nations predates the modern international system, albeit on a relatively small scale. History tells that Jason had only a single ship in his search for the Golden Fleece, and camel trains – the ships of the desert – had a similarly limited capacity. However, the onset of the industrial revolution initiated an expanding need for secure supplies of raw materials, and the need to secure markets for the manufactured goods. For states that were early into the industrial revolution, the solution to these needs was met through the concept of Empire wherein states used technological superiority – manifest in military power – to capture foreign territories for the purpose of exploiting materials and manpower. Colonies were acquired to bolster the ego of the sovereign in addition to their economic significance and the recognition that access to raw materials was an important part of the power equation.

In order to service the needs of developing international trade a number of international organizations developed to manage, and sometimes regulate, the shipping and communications interactions of states, such as the International Postal Union of 1874. Similarly, private institutions developed to serve the same trade – Rothschild's Bank from France is a much quoted, early example of a private institution operating on the international political scene. Private institutions had a similar but separate interest in the development and conduct of foreign policy, and over time private institutions began to develop in their authority and influence that marked the beginning of the international monetary system.

As with military power, economic power operates under a hierarchy. The very great size of the economy of the USA, for example, translates into power and influence. The US currency has large resources to draw upon, an advanced manufacturing sector, an established banking system and a liberal yet effective regulatory system and consequently has huge global impact. Thus, the US dollar will be far more likely to have a regional and global impact than the currency of a small, newly created state. As has proven to be the case throughout human history: the rich are powerful, the poor are not. Often, powerful currencies such as the US dollar, the Swiss franc (for historical reasons the Swiss were bankers almost before banking was invented), the euro, and at one time the British pound sterling, are held by weaker states in order to give stability to their own currency and to enable them to trade freely. Unlike military power (that is more or less unfettered) there has been a lengthy and concerted effort to ensure that financial power is used in responsible ways – partly, of course, because it suits the national interest of all parties to have a stable and relatively predictable international economic order.

Of course, whether financial power is managed effectively is open to doubt, and whether states have the authority, power or ability to regulate the international financial system is equally questionable. To control considerable financial resources is to wield considerable power, and private (profit-oriented) individuals or companies control a significant amount of financial resources. In early 2007 capital funds are estimated to have resources available to them equivalent to the size of the whole of the economy of the USA. This means that largely unregulated individuals have the capacity to make or break the global economy. This is a very significant development and presents a major challenge to the power of the state.

The study of the international political economy

To date, scholars have not given great attention to the element of economic power in the international political system. Indeed, the study of the international political economy is a phenomenon dating from the 1950s and some aspects of the international money market go back only to the 1990s. The main reason for the lack of scholarly interest, however, lies in the fact that the USA dominates and operates the system in a relatively benign manner and there is no obvious threat to equate to tanks and ICBMs. It is equally true, however, that the USA operates the system to its own benefits – and to a lesser extent the UK and the City of London follow the same path. Additionally, banks and other private financial institutions operate in a discrete manner and are less open to public scrutiny than most governments. Or it may be that states did not have, or do not have policies on the international political economy and therefore it is extremely difficult to pinpoint where power lies and how it is being exercised.

Regulation of the international political economy

The main players in the spectacular growth of the international political economy since the 1990s have been private companies using private networks. Furthermore, states have proven to be unable to control the international political economy. For instance, the British pound sterling used to be one of the strongest currencies in the world, but as the UK struggled to maintain the strength of its currency the British government attempted to manipulate exchange rates by using its own reserves and in 1971 this edifice collapsed to reveal the real weakness of the currency. As a consequence, a fixed exchange rate for currencies became a thing of the past and the state became powerless to alter that situation. Governments gradually lost control of the international political economy – not necessarily because banks and other financial institutions pushed to take control but because states found it convenient and did not resist such developments. Capital markets became increasingly open and the ability of companies to raise funds on a global market made it much easier for companies to become multinational, bringing with them not just a market for goods and services but also for capital. The state, with its focus on a finite territory, lost the power to control or influence.

Until the end of the twentieth century financial regulators expected, at the very least, to be able to monitor flows of capital even if they could not formally regulate it. Such monitoring was possible because the major capital flows were through regulated banks. However, in 2007 it was estimated that up to 25 per cent of all capital agreements are made between unregulated hedge funds, resulting in significant volumes of financial activity taking place outside any forum that the state can control or even monitor, and such a situation has very considerable implications for the power of the state.

The multinational corporation

Multinational corporations have become at least as important as states in the international political economy. The financial turnover of many twenty-first-century multinational corporations exceeds that of the GDP of a substantial number of states and consequently many states have become suppliants in endeavouring to attract multinationals to establish links with them. The state no longer regulates the supply and cost of capital or provides the regulatory regime in which it is supplied. It is not only the manufacturing companies that have become global in their operations, so too have the companies that supply them with services. Local banks survive only as a consequence of protectionism, as in the USA, or by virtue of having a high degree of specialization, usually in catering for the needs of clients with very high net wealth. Indeed, banks have been forced to become multinational corporations in order to keep pace with their clients.

Manufacturing companies now manufacture very close to their markets, or where labour, raw materials, taxation or production costs are lowest. Developments in logistics, especially in sea and airfreight, have also contributed to the transfer of power from the state to the private sector. Investment banks, offshore funds and private equity may be glamorous, but super container ships, supertankers and 747 freighters have played an equally pivotal role.

Multinational corporations do not operate in isolation but need to negotiate with governments and with each other. In so doing, and in pursuing the interests of the company, multinational corporations are increasingly acquiring some of the roles of the state. Although no multinational corporation is recognized as a state, many such corporations wield far more power and influence than actual states. Similarly, the multinational corporation raises the question as to whether any state can act autonomously in either the international political system or the international political economy. To a significant degree, the state has surrendered power to the multinational corporation. However, rather than see the relationship between the state and the multinational corporation as a zero sum game, it is better to regard the relationship as one of shared power and mutually increased dividends. The state does, of course, seek to retain the monopoly of coercive power and retains the theoretical capacity to regulate the finance sector. However, the finance sector has become so powerful and significant that there is now a power struggle between states seeking to regulate tightly and effectively and those less scrupulous states that operate more relaxed regulatory regimes. This dilemma is exacerbated by the nature of modern electronic communications that permit financial movements from one jurisdiction to another, quite literally at the touch of a button.

BOX 5.6 THE MULTINATIONAL CORPORATION (MNC)

- *MNCs*: Any corporation that is registered and operates in more than one state, but has headquarters in one state

TERRORISM

Terrorism presents another threat to the traditional power of the state. Terrorism is not a new phenomenon – following the French Revolution the Jacobins ruled the French Assembly (and France) through the creation of fear – but since the 1950s the phenomenon of terrorism as a means of exercising power has become painfully familiar. Like all forms of power, terrorism is directed towards changing policy, or indeed the whole nature of society. In terms of power, terrorism is essentially an action of the weak against the powerful. The liberal societies of the West provide not only the milieu in which the terrorist is able to operate, but also provide a wide range of high-value, high-profile targets such as airports, civic buildings, power stations, cruise liners, gas and oil tankers. The challenge of the terrorist to the power of the state is considerable and cannot be ignored, but eliminating terrorism is not easy. Indeed, Mao Tse Tung characterized the terrorist as being as indistinguishable as the fish that swims in the sea.

Power, as it is presently conceived, cannot counter the terrorist and 'the fish that swims in the sea' does not present a target. Terrorists are inherently difficult to identify and use their power as such to create fear. The role of the state to counter both terrorism and the fear created by terrorists, and to eliminate the terrorist threat is a difficult and delicate affair. Rather than utilizing conventional power sources, the state is required to deploy intelligence and to be prepared for a long haul of political, social and economic reforms and for the possibility that such measures may be inadequate to respond to the ideological terrorist or the radicalized believer. It is tempting for the state to use its capacity to change the law in order to counter terrorism, but in changing values, the state merely empowers terrorism as a vehicle for change. The values of liberal democracy – the targets of terror – have to be upheld, especially the rule of law. Once the rule of law is abandoned – as many commentators feel is happening under US rule at the Guantanamo Bay detainment camp – the moral high ground is lost and with it the purpose of resisting the terrorist onslaught.

BOX 5.7 GUANTANAMO BAY

The United States established Guantanamo Bay detainment camp in 2002 to hold foreign terror suspects during the war in Afghanistan. At Guantanamo, up to 750 suspects are not permitted prisoner of war status, or US citizen prisoner status. The camp is located in southern Cuba, on a disputed permanent lease

Counter-terrorism poses a new problem for many states and may in fact make redundant many existent mechanisms of government. For example, power as a means of coercion has traditionally been channelled through a Defence or Security Ministry. Internal threats are the purview of the Home Office or Ministry of the Interior. Consequently, a threat that does not easily fall under the purview of either but draws on both requires that new and difficult-to-construct mechanisms are necessary to bridge foreign and domestic policy.

RESOURCE CONTROL AND DISTRIBUTION

Oil, like many other minerals, is a global commodity. Uniquely, oil is a key element in economic development in every country in the world, yet the distribution of oil reserves is uneven and the major consumers are not the major suppliers. To control the means of oil production is to wield a very considerable power to regulate supply and pricing and to impact the economies of the purchasing states. Producer cartels such as OPEC work to regulate supply and to align it with demand in such a way as to give economic benefit to all concerned. Such regulatory mechanisms work well in times when supply and demand are in equilibrium, but the situation for most of the twenty-first century has been that demand for oil resources has risen faster than supply, benefiting the producer with massive revenue flows to the producer states. Such revenues have been used wisely and unwisely (and sometimes bizarrely such as when the Lord Mayor of London and President Chavez of Venezuela entered into agreement to supply cheap oil for running London's buses), but however it is used, oil revenue contributes to the vast capital sums in the international economic system.

BOX 5.8 OPEC

The Organization of Petroleum Exporting Countries (OPEC) was created in 1960 to coordinate and unify petroleum policies, to secure fair and stable prices and to ensure regular supply to consumer states

Natural gas shares many characteristics with oil, except that it is more difficult to distribute. Very large cryogenic supertankers – in which gas is chilled in liquid form – offer one mode of distribution, but a pipeline is a more favoured, and much simpler means. Pipelines, however, are vulnerable to external attack and lend themselves to interruption of supply. The ability to control the flow of gas along a pipeline gives considerable power to the controlling state, as has been demonstrated by Russia's use of oil pipelines as an instrument of power to impose its will on the littoral states, and there is apprehension in Western Europe that similar pressure could be applied to the European Union once a new gas pipeline from Russia is completed.

Water is frequently cited as the subject of the next resource war. Any conflict over water, however, will be concerned with distribution rather than availability. The United Nations has identified inadequate water supplies as being the consequence of mismanagement, corruption, lack of institutional initiatives, inertia and low investment. Despite this rather sanguine assessment, a state that controls the headwaters of a major river that flows through other states has a significant power position vis-à-vis its neighbouring states who share the river, especially in low rainfall areas.

INFORMATION TECHNOLOGY

The power of the Internet grows daily and as a means of communication the World Wide Web is without parallel. Instantaneous communication has revolutionized the way in which business is conducted, and with a high proportion of business and trade being conducted over the Internet those with a capacity and a will to target and disrupt the business of any one state have a newly emerging form of power – the power of economic and social disruption. Before 2007, attacks were generally targeted on companies or particular departments of state and emanated from a variety of sources. Organized crime had also become Internet savvy, targeting gambling and pornography companies to extract ransom payments. In early 2007 this element of power was adopted as means of demonstrating state power when Estonia became the target of a full-frontal web-based attack from Russia following a disagreement between the two states regarding the location of Second World War memorials. Russia's attempt at cyber-attack – to swamp banks, government departments and the media – came close to success and demonstrated a new form of power that could be exploited by the powerful against the weak. It is unlikely that the state-led cyber-attack on Estonia will be the last.

CONCLUSION

Considerations of power in conventional literatures are still dominated by concepts of military power. However, the end of the Cold War and the liberalization of trade have resulted in a significant rise in economic power. Vast increases in world trade, allied to multinational companies procuring raw materials and manufacturing on a global scale, have transferred power away from the state to poorly regulated, or unregulated, bodies and individuals. The staggering rise in electronic communication has additionally created a wholly new vulnerability for companies and states. Those that can attack the electronic medium wield very great potential power.

The nature of power is changing rapidly and becoming ever more diffuse. Power is moving away from the state towards corporations and even individuals – many would argue that Microsoft founder Bill Gates is more powerful than the US President.

Power, however it manifests itself, can no longer be wholly controlled by the state and non-state actors are gaining ever greater significance. As a result, the twenty-first century is likely to be increasingly difficult to manage.

FURTHER READING

Carr, E.H. (1939) *The Twenty Years Crisis*, Oxford: Oxford University Press.
Morgenthau, H.J. (1954) *Politics Amongst Nations: The Struggle for Power and Peace*, New York: Knopf.
Stange, S. (1988) *States and Markets: An Introduction to International Political Economy*, London: Pinter.
Strange, S. (1996) *The Retreat of the State: Diffusion of Power in the World Economy*, Cambridge: Cambridge University Press.
Strange, S. (1998) *Mad Money*, Manchester: Manchester University Press.
Sun Tsu (1971) *The Art of War* (translated by Lionel Giles), Oxford and New York: Oxford University Press.
Thucydides (1954) *The Peloponnesian Wars* (translated by Rex Warner), Harmondsworth: Penguin.
Waltz, K. (1959) *Man, the State and War*, New York: Columbia University Press.

CHAPTER 6

Force and Security
James Wyllie

Any glance at the history of the modern international system reveals an important and enduring fact: that states are the primary actors on the international stage. Whether acting alone or in forms of cooperation with other countries, the behaviour of states is the key factor in determining whether populations exist in peace or at war. Despite numerous competitors for the allegiances of state populations, it is clear that states constitute the most coherent, efficient and legitimate concentrations of identity, loyalty and power. Contemporary states emerged from the demands and the turmoil of centuries of conflict, and maintain a vigilant security alertness in order to protect and preserve this status. The anarchical nature of the international system – where there exists no higher, hegemonic global authority – results in a global condition where all states are 'structurally insecure – their existence suffused with risk' (Morgan 2007: 17) and consequently the provision of the security of the state, commonly known as national security, is the primary purpose of the government of any state.

NATIONAL SECURITY

National security is normally considered as 'the absence of threat to major values' (Nye 2005: 222–3). In other words, for the nation to be secure, the territorial integrity of the state, its sovereignty, its population, its culture, and its economic prosperity should be deemed safe from destruction or major damage. As with all public goods, national security can never be achieved absolutely and what is taken to be satisfactory in terms of national security is always relative. Indeed, the advanced industrial states of North

America and most of Europe are currently experiencing one of the most prolonged periods of inter-state peace and security that has ever existed for them, but there remain major challenges to the national security of such countries from turbulent non-traditional sources outside their communities. Additionally, the condition of national peace and security enjoyed by advanced industrial democracies is not the global norm and is experienced by few other states. Any review of the Middle East, much of East Asia and sub-Saharan Africa reveals security conditions often far removed from the relatively benign situation enjoyed by members of NATO and the EU (Kissinger 2002: 25–6).

BOX 6.1 STATE ASSETS PROTECTED BY NATIONAL SECURITY

- Territory
- Sovereignty
- Population
- Culture
- Economic prosperity

Indeed, global terrorism such as the events of 9/11 serves as a graphic reminder that any semblance of national security achieved by even the most powerful states 'within modern international society is precarious and imperfect' (Bull 1978: 52). In all but the most rare exceptions, states cannot abrogate responsibility for their own protection. Rather, the level of security attained by any given state is dependent on the policies devised by the government of that state. Security may be a 'contested concept' (Buzan 1991: 35) but national security is the linchpin upon which all other achievements and values of the state are dependent.

Distrust and suspicion between states has been an unchanging characteristic of international society, based on the principle that any single state's perception of security is most often at the cost of other states' insecurity which, in turn, perpetrates a vicious circle of national security anxiety (Mingst 1999: 166). Since the end of the Cold War the sub-discipline of Security Studies has evolved to address legitimate security issues such as gender, societal and environmental security. However, such issues can only ever be considered in the context of national security when states, the primary actors in the system, are already relatively secure. Without a high degree of national security, issues such as oppression, injustice and other related domestic insecurities, cannot be addressed with real prospects of success.

Security is an ambiguous and flexible concept, open to wide interpretation subject to a distinct psychological dimension (feeling safe from attack is a crucial element of security even when objective realities could suggest great vulnerability). Consequently, it will always be difficult for states to qualify and articulate their levels of security. States normally consider the capabilities and the intentions of a possible rival when making a threat assessment and usually find it prudent to attach more weight to capabilities that can inflict severe damage. However, such analysis can be expensive and time-consuming to devise and procure. Additionally, good intentions and good interstate relations can often be transient and subject to sudden change (following an election, a *coup d'état* or a miscalculated political dispute). Threat assessment can never truly be measured or predicted. Analysed by objective criteria Canada ought to feel extremely insecure vis-à-vis the United States – Canada's military and economic capabilities are dwarfed by their superpower neighbour – but Canada and the United States share a secure and prosperous relationship based on a history of benign intentions by the United States towards Canada. Indeed, security is generally assumed to comprise an absence, or at least a manageable level, of physical threat coupled with the confidence that any level of threat to the state can be defeated. However, any threat assessment hinges on a correct assessment of the character of any animosity and an honest measurement of ability of the state to defend itself against such animosity. History is littered with wars fought as the direct result of a miscalculated threat, such as the West European democracies in the 1930s failing to fully comprehend the threat posed by Hitler's Nazi Germany, and Iraq's 1990 misapprehension of the international response to their Kuwaiti invasion. Conversely, there have been many instances when states overestimated threats and subsequently wasted valuable national resources on needlessly high defence budgets. However, the security paradox is that it is difficult to prove the viability of a threat without letting the threat develop to the stage where it is unmanageable. Nonetheless, records show that in times of peace states are often unsure of their national security level, but in times of war or perceived jeopardy, no such uncertainties exist.

BOX 6.2 MEASURING THREAT ASSESSMENT

- Capabilities
- Intentions

The subjective nature of security results in a multiplicity of security factors, some of which are shared by all states and some of which are specific to a particular state at a particular time. Indeed, the same elements that make one person or state feel secure may serve to make another feel insecure, such as the much debated virtues and vices of the Cold War nuclear deterrence strategy. Identifying all the relevant variables in assessing national security is problematic; measuring them even more so.

Military considerations have traditionally been deemed the most important variable in analysing national security with military force being the only governmental instrument sustained specifically and uniquely for the purposes of attack or defence. Military power is the only instrument that can be used to conquer another state and is solely available to the government. A state may be secure in political, economic and social terms, but failure to maintain and project a strong military could compromise all these security achievements. However, overall relative security requires more than a military capability. In the modern world national security also requires a strong, technological base to provide advanced military hardware and software, and a strong economic base to finance such endeavours. Additionally, a legitimate political system and popular support for any national security policy is vital for a robust, durable level of security. Other factors such as whether a state is homogeneous or multi-ethnic can also contribute to the functionality, and consequent security of the state.

Ancillary variables such as strong allies, access to raw materials, sea borders or undefended borders with historically friendly neighbours, a free trading system, and shared cultural values with other contiguous states may all additionally contribute to national security or national insecurity. A holistic view of security would argue that as well as defence and foreign policy, domestic policy such as social welfare and education have crucial national security functions. In effect, all government policy carries national security implications. Such thinking is particularly popular in many West European societies, especially Scandinavia. Indeed, all states have their own national security cultures that reflect their histories and strategic circumstances and in turn, by way of reputation, govern the security perceptions of their neighbours and the wider world. For instance, Russia is often perceived as being expansive, belligerent and proud. The United Kingdom lends itself to the expectation of non-hesitancy to use military force to address core interests when necessary. Others such as Canada and Denmark generally wish to identify with a more collectivist, liberal, low-cost national security culture. The self-perception of states, as well as the prism through which the rest of the world views individual states, is a vital factor in assessments of national security (Jepperson, Wendt and Katzenstein 1996).

BOX 6.3 VARIABLES CONTRIBUTING TO NATIONAL SECURITY

- Military capabilities
- Economic and technological base
- Legitimate political system
- Homogeneous population
- Strong allies
- Sea or undefended borders with friendly states
- Free trade
- Cultural similarity with contiguous states
- Stable domestic social and welfare system

Security, however, is not a framed set of objectives and inflexible strategies but a condition. To be effective, national or collective security policy must be allowed to be dynamic. Just as power is a relative concept, and meaningless unless related to countervailing power, then so is security. Perceptions of security differ depending upon the threat to which it is related, and the constantly changing levels and severity of threat posed by other states and non-state actors. In the international system, nothing is immutable and as the nature of challenges changes, so do capabilities and allies. States may use a variety of policies to seek security, not all of which are military in nature. If insecurity results from access to foreign raw materials, then stockpiling reserves, the use of substitutes, conservation and diversifying suppliers could be a more cost-effective way of improving security than deploying a military expeditionary force to a potentially hostile and distant environment. If a state is deemed to be relatively weak, diplomatic arrangements with likeminded states should be pursued. Formal alliances, informal coalitions, collective security agreements, and balance of power manoeuvres all have particular visions of security as the goal. According to classical Realist theory, security regimes will survive as long as the interests of the members correspond. When interests diverge in a serious manner, alliances, balances of power and other such collective security arrangements disintegrate and change (Walt 1997: 163).

It should not be assumed, regardless of the popular view, that security and peace are the same condition. Circumstances may sometimes compel states to pursue war in pursuit of greater security, and states perceiving threats may see war-making as an opportunity to defeat enemies and establish longer-term security (Mearsheimer 2001: 32–3). Such perceptions influenced the German decision to wage war against French and Russian encirclement in 1914, and Japan's decision to enhance the security of its expanding empire by attacking the United States in 1941. Historically, nearly all states have regarded independence and well-being as more important than the absence of war (Bull 1978:18). Furthermore, perceptions of national security do not always coincide with sustaining the status quo, and vulnerabilities may be addressed through conquest, creating buffer zones, seeking regional hegemony, and forming alliances to redress perceived power balances.

National security is an amorphous and elastic concept. Security may be conceptualized in a narrow way, restricted to military threats, which remains valid if safety from military attack is the primary consideration of national security. However, the modern world demands a re-conceptualization of security to include, at least, economic considerations. No matter how national security is defined, no state can ever be absolutely secure, or even precisely aware of how secure it is, as long as the independent system is comprised of independent and sovereign states.

STRATEGY

If the security of states, both individually and collectively, can never be accurately assessed or absolute it is the responsibility of governments to adapt and amend strategies in response to prevalent demands. At any time, the degree of security attained by any state is a direct result of government policies and strategies based on 'the ever-present threat of conflict' (Baylis and Wirtz 2002: 6). Strategy as a concept is derived from the ancient Greek *strategos*, translated as 'generalship'. Today the concept of strategy has moved beyond tactics and battlefield manoeuvre, but neither is strategy just a big plan or a worldview. For nearly two hundred years, strategy has been informed by the popularized Clausewitzian dictum that 'war is the continuation of policy by other means'. To employ strategy is to employ a specific mode of behaviour, always related to politics, with serious and often costly implications (Paret 1986: 200–1). Strategy is 'the use that is made of force and the threat of force for the ends of policy' (Gray 1999: 17) or 'the art or science of shaping means so as to promote ends in any field of conflict' (Bull 1968: 593). Measured, well-ordered use of coercion in the context of conflict lies at the heart of any good strategy, and to use the term otherwise is misleading and may have outcomes contributing to costly insecurities. For instance, leaders may wittingly or unwittingly lead the public to believe that threats have been rigorously assessed and responsive forces procured and deployed, when in reality, all that has been declared is a preferred view of the world and how it should work, and this *weltanschauung* (world-view) has been labelled as a strategy. Frequently 'the noun and adjective, strategy and strategic, are purloined by the unscrupulous or misapplied by those who are careless or ignorant. Such sins or errors can have dire consequences' (Gray 1999: 16). Indeed, the Cold War proffered the notion that 'there is no other science where judgements are tested in blood and answered in the servitude of the defeated' (Brodie 1959: 21).

Strategy considers power capabilities (predominantly but not exclusively military capabilities) and connects such capabilities to political ends. Strategy is the method by which all the necessary assets of the state are managed to deliver crucial objectives, the most vital of which is national security. A state may be in possession of impressive capabilities that count for very little if they cannot be brought to bear on the target. Strategy is frequently used to describe either strategic theory or strategic doctrine. Strategic theory attempts to prescribe the outcome of the application of (usually military) power in any given situation, and attempts to construct a body of timeless behavioural principles to guarantee specific outcomes to specific circumstances, regardless of the ethical or moral values of the actors or objectives. The durability of any strategic theory is dependent upon whether or not the vital elements of the theory are identified and put into practice effectively. For example, in the case of a corrupt and wicked regime attempting to deter righteous adversaries, if capabilities are accurately calculated, if warnings are issued clearly, and if threats are rational and credible, then opponents should be deterred and conflict avoided. Of course strategic theory cannot always be as precise and predictive as in the deterrence case. Although strategic theory strives to be scientific, unquantifiable variables (such as credibility of threat) mean that it remains largely an art form. The application of strategic theory remains very much a leadership call, or matter of judgement. Various theories of strategy exist and are available as required or requested to policy-makers and the private businesses. Such strategic theories present a range of instrumentalities such as alliance, deterrence, compellence, and military intervention, which allow the best use of coercion (Moran 2002: 18).

BOX 6.4 COMPONENTS OF STRATEGY

- Strategic theory
- Strategic doctrine

Strategic doctrine concerns the implementation of specific strategic theories in particular circumstances and in pursuit of particular ends. For example, NATO's flexible response strategic doctrine, in practice from the late 1960s until the end of the Cold War combined elements of deterrence theory and limited war theory in a manner appropriate to the political and military circumstances prevalent in Europe at the time. For reasons of political cohesion, the NATO strategy had to be defensive in nature, but could not be interpreted as encouraging any kind of large-scale conflict by what were perceived to be the superior conventional forces of the Soviet bloc. US nuclear forces provided an obvious deterrent to such an eventuality but US leadership, aware of the prospect of a retaliatory strike on US homeland, was reluctant to commit to a large-scale nuclear response at the beginning of any conflict. The flexible response doctrine allowed for some limited and deliberately contained war fighting early in any conflict, but surpassing previously agreed acceptable levels of fighting would trigger a gradual escalation of clearly communicated NATO military responses, the end-line of which was a nuclear response. Thus the NATO doctrine guaranteed an escalation of conflict at a specific and forewarned time, culminating in the use of nuclear force, as a deterrent and incentive against large-scale fighting or insurgency

An effectively constructed strategic doctrine should deliver both a lucid projection of foreign policy goals and the repercussions to be expected in the event of hostility. Strategic doctrine should also assist in an appropriate and cost-effective choice of appropriate military technology. For example, a strategic doctrine based on forward deployment of light, flexible forces should prioritize purchase of transport aircraft, light armour and attack helicopters over state-of-the-art heavy battle tanks. Furthermore, strategic doctrine must be compatible with the diplomacy of the leadership and serve foreign policy objectives, otherwise problems can arise that lead to more, not less, conflict. For example, the primary French foreign policy goal of the 1930s was to oblige Germany to abide by the territorial and armaments stipulations of the Treaty of Versailles following the First World War. However, following the experience of that war, French strategic doctrine was heavily defensive, precluding from French diplomacy the threat of forward deployment that would allow them to prevent the breaching of the Versailles arrangements by the Nazi regime. To maximize effect, a strategic doctrine should be rapidly applicable to most parts of the international system, should not be too complicated or abstruse, should be enthusiastically supported by those who promulgated it, and should be accepted by the public as relevant rather than purposeless. In democracies, this last requirement is especially important. If the public are not persuaded that the doctrine contributes to national security the voting public can object to paying for it and can vote the government out of office to render the doctrine dysfunctional (Howard 1983).

BOX 6.5 PURPOSES OF STRATEGIC DOCTRINE

- Convey foreign policy goals
- Signal costs for aggressor
- Assist the choice of military technology
- Serve diplomacy
- Be applicable elsewhere in the system
- Engage allies
- Carry public support

Strategy has been described as 'a process, a constant adaptation to shifting conditions and circumstances in a world where chance, uncertainty and ambiguity dominate' (Murray and Grimsley 1994: 1). During the pre-nuclear era the focus of strategy, theory and doctrine, was to win battles and wars. During the Cold War, the strategic purpose was to achieve objectives without escalation to nuclear war and if coercion was unavoidable every effort was made to control it tightly. Consequently, the Cold War saw theories of deterrence, arms control, crisis management and limited war developed and articulated as rarely before. The modern era has witnessed a particularly dynamic character to the condition of international security. The Cold War model of containment of quantifiable threats with timely recourse to warnings and to limited, last-resort coercion is no longer feasible. There is now a trans-national geography of security wherein national frontiers no longer define threats, as Germany did for France between 1870 and 1945 and the Soviet Union for the West between 1947 and 1990. The major threats of the modern era stem not from states, nor from groups that aspire to become states, but from hostile trans-national groups that often have relationships with states, thereby compounding the uncertainty and unpredictability of the threat (Gaddis 2005: 4). Preparedness for an attack is a function not just of identifying an enemy, but also having some degree of warning, but modern mass terrorism is based on unpredictable and sudden attacks leaving little time to identify the aggressor's target, take specific defensive measures and deploy forces (Zekilow 2003: 25–6). Even assuming that some time is available the aggressor may often be difficult to locate and will not be willing to negotiate. Al Qaeda, for instance, represents a new type of trans-national threat very different to traditional terrorist groups such as the IRA or Hamas. Al Qaeda has potentially thousands of members and no interest in bargaining with the United States or its allies. Instead Al Qaeda seeks to cripple their enemies through a process of inflicting mass casualties that may, potentially, include the use of weapons of mass destruction (Stevenson 2003: 77).

BOX 6.6 DYNAMIC SECURITY ENVIRONMENT

- Many threats no longer defined by borders
- Some state regimes irrational
- High anxiety over proliferation of weapons of mass destruction
- New time and direction dimensions to surprise attack
- Some redundancy of multilateral institutions and international law

The strategic doctrine of any state is usually accepted without the undue constraints that would inhibit unilateral or extra-alliance multilateral action. However, international law serves as one primary constraint on the flexible utilization of strategy. International law is based on interpretations of past statutes and is derived from conventions reflecting past conditions that have become revered as a consequence of their historic functionality towards national security. The challenges of a dynamic twenty-first century 'globalised insecurity' (Bertram in Bertram *et al.* 2002: 142) environment are reflected in the debates concerning the continuing efficacy and appropriateness of certain international law conventions, specifically regarding the legitimate use of force and anticipatory self-defence by states anxious about new forms of surprise attack. International law, including the pre-nuclear, pre-trans-national mass terrorism UN Charter framework, has developed historically. Traditionally, in custom as well as statute, international law has addressed the use of conventional weapons in inter-state conflict. However, such customs are changing and an evolutionary fusion of new custom with reformed statute is emerging to reflect the age-old principle that states have the sovereign right 'to use force to defend themselves effectively' (Arend 2003: 98).

Not international law, nor distance nor deterrence are capable of meeting the contemporary requirements of national security against non-state and state adversaries who employ mass killing, eschew risk-averse behaviour, and often advance ideological agendas beyond rational negotiation (Levite and Sherwood-Randall 2002–3: 81; Freedman 2003: 105). Paradoxically, it seems that while Western military and economic superiority may provoke such adversaries, it is the utilization of such strengths that are required to address the resultant security conditions. The East/West nuclear balance-of-terror security arrangements of the Cold War necessitated careful, rational strategic decision-making on the part of the rival great powers to protect core values while avoiding conflict. However, caution and rational policy may not factor in the strategic doctrine of current adversaries that will, in turn, require a strategic rethink on the part of Western states.

The emergence of new strategies and strategic doctrines does not necessarily mean that past strategies should be abandoned. The lengthy and vigorous debates of recent years concerning Unites States strategic doctrine suggest that there remains a role for traditional deterrence. The controversial US National Security Strategy of 2002, developed in the aftermath of 9/11, was criticized for establishing a strategy of pre-emptive war but it nonetheless stated that US forces 'will be strong enough to dissuade potential adversaries from pursuing a military build-up in hopes of surpassing, or equalling, the power of the United States' (White House 2002: 30). However, there remain concerns that contemporary adversaries may be immune to deterrence, and maximum strategic flexibility unimpeded by anachronistic political and legal features of institutionalized multilateralism is deemed essential to any contemporary strategic doctrine. The clear and present danger for advanced industrial democracies lies with anti-Western trans-national terrorism, weapons of mass destruction proliferation, and rogue and/or failing states. In such cases, 'it is difficult to argue with the principle that it is better to deal with threats as they develop rather than after they are realized' (Freedman 2003: 105). While the concept of pre-emptive war is a relatively simple strategic instrument, the implementation of pre-emptive war is a much more difficult strategic decision. The practice of strategy remains an art much more than a science.

THE MILITARY INSTRUMENT

The term 'military instrument' refers to both military power and military force. Military power refers to the degree of influence, derived from relative military capabilities, held by one state over another. Clearly, the United States has much greater military power over Guatemala and Kenya than over India and Russia. Military power can also be subject to sudden and dramatic change in relative military capabilities, as would be the case if a weaker state acquired weapons of mass destruction in relation to a non-WMD-capable stronger state, as has been demonstrated by North Korea's and Iran's nuclear weapons policies. For North Korea and Iran, the possession or near-acquisition of nuclear weapons significantly changes their relationship with the United States and dilutes the military pressures that the United States can exert towards them. Military power comparisons also explain the Cold War nuclear weapons policies of Britain and France both of which resulted from an acute awareness of relatively weak power status vis-à-vis the American and Soviet superpowers. Britain and France felt severely vulnerable to Soviet power; and over-dependent on American power. Military force refers to the point when military power has failed and coercion is adopted. Similarly, the utility of military force must be viewed as a relative concept, subject also to the impact of sudden and dramatic change. For example it would be anticipated that there would be a high expectation of success in the case of British military force against Sierra Leone compared to the inhibited expectations that would likely pre-suppose any British military force in Iran. However, such analysis can never be a perfect science and there have been numerous cases throughout history when expect-ations concerning a rapid victory or defeat were confounded, such as in Israel's victories against Arab coalitions in 1948, 1967 and 1973, wherein qualitative differ-ences in command, strategy and political commitment usurped victory from a stronger military force. However, modern military interventions, or 'military oper-ations other than war' such as counter-insurgency, coercive diplomacy, peacekeeping and peace-making, demand considerable interface between military power and force. When civil war is more common than inter-state war it is often difficult to sustain any viable distinction between the military power and military force. As such, there exists a symbiosis between military power and military force that enables a functional value in considering them together as the military instrument.

BOX 6.7 ELEMENTS OF THE MILITARY INSTRUMENT

- Military power
- Military force

Despite caveats concerning relativity there remain certain fundamental components – such as maintaining a disciplined, well-equipped and adaptable armed force – to ensur-ing the effectiveness of any military instrument. Even in small states where national resources may be relatively limited there needs to be an accurate awareness of the strategic environment and an astute understanding of procurement and training requirements. In addition to ensuring the best possible defences for the state, such measures will make the state a valuable ally to stronger states. Additionally, techno-logical, economic and educational advances play a crucial role in a modern military. Modern soldiers can deliver immense, precise firepower compared to the mass armies of previous generations, but such advancements rely on sophisticated transport, engineer-ing, intelligence, education and administrative personnel. More traditional power fac-tors such as a big population and a large territorial base still allow certain advantages in the modern military environment. Large populations allow for a greater pool of poten-tial soldiers, a hugely significant factor in societies where there are legal restraints on conscription or a large amount of attractive career alternatives to the military. Also, large societies are often more tolerant of casualties. If contiguous to antagonistic neighbours, large areas of territorial buffer zones provide security reassurance. Indeed, the lack of such a buffer in Israel has contributed significantly to the intense security problems with neighbouring states and has been a driving element of Israeli strategic policy. The size of a state's territory can also provide a military advantage in the event of a strategic nuclear weapons crisis or conflict between states, for the very simple reason that the greater the distance weapons have to travel, the more time there is for decision-making. A state with concentrated military, industrial and population centres is at a severe disadvantage to a state with a spread of targets over great distances. However outdated such crude assessments may seem they remain vital to strategic policy-makers in certain parts of the world such as India and Pakistan, and Iran and Israel, and there is no guarantee that the twenty-first century will be the first century in recorded history free from major conflict between states using the capital weapons systems of the day (Gray 2006).

BOX 6.8 COMPONENTS OF AN EFFECTIVE MILITARY INSTRUMENT

- Modern, well-trained armed services following the correct strategy
- Advanced technological, economic and educational society
- Adequate population
- Territory appropriate to military posture
- Military reputation
- Public will and resolve

Additional, less tangible elements should also be borne in mind when considering the components of an effective military instrument. A state's reputation for gritty resolve, persistent commitment to success despite setbacks, and the excellence of the quality of the military is deemed to provide a national security dividend. Another intangible component, vital in the modern media world, is that of public will. In asymmetric war, where much weaker states or non-state actors avoid direct military battle, the will of the public of the stronger state is deliberately targeted. The liberal sensitivities of the democratic publics are seen as the Achilles Heel of the advanced industrial societies (Luttwak 1994). In such scenarios, terrorism is used with the intent to horrify the viewing public with images of mass civilian casualties and a steady stream of military fatalities. To date, the resilience of Western publics to such tactics is mixed. In 1983 and in 1993, the United States withdrew from deployments to Lebanon and Somalia respectively in the face of such tactics but, in Iraq since 2003, the American public has absorbed over three thousand military casualties and withstood the images of huge terrorist outrages against much of the Iraqi population. The Vietnam War is often used as an illustration of weak public will leading to military defeat. However, the United States elected a pro-war president in 1968 and 1972 – an era over which the United States sustained 55,000 fatalities. It was not until South Vietnam fell to a conventional *blitzkrieg* attack by North Vietnam in 1975 and the Sino-Soviet split became clear the same year that public will changed concerning the Vietnam conflict. Thus the Vietnam War of 1965–73, and the Iraq operation since 2003, suggest that if the public consider the conflict worthwhile, the public can be very resilient.

The military instrument may be noted for its versatility, but it is for the physical defence or protection of vital interests that the military instrument is most valuable. States may not always succeed when they use military force, indeed, states have often incurred setbacks or made costly mistakes in relation to the use of armed force. However, analyses suggesting the military instrument is redundant must examine the bigger picture. To measure the utility of the military instrument on a win/lose basis does not account for the viability of the military instrument as a whole – the loser's military instrument may seem redundant, but the victorious side will almost certainly be celebrating the strength of their military instrument. Nuclear deterrence is another condition that may appear to contribute to the supposed redundancy of the military instrument. No party wishes to deploy nuclear weapons because of the obvious costs to both the perpetrating and the victim society, thus rendering nuclear weaponry useless. However, this simplistic analysis does not consider that nuclear weapons may be used without actually being fired. Nuclear weapons power lies in the threat of their use, not in their deployment, and it is such a nuclear threat that has, so far, delivered peace between nuclear weapons states. Such would not be possible without a credible nuclear 'force in being' (Martin 1979: 15). The use of military force in matters of internal security such as assisting police forces to counter insurgency and terrorism, is another vital aspect of maintaining national security. The British army played a vital role against the Provisional branch of the Irish Republican Army, leading a counter-terrorism campaign that endured for approximately thirty years and required the deployment of twelve thousand troops. The Sri Lankan army have also used military force for over twenty years to counter the terrorist activities of the Liberation Tigers of Tamil Eelam (LTTE).

Military power also serves a vital role in setting the framework for diplomacy. Regardless of how large or small a state may be, the resort to military force, not least when there is little prospect of battlefield success, is a clear and shocking measure of the limits to which a state may be pushed in negotiations. All diplomacy is conducted in the context of military power, though in most instances of low- and middle-level diplomacy the contemplation of recourse to military means as part of that diplomacy is not a real consideration. Nonetheless:

> [If] no such limits existed, if it were known that there were no extremes of surrender or humiliation beyond which a state could not be pressed, the maintenance of international order would surely be, not easier, but incalculably more difficult. It is significant that nearly every one of the new states which has emerged since the Second World War has considered it necessary to create at least a token military force.
>
> (Howard 1972: 46–7)

Other important contributions made by the military instruments may be less tangible, but remain important in terms of being a manifestation of the state's duty of national security towards its population. In many countries the military arm of the state has been in existence as long as the state; it is the oldest institution, the repository of tradition, culture and often ideology, and the embodiment of what is perceived to be virtue, loyalty and courage. Military culture is often part of the very fabric and foundations of the state, and to be without it would signal the end of the state. In terms of soft

BOX 6.9 CONTRIBUTION OF THE MILITARY INSTRUMENT

- Physical defence or protection of vital interests
- Deterrence
- Internal security
- Essential framework for diplomacy
- Manifestation of the state
- International duties, such as peacekeeping and humanitarian assistance
- Socialization, training and education of personnel
- 'Military aid to the civil power'

military roles such as international peacekeeping, crisis management, and humanitarian missions, the military instrument can bring pride and prestige to the state. Usually, the armed services also act as a vehicle for socialization and excellent training and education for all who serve. This is generally accepted as being of considerable benefit to the economy and society at large. Additionally, a low-key role for the military exists in what the British call 'military aid to the civil power' where in times of natural disasters or the breakdown in civic utilities (such as fire-fighting) the military instrument is present to provide assistance. All of the military instrument's contributions, from crucial issues of war and peace to providing ambulances during civilian labour relations disputes, address a core interest of national security.

HIGH STAKES

In whatever kind of collective unit humankind exists, the safety of that unit from destruction or conquest has been the oldest preoccupation of leaderships. This has been the case throughout history from small tribes to city-states, or empires and modern states. National security may be an elusive and controversial concept that can never be met absolutely, but it will always be a fundamental responsibility of government neglected only at great risk. Being secure, whether as a state, a race, or an individual, is always a dynamic condition – security is always relative to the nature and capabilities of the possible threat. The strategies selected to address acute security challenges must be appropriate and subject to constant evaluation. The instruments utilized, normally military, should be commensurate with the strategy of choice and also open to continuous review in the light of changing technologies and the strategic innovations of opponents. National security, strategy, and the military instrument comprise a high-stakes enterprise the failure of which may have catastrophic consequences.

REFERENCES

Arend, A.C. (2003) 'International Law and the Pre-emptive Use of Military Force', *Washington Quarterly*, 26 (2): 89–103.

Art, R. (2007) 'The Fungibility of Force', in *International Politics: Enduring Concepts and Contemporary Issues*, New York: Pearson Longman.

Baylis, J. and Wirtz, J. (2002) 'Introduction', in J. Baylis, J. Wirtz, E. Cohen and C. Gray (eds), *Strategy in the Contemporary World*, Oxford: Oxford University Press.

Bertram, C., R. Kagan and F. Heisbourg (2002) 'One Year After: A Grand Strategy for the West', *Survival*, 44 (4): 135–56.

Brodie, B. (1959) *Strategy in the Missile Age*, Princeton, NJ: Princeton University Press.

Bull, H. (1968) 'Strategic Studies and its Critics', *World Politics*, 20 (4): 593–605.

Bull, H. (1978) *The Anarchical Society*, London: Macmillan.

Buzan, B. (1991) 'Is International Security Possible?, in K. Booth (ed.), *New Thinking about Strategy and International Security*, London: HarperCollins Academic.

Collins, A. (ed.) (2007) *Contemporary Security Studies*, Oxford: Oxford University Press.

Freedman, L. (2003) 'Prevention, Not Pre-emption', *Washington Quarterly*, 26 (2): 105–14.

Gaddis, J.L. (2005) 'Grand Strategy in the Second Term', *Foreign Affairs*, 84 (1): 2–15.

Gray, C. (1999) *Modern Strategy*, Oxford: Oxford University Press.

Gray, C. (2006) *Another Bloody Century*, London: Phoenix.

Howard, M. (1972) 'Military Power and International Order', in J. Garnett (ed.), *Theories of Peace and Security*, London: Macmillan.

Howard, M. (1983) 'The Forgotten Dimensions of Strategy', in M. Howard, *The Causes of Wars*, Cambridge, Mass.: Harvard University Press.

Jepperson, R.L., Wendt, A. and Katzenstein, P.J. (1996) 'Norms, Identity, and Culture in National Security', in P.J. Katzenstein (ed.), *The Culture of National Security*, New York: Columbia University Press.

Kissinger, H. (2002) *Does America Need A Foreign Policy?*, London: Free Press.

Levite, A.E. and Sherwood-Randall, E. (2002–3) 'The Case for Discriminate Force', *Survival*, 44 (4): 81–97.

Luttwak, E. (1994). 'Where Are the Great Powers?', *Foreign Affairs*, 73 (4): 23–8.

Martin, L. (1979) 'The Role of Military Force in the Nuclear Age', in L. Martin (ed.), *Strategic Thought in the Nuclear Age*, London: Heinemann.

Mearsheimer, J.J. (2001) *The Tragedy of Great Power Politics*, New York: Norton.

Mingst, K. (1999) *Essentials of International Relations*, New York: Norton.

Moran, D. (2002) 'Strategic Theory and the History of War', in J. Baylis, J. Wirtz, E. Cohen and C. Gray (eds), *Strategy in the Contemporary World*, Oxford: Oxford University Press.

Morgan, P. (2007) 'Security in International Politics: Traditional Approaches', in A. Collins (ed.), *Contemporary Security Studies*, Oxford: Oxford University Press.

Murray, W. and Grimsley, M. (1994) 'Introduction: On Strategy', in W. Murray, M. Knox and A. Bernstein (eds), *The Making of Strategy Rulers, States and Wars*, Cambridge: Cambridge University Press.

Nye, J.S. (2005) *Understanding International Conflicts*, London: Pearson Longman.

Paret, P. (1986) 'Clausewitz', in P. Paret (ed.), *Makers of Modern Strategy from Machiavelli to the Nuclear Age*, Oxford: Clarendon Press.

Smith, R.S. (2005) *The Utility of Force*, London: Allen Lane.

Stevenson, J. (2003) 'How Europe and America Defend Themselves', *Foreign Affairs*, 82 (2): 75–90.

White House (2002) *The National Security Strategy of the United States of America*, White House: Washington, D.C.

Walt, S.M. (1997) 'Why Alliances Endure or Collapse', *Survival*, 39 (1): 156–79.

Zekilow, P. (2003) 'The Transformation of National Security', *The National Interest*, 71 (spring): 17–28.

International Law and the Use of Force

Steven Haines

It is close to being a truism to say that the legality of the use of force is a current issue in international politics. The use of the military as an instrument of state policy has been one of the constant themes of international relations and remains so, as current operations in Afghanistan and Iraq well demonstrate. It is also necessary today to assume that such uses of force are only fully justified if they satisfy certain legal requirements. This has not always been the case, however.

In pre-Westphalian Europe, the principal normative framework for legitimizing resort to force was the moral doctrine of Just War, a feature of faith-based Natural Law. War was permissible if it was just and, to be so, certain criteria had to be met. War could only be initiated by a sovereign prince, had to be for a just purpose with just intent, could only be resorted to after other means of achieving the desired result had failed or if other methods would be manifestly inadequate, had to be a proportionate response in the circumstances, could only be justified if it was likely to succeed, had to be declared formally, and needed to be conducted in accordance with the laws of war. This doctrine was as reflective of profoundly practical concerns as it was derived from moral and ethical bases. It greatly influenced early international lawyers, most notably the Dutchman Hugo de Groot (Grotius), the so-called father of international law. Grotius was significant in moving Natural Law thinking from a faith-based foundation to one based on reason and rational analysis. Nevertheless, the fundamental assumption of Natural Law – that there are norms of international behaviour that sovereigns, either individually or collectively, do not control but to which they are themselves subject – remained a part of the Grotian tradition.

Although the Peace of Westphalia that ended the Thirty Years War in 1648 was

BOX 7.1 CRITERIA OF JUST WAR

- Be authorized by a sovereign prince
- Be waged for just purpose
- Be pursued for just intent
- Only be waged as an ultimate resort
- Be proportionate
- Only proceed if there is a good chance of success
- Be formally declared
- Be conducted in accordance with the laws of war

arguably not as massively significant and as obvious a watershed as it is frequently claimed to be, many of the features of the modern state system certainly developed in distinctive ways from the mid-seventeenth century onwards. One such development was the relative decline in the Natural Law approach to international law and the rise of Positive Law. Whereas the former held that there were 'higher' norms to which states were entirely subject – derived originally from God but latterly through reason – Positivism defined law as merely those rules by which rulers (or states) had expressed a willingness to be bound; there was no 'higher' law. The Just War doctrine was one of the casualties of this shift from Natural to Positive Law.

During the high period of balance of power politics, in eighteenth- and nineteenth-century Europe, the use of force was justified, if justification was required at all, by reference to the strategic need to maintain that balance and, by so doing, enhance security. War, as Clausewitz so famously remarked, was merely the continuation of politics by other means. It was principally the experience of European great power rivalry in this period that established Realism as the default position in the modern practice and academic study of international relations. For international lawyers, the closest jurisprudential equivalent to Realism was Positivism. Pragmatic Realism in international politics generated the right conditions for Positivism in international law; Realism and Positivism are natural bed-fellows. In its Positivist period international law virtually ignored the reasoning behind the decision to use force; it tended merely to acknowledge the distinction between the legal conditions of 'war' and 'peace' and posited the rules of the game that gave some semblance of order to the transition between the two.

Things began to change, however, with the outbreak of great power war in Europe in 1914. As a result of the devastating effects of modern mass warfare, Liberal opinion in favour of restraints on resort to war became increasingly influential. Legal, ethical and moral concerns of a Natural Law character, that had progressively lost their significance throughout the development of the modern international system to that point, began to challenge the Positive Law assumptions that had chimed so well with the profoundly pragmatic Realist approach to international politics.

The post-war establishment of the League of Nations and the later negotiation of the 1928 Pact of Paris (or Kellogg–Briand Pact) represented Liberal attempts to control recourse to war. The aim was to replace balance of power politics with collective security and, by so doing, reduce reliance on force or, better still, dispense with war altogether. This Liberal ideal almost foundered, however, as the world witnessed a further descent into a state of global great power war in the late 1930s and early 1940s. The subsequent emergence of ideological conflict during the Cold War further reinforced Realism's position as the default approach to international politics. Nevertheless, the creation of the United Nations and the attempt to regulate recourse to war through the application of new rules incorporated in the UN Charter served to maintain a challenge to Realism. Indeed, the UN Charter established a normative framework that remains, over half a century later, the obvious starting point for a consideration of the legitimacy of force.

The UN Charter represents a compromise that serves to accommodate the major contrasting international political and legal traditions. Politically, it reflects both Realist and Liberal Internationalist influences. In legal terms it has something for both Natural and Positive lawyers. While it is an especially significant one, the UN Charter is but a treaty and states willingly choose to become members of the UN presumably, in Realist terms, because they regard membership as being in their national interest. Their support for the UN Charter is evidence of a Positivist acceptance of the rules contained therein. But there is more to the UN Charter than this Realist conclusion suggests. Importantly, it salvaged the notion of collective security from the ruins of the League of Nations; a clear achievement for Liberal Internationalist opinion. Additionally, the formal emergence of the need for the universal protection of human rights, as a key purpose of the UN, paved the way for a general acceptance that not even sovereign states could with impunity subject their own peoples to widespread and extreme abuse. The increasing acknowledgement, most notably by the International Court of Justice (ICJ) (especially in its 1970 judgement in the *Barcelona Traction* case), that there are certain peremptory norms of international behaviour binding on all states, regardless of their expressed consent, signalled an important shift from Positive to Natural Law assumptions about the nature of international law. Limits were placed on sovereignty, with states clearly subject to some form of 'higher' law. The result of this shift, and the incorporation of contrasting and, in many ways, incompatible approaches to the management of international security within the UN Charter, has been the cause of differing interpretations of the international law relating to the use of force ever since.

The end of the Cold War created an international political climate more conducive to normative influence. Both Realism and the Positive approach to international law have suffered as a result. There has also been a significant increase in the number of military deployments in response to crises, many of which have had humanitarian concerns at their core. This has generated a good deal of debate about the lawfulness of resort to force and arguably caused certain shifts in the law through the development of state practice, including practice in evidence as a result of decisions made in the Security Council, the key organ of the UN.

Two areas of the law on the use of force constitute matters of particular note in this volume about current issues in international relations. The first is to do with self-defence and the extent to which states may use force in anticipation of threats to their own security, including that posed by international terrorism. The second is to do with the legality of humanitarian action and the balance between the well established

BOX 7.2 INFLUENCES OF NATURAL AND POSITIVE LAW

Period	Natural Law	Positive Law
Pre-Westphalian Europe	Dominant	Slight
Eighteenth and nineteenth centuries	Much reduced	Dominant
Versailles Treaty to 1930s	Slight increase	Dominant
Cold War	Increasing	Dominant
Post-Cold War	Increasing	No longer dominant

principle of non-interference in the internal affairs of sovereign states and the responsibilities of states to protect both their own people and those being threatened elsewhere. Before going on to discuss these two issues in detail, it will be useful briefly to describe the overall framework in international law for the use of force within the international system, the starting point for which must be the UN Charter.

THE UNITED NATIONS CHARTER FRAMEWORK

As already mentioned, the UN Charter is a document within which one can discern contrasting, and at times conflicting, influences. It combines a degree of political idealism in the Liberal tradition (the Wilsonian ideal of collective security previously incorporated in the Covenant of the League of Nations) with a dose of Realism most obviously manifest in the acknowledgement of a hierarchy of states through the inclusion in the Security Council of five great powers as Permanent Members with the power of veto. It also contains thinking that corresponds with both Natural and Positive Law approaches to international law. From Natural Law is drawn the notion of human rights (Article 1(3)). From Positive Law is drawn the idea of the sovereign equality of states (Article 2(1)) and the principle of non-interference in their internal affairs (Article 2(7)).

Article 2(4) requires states to refrain from the threat or use of force against the territorial integrity or political independence of any other state. In other words, war is no longer to be a necessarily legitimate way of continuing politics by other means. In accordance with the UN Charter, states can only legitimately use force in self-defence (Article 51) or when contributing military forces for the enforcement of UN Security Council resolutions by way of collective military sanctions authorized under Article 42. This, briefly stated then, is the law of the UN Charter: states are to refrain from the use of force except in self-defence or when authorized by the Security Council. In accordance with the law of the UN Charter, all other uses of force against other states would *prima facie* constitute aggression and are to be regarded as unlawful.

This UN Charter framework is universally acknowledged. Even the US, British and Australian arguments justifying what a great many regarded as the unlawful invasion of Iraq, relied on this to defend their decision. They argued that they were engaged on UN authorized enforcement action following Saddam Hussein's failure to comply with a succession of binding Security Council resolutions. Quoting Resolutions 678(1990),

BOX 7.3 UN CHARTER FRAMEWORK FOR THE USE OF FORCE

Article 2(4) All states are to refrain from the use of force

Article 2(7) Codifies the principle of non-interference within the domestic jurisdiction of any state

Chapter VII Exceptions to the ban on the use of force:

Article 7(51) Right to self-defence as an exception to Article 2(4)

Article 7(42) Allows the Security Council to initiate military sanctions for enforcement purposes

687(1991) and 1441(2002) they claimed that their use of force was derived from the authorization in 678 that had been suspended conditionally by 687 but then effectively re-activated by 1441. Massively controversial though the Iraq War was, the states concerned were careful not to depart from the UN framework in justifying their actions. It is, of course, a matter of judgement whether their decision was in fact lawful or not.

Interestingly, the shift during the twentieth century back towards some measure of moral justification for the use of force may well have resulted in the resurrection of the pre-Westphalian doctrine of Just War. The Security Council is now the legitimate authority for resort to force, with member states transferring their traditional sovereign authority to the Council, which is required to consider the appropriateness of force in the specific strategic circumstances. The Security Council must weigh up the purpose and objectives of military action, only using force if economic or diplomatic sanctions have either already failed or been assessed to be almost certainly ineffective. The Council must itself act within the law and must not authorize a disproportionate response, it must only resort to military sanctions if they have a high chance of success, and military forces acting on behalf of the UN must conduct operations fully in accord with the relevant operational law, including the law of armed conflict when appropriate. The intention to use force will invariably be announced in a UN Security Council resolution (the modern equivalent of a declaration of war) which will outline the conditions that must be met by the recalcitrant state if it is to avoid military sanction. All of these conditions correspond with Just War criteria outlined earlier. The conclusion one is inexorably drawn to is that the UN Charter is the modern day manifestation of Just War doctrine.

THE LAW OF SELF-DEFENCE

The most obvious exception to the ban on the use of force relates to the legitimate reaction to acts that threaten the security of the state. Ultimately, in accordance with the UN Charter, states subjected to armed attack may respond themselves, without prior Security Council approval, but only until the UN is able to take effective collective action itself. Article 51 of the UN Charter upholds the inherent right of self-defence 'if an armed attack occurs'. On a first and cursory examination of the wording of this article, the law seems clear. An attack justifies a response. However, if anyone needs to illustrate the potential for ambiguity in treaty law, Article 51 is a prime example. In deconstructing its wording, one is prompted to ask several questions. What constitutes an 'armed attack'? What if the attack is clear but falls some way short of the definition of 'armed attack'? Is an act in self-defence only lawful once an attack has occurred or is it possible to respond to an attack before it has materialized – in other words, is it possible to act in anticipation of an attack that is certain to occur (if one state is mobilizing to attack another, can the potential victim of that attack act first to protect itself)? Article 51 is far from providing a clear and unambiguous answer to these questions, and yet they are profoundly important because they go to the heart of the issue of legitimate self-defence.

International law is derived from an examination of various sources, the most frequently cited list being that contained in Article 38 of the Statute of the International Court of Justice. The two most important sources of law are treaties and customary law. To understand the controversy at the core of Article 51, one needs to understand the relationship between treaty and custom. Treaties contain words that are agreed by those states that are parties to the relevant treaty. Very often, the words will require amplification. This may be achieved by reference to what is customarily regarded as lawful and unlawful. Treaties have proliferated in recent times and there is a tendency to assume that the body of treaty law represents the ultimate statement of what the law is. However, this is far from being the case. If states habitually adopt a practice and regard this as a legal obligation or right, the rule derived from practice can be more powerful than the often ambiguous nature of treaty provisions. This is especially relevant when one recognizes that the words of a treaty may contain deliberate ambiguities arising from the need to achieve formal agreement.

One vitally important aspect of self-defence that is not expressly dealt with in the UN Charter is that to do with the two fundamental customary law limitations placed on defensive action: necessity and proportionality. (Arguably, a further limiting principle relates to the immediacy of the threat of attack, but this is best dealt with under the 'Anticipation, Pre-Emption and Prevention' heading below.) A military response to attack is only lawful if it is necessary and the attack cannot be avoided by other means (diplomatic, for example). Once a military response has been initiated, it must be proportionate to the act giving rise to that response (though not necessarily equal to it). To use an extreme example, it would have been wholly out of proportion for Britain to have used nuclear weapons against Argentina as a result of the latter's invasion of the Falkland Islands in 1982. Self-defence was permitted but within limits. To use a more recent actual example, the defence of Kuwait following the Iraqi invasion of 1990 was limited to the restoration of Kuwait's territorial integrity and political independence. Whatever the political and strategic arguments and consequences, if the Coalition forces had gone on to occupy Iraq and depose Saddam Hussein's regime, they would have exceeded their mandate through a disproportionate response. Even for those who believed that this would not have been disproportionate (and some did not), it was arguably not necessary to do this to ensure the future political independence and territorial integrity of Kuwait. Either way, to have effected regime change in Iraq would, in the opinion of a great many international lawyers, have breached the limitations imposed on legitimate self-defence (limitations implicit in UN Security Council Resolution 678 of 1990).

BOX 7.4 CRITERIA FOR SELF-DEFENCE

Cardinal principles:

- The use of force must be necessary
- The use of force must be proportionate

Secondary principle:

- If force is used in self-defence in anticipation of an attack, that attack must be imminent for defence to be lawful

Article 51 is based on this customary understanding of the twin principles of legitimate self-defence. What it effectively authorizes, nevertheless, is the decision to resort to the level of force traditionally associated with war. It does not grant a state the right to use force (go to war) in self-defence in all circumstances in which it experiences some measure of assault, however. Unless the assault constitutes an 'armed attack', resort to force under Article 51 will, in all probability, be unlawful. In both the Nicaragua and Oil Platforms cases, the ICJ distinguished between the most grave forms of the use of force that do represent armed attacks, and those that are insufficiently grave to do so. A minor border incident, even one involving an exchange of fire between forces on either side, would not automatically justify use of force in self defence. It is, of course, a matter of judgement based on the facts of individual cases whether or not the gravity of an incident would create a right of self-defence for the wronged state under Article 51. This is fully consistent with the principle of proportionality.

This issue was most recently highlighted in the Middle East in the summer of 2006, when Israel responded to actions by Hizballah based in southern Lebanon by the invasion of Lebanese territory. This example was, of course, complicated by the fact that Hizballah, while occupying and controlling a substantial proportion of the southern part of the state, was not acting on behalf of the Lebanese government. Ambiguity as to the nature of the relationship between Hizballah and the Lebanese government (which included representatives of Hizballah) certainly confused matters, not least because the latter was not sufficiently powerful in its own territory to prevent the former from acting in the way it did against Israeli territory and forces. Was the state of Lebanon responsible for the actions of Hizballah nevertheless? Regardless of how one answers that question, Israel was not under an obligation merely to accept without any response the attacks launched by Hizballah (which included the firing of indiscriminate Katyusha rockets into Israeli controlled territory). Arguably, Israel was entitled to exercise its right of self-defence under Article 51, but its invasion of Lebanon and the targeting of establishments as far north as Beirut was widely regarded as disproportionate under the circumstances.

'Armed attack' defies precise definition for the simple reason that the circumstances on each occasion need to be considered in evaluating the gravity of the assault. There has also been some doubt as to the ability of non-state actors to be responsible for launching an armed attack. Despite this, the UN Security Council in its resolutions following the terrorist attacks on New York and Washington in September 2001 (resolutions 1368 and 1373), authorized the US to exercise self-defence under Article 51. These resolutions were almost universally supported. Implicit in them was the acceptance that the terrorist attacks had constituted armed attacks, otherwise Article 51 self-defence would not have been possible in law. The subsequent military actions by the US, Britain and others in Afghanistan against both Taliban and Al Qaeda (a further example of a relationship between a state and a non-state actor operating out of its territory) were essentially uncontroversial in their justification. Whatever the degree of doubt prior to 2001, about the ability of non-state actors to launch an 'armed attack' initiating Article 51 self-defence, the Security Council, with universal support, appears to have clarified the situation.

Although there will continue to be some measure of uncertainty about what constitutes an armed attack and what does not, the most controversial issue to do with self-defence raised in recent years has been concerned with the legality or otherwise of action in self-defence before an armed attack has actually materialized. This is the issue of anticipatory and pre-emptive self-defence and, more controversially, the notion of preventive war.

ANTICIPATION, PRE-EMPTION AND PREVENTION

Article 51 of the UN Charter was an attempt to codify the law on self-defence as it existed in 1945. At that time, the pre-existing law on self-defence accepted the legitimacy of an anticipatory element, most frequently argued on the basis of an exchange of letters between the United States and British governments following the destruction of an American vessel called the *Caroline* by British agents in 1837. The *Caroline* was destroyed (it was sent over the Niagara Falls) in anticipation of it being used to launch attacks on Canadian territory. The American Secretary of State, Daniel Webster, argued that such anticipatory action could only be justified if the expected attack created a 'necessity of self defence, instant, overwhelming, leaving no choice of means, and no moment for deliberation'. Today we refer to this condition as that of 'imminence'. An attack must be imminent for an act of anticipatory self-defence to be lawful. This was broadly accepted as lawful in 1945 (though not universally so). While Article 51 stated that self defence was only lawful 'if an armed attack occurs' (implying on one interpretation that an act of self defence would be unlawful unless or until an attack materialized), the same sentence earlier stated that 'Nothing in the present Charter shall inhibit the inherent right of . . . self defence'. In 1945 the inherent right arguably included anticipation; the other words in Article 51 suggested that no anticipation was permitted. International lawyers have been arguing about the actual meaning of Article 51 ever since. One prominent international lawyer (the Israeli academic, Yoram Dinstein) has opted for the more restrictive interpretation disavowing anticipation, but has effectively allowed for what others would describe as anticipation by arguing that an armed attack begins once military forces deploy in preparation for the actual attack. For Dinstein, what he refers to as 'interceptory' self-defence is lawful. Overall, therefore, anticipatory self-defence is generally regarded today as lawful, as long as an armed attack is considered 'imminent', borrowing from the Webster criterion mentioned above. This does not entirely resolve the issue as there remains some dissent, as well as doubt as to what is meant precisely by 'imminent' in all circumstances.

BOX 7.5 CONTRASTING INTERPRETATIONS OF ARTICLE 51

Nothing in the present Charter shall impair the *inherent right* of individual or collective self defence *if an armed attack occurs* against a Member of the United Nations.

UN Charter, Chapter VII, Article 51

- *Inherent right* implies that the pre-existing customary right of anticipatory self-defence is incorporated in the Article
- *If an armed attack occurs* implies that the right to self-defence is conditional on the attack having actually materialized

Notwithstanding the lack of full agreement as to anticipation, there are two areas of particular current controversy. One is to do with defensive acts following armed attacks but in anticipation of possible further similar acts, principally those of a terrorist nature. The other is to do with the nature of threats posed by modern weapons with massive destructive potential and the need, perceived by some, to re-evaluate what is meant by 'imminent'.

Defensive acts following armed attack

The first of these is well demonstrated by the US reaction to the terrorist attacks on its embassies in the East African states of Kenya and Tanzania in 1998. Following those attacks, in Nairobi and Dar-es-Salaam, the Clinton administration launched cruise missile strikes on what it assumed to be Al Qaeda bases in both Afghanistan and Sudan. Clearly these US responses were not designed to defend the already attacked embassies; they were initiated after the events that triggered them. On one interpretation, the US responses could be regarded as reprisals or punishment for acts already perpetrated. However, the less controversial interpretation was that they were intended to pre-empt further attacks launched by the same organization.

Reprisals as punishment are generally regarded as unlawful. But was the US response strictly in accordance with the imminence criterion that legitimizes anticipatory self-defence? It must be said that examples such as this lend themselves to either interpretation and make it difficult to distinguish between unlawful reprisals and lawful self-defence. One particular difficulty is to do with the criterion of imminence – does one attack necessarily indicate the imminence of further attacks? Nevertheless, while such responses would have been generally regarded as unlawful in the past, state practice combined with evidence of growing international opinion in sympathy with them seems to have caused a shift in the law, culminating in the UN Security Council's authorization of the use of force in self defence following 9/11.

The trail of state practice in relation to armed responses to terrorist attack can usefully start in 1968, when Israel launched an attack on Beirut airport following a terrorist attack on an Israeli aircraft at Athens airport. The Israeli action was unanimously condemned by the Security Council. In 1985 the Israelis once again launched an attack in response to Palestinian terrorist attacks on Israeli citizens. On this occasion the Israelis attacked the Palestinian headquarters in Tunis. Again, the UN Security Council condemned the Israeli action. In 1986 the US launched an attack on Libya using aircraft that took off from air bases in Britain. The US was responding to terrorist attacks against its citizens abroad. On this occasion, while the action attracted much criticism, both Britain and France (as well as the US) vetoed a Security Council resolution condemning Washington's action. In 1993, the US launched an attack on the Iraqi Intelligence Headquarters in Baghdad in response to an attempt on the life of former President Bush while he was on a visit to Kuwait. This US response attracted a significant amount of support within the Security Council. By the time President Clinton launched the attack on Sudan and Afghanistan in 1998, the Security Council did not even consider it necessary to become substantially seized of the matter, despite a request for it to do so from Sudan.

All of these responses, argued as being on the basis of self-defence by the states concerned, occupy a position on the spectrum of legality that can be interpreted as either unlawful punitive action for acts previously committed or defensive measures intended to deter further similar attacks. While a degree of uncertainty as to the nature of the response might also have been possible following the 9/11 attacks, the profound nature of the terrorist attacks on New York and Washington, coupled with the growing tendency for the Security Council to look with sympathy on such responses, produced UN Security Council Resolutions 1368 and 1373, fully supporting the subsequent invasion of Afghanistan. From 1968 through to 2001 there would appear to have been a shift in the law relating to self-defence in this important area. In the current climate, it is perhaps difficult to imagine terrorist attacks originating, directed or ordered from the territory of another state not being met by some measure of armed response in self-defence – even if the response still appears to many as a punitive action.

Weapons of mass destruction and preventive war

Although the question of imminence has been controversial since Article 51 was drafted in 1945, more recently it has received a good deal of attention as a direct result of the US National Security Strategy of 2002. Following 9/11, the Bush Administration conducted a thorough review of its security strategy. One of its conclusions was that decisive strategic action needed to be taken to deal with the threat of nuclear weapons and other so-called weapons of mass destruction (WMD) in the hands of what it regarded as 'rogue states'. The core problem it addressed is simply stated. Nuclear weapons, in particular, are so potentially destructive that the pre-existing understanding of legitimate anticipatory action based on evidence of imminent attack is no longer adequate. Once a 'rogue state' obtains such weapons it is arguably too late to take decisive military action to neutralize the capability. Action must therefore be taken to prevent such weapons ever getting into the wrong hands. By definition, therefore, the criterion of imminence is quite inappropriate, and dangerously so. With an eye on Saddam Hussein's Iraq in particular (but also of relevance to states like Iran, Libya and North Korea), Washington argued that military force ought to be used if necessary to destroy a 'rogue state's' ability to develop or obtain the capability. Relatively benign approaches, such as the US initiated Proliferation Security Initiative (aimed at intercepting the supply of nuclear materials to 'rogue states') would be helpful but, ultimately, an attack on embryonic nuclear facilities should be considered.

There is a previous example of such an attack. In 1981, Israeli aircraft attacked and destroyed the Iraqi nuclear reactor at Osirak. There was no question at the time that this preventive attack was unlawful; it was roundly condemned by the Security Council, including the US. By 2002, however, the situation had changed markedly as far as Washington was concerned. For a start, the threat from international terrorism was profoundly manifest following 9/11. Additionally, Iraq was assumed to be a potential nuclear power hostile to the US and its allies, and capable of providing terrorist groups with the wherewithal to deploy WMD. The combination of suicide terrorism and nuclear capability presented a massive threat, regardless of the individual intentions of the potentially nuclear armed 'rogue states' themselves. Although the US did not use preventive war arguments to justify the subsequent invasion of Iraq in 2003, there is little doubt that the inclusion of such an idea in the National Security Strategy was motivated by that possibility. The White House argued that the overwhelming nature of this new threat demanded a review of the legal basis for anticipatory action. Unsurprisingly, this has generated a considerable amount of controversy, both political and legal.

It is far too easy to dismiss the Bush Administration's concerns in this respect as the dubious conclusions of an irresponsible group of ideologically motivated neo-conservative zealots. Unfortunately, such assumptions have characterized much of the criticisms levelled at Washington for raising this possibility. The fact is, however, that there is a disturbing potential at the heart of this issue. What is the international community going to do to ensure security in the face of such a threat? This problem is a serious one and is likely to remain a concern of substance for some years to come. What is often forgotten, or conveniently dismissed, by arch critics of George W. Bush, is that the National Security Strategy did not posit the view that the existing law should simply be ignored. On the contrary, it stressed that this was a clear legal issue and that it would be necessary to review the law in order adequately to deal with the threat. While one can responsibly disagree with this view and argue that diplomatic initiatives based on the existing non-proliferation regime should prevail over precipitate and unilateral military action (the approach to Libya and North Korea being recent and current examples of a tangible alternative), there is also a clear and responsible need to think through contingencies if the worst predictions come to pass.

In current international law, preventive action would not necessarily be unlawful. If a clear threat emerged that was deserving of decisive action, the existing lawful route would be to secure UN Security Council support for action. Obviously, there are many critics of the UN who would, with due cause, argue that the Security Council would never deliver an appropriate mandate. Nevertheless, a legal solution theoretically exists. Importantly, however, a unilateral decision by the US, to attack Iran for example, would, under current international law, be manifestly unlawful. Of that, there is no doubt and it is submitted that this is not a responsible way forward. But ignoring the substantial strategic – and systemic – security issue that the National Security Strategy raises is not responsible either.

So where does the law stand overall in relation to defensive responses to threats that have yet fully to materialise? At present the law on anticipation, pre-emption or prevention can probably best be illuminated by reference to the standard threat equation:

$$Threat = Capability + Intent$$

A threat is only manifest when its two elements exist together. It is only when this condition is met that the criterion of 'imminence' comes into play. Capability takes time to acquire; intent can change overnight. Russia has the capability to launch a nuclear attack on the US but is not considered at present to have the intention so to do. The US retains its nuclear capability in order to deter Russia from changing its intentions in that respect – but, importantly, Russia is not currently a threat to the US. When capability is combined with immediate intent, anticipatory self-defence is permitted. Even if a potential aggressor with whom a state has fractious relations has the capability to attack, the conditions for lawful anticipatory self-defence must be absent if immediate intent is not in evidence.

Although in the past, the phrases 'anticipatory' and 'pre-emptive' have been regarded as entirely synonymous, it may be useful to distinguish between them now by using the former to describe a defensive attack when an immediate threat has materialized, reserving the latter for a defensive response in the absence of a potential aggressor's immediate intent. Given this distinction, anticipatory self-defence would be lawful; pre-emptive self-defence would not be. (Although suggested here as a useful formula, it must be stressed that this distinctive use of the two phrases is not common.)

In the case of preventive war, the capability to attack does not yet exist. In this instance there can be no immediate intention on the part of a potential aggressor to attack. If intent exists at all, it is not the intention immediately to attack but merely the intention to obtain the capability. Even if a 'rogue state' like Iran obtained nuclear weapons, there is no convincing evidence leading us to conclude that it would actually deploy them against any other state. Indeed, an Iranian nuclear weapon may merely serve the purpose of deterring an attack on Iran by another nuclear weapon state, either regionally (Israel or Pakistan, for example) or systemically (the US). As the US National Security Strategy pointed out, for any use of preventive war on the basis of self-defence to be rendered lawful it would require a substantial shift in the law. Preventive war as a method of enforcement, however, with UN Security Council authorization, could be lawful, although admittedly both controversial and most unlikely. The question at the heart of this issue (what can be done legitimately and ultimately to prevent the acquisition of nuclear weapons by 'rogue states') is likely to remain an important one for some time to come.

HUMANITARIAN INTERVENTION

Immediately prior to 9/11, by far the most contentious issue to do with the law relating to the use of force was that associated with humanitarian intervention. While now

BOX 7.6 ANTICIPATION, PRE-EMPTION AND PREVENTION

Capability + Immediate intent = Imminent threat	Anticipatory self-defence (lawful)
Capability + No immediate intent = No imminent threat	Pre-emption (unlawful)
No capability + Intent to obtain = No threat	Preventive war (unlawful unless authorized by UN Security Council)

overshadowed somewhat by the legal debates about responses to international terrorism and the ongoing controversy about the legality of intervention in Iraq, the subject of humanitarian intervention has by no means disappeared from the legal agenda. As this chapter is being written, the UN is putting together the force necessary to give substance to UN Security Council Resolution 1769(2007) relating to the Darfur region of Sudan. Humanitarian missions are as important today as they were prior to 9/11.

Particular controversy over humanitarian intervention was generated by the NATO decision to launch a military campaign against Serbia in order to prevent what it expected to become widespread humanitarian abuse of ethnic Albanians in the Serbian province of Kosovo. What made NATO's action particularly controversial was the absence of a UN Security Council mandate authorizing the use of force. In effect, while the nature of the operation was enforcement, NATO took the law into its own hands when it became obvious that no UN mandate would be possible (principally because of a probable Russian veto in the Security Council).

While the NATO action over Kosovo was the 'grit in the oyster' that stimulated the controversy, it was by no means the beginning of the substantive debate over humanitarian intervention. The core issue here is to do with the balance between two conflicting ideals. The first of these is the principle of non-intervention in the internal affairs of sovereign states, a principle acknowledged in Article 2(7) of the UN Charter. The second is the need to protect all peoples from widespread abuse breaching fundamental human rights standards (including genocide), a responsibility of states under, for example, Article 1 of the Genocide Convention.

A traditional and extreme Positive Law approach would stress the absolute nature of sovereignty, granting states the right to behave with impunity within their borders and placing on all other states a correlative obligation not to interfere. This is not to say that humanitarian concerns were entirely absent from the international system during the high period of Realism and Positive Law. One example of an arguably humanitarian intervention was that of Britain, France and Russia in Greece between 1827 and 1830. So Natural Law influence was not entirely absent. As we have noted already in this chapter, however, it is the period since the middle of the twentieth century that the Positivist approach has come under increasing challenge from Natural Law influences. In the Cold War period (in which Realism retained its influence) there was considerable reluctance to shift towards an undermining of absolute notions of sovereignty, in particular in relation to the issue of non-intervention. In 1965, for example, the General Assembly adopted a Declaration on the Inadmissibility of Intervention and followed this up with a further non-interventionist resolution in 1970 (the Declaration of Principles of International Law Concerning Friendly Relations and Cooperation Among States). Nevertheless, interventions did take place that had positive humanitarian consequences. India applied force in East Pakistan (now Bangladesh) in 1971, Tanzania intervened in Uganda in 1978 and Vietnam intervened in Cambodia in 1979. All of these interventions were unilateral and without authorization from the UN Security Council. In general they were justified, not by reference to humanitarian objectives but under the rubric of self-defence.

The Security Council in its practice has itself tended to shift in favour of humanitarian intervention. By defining the effects of humanitarian abuse as a threat to international peace and security (by reference to its cross border consequences) it opens up the prospect of Chapter VII action and the imposition of sanctions, including military enforcement. It is now widely regarded to be the case that sovereignty brings with it responsibilities as well as rights and these impose some restrictions on what states can and cannot do in the exercise of their sovereignty. Genocide, in particular, is not only dealt with in treaty law, with parties under an obligation to both prevent and punish the crime, the crime itself represents non-compliance with a peremptory norm of international law (or *jus cogens*) that no state is at liberty to breach under any circumstances (although it must be said that the record of the international application of the Genocide Convention has been lamentable, with virtually no instance of mass human rights abuse having been formally declared as genocide).

Following the end of the Cold War, the debate began noticeably to move forward. The break-up of the Federal Republic of Yugoslavia, and the horrific instances of ethnic abuse that this precipitated, began to shift opinion markedly. While this was creating grave concern within Europe, genocide on an appalling scale was perpetrated in Rwanda in 1994. The lack of effective international action to prevent this is a profound indictment of the international community, the UN and the major states that could, and should, have acted. The following year, the massacre in Srebrenica demonstrated the depths to which the former regular holiday destination of countless European families had descended. All of this provided the backdrop to Kosovo four years later, when political leaders within NATO were galvanized into taking action to prevent a further genocide occurring in Europe.

By the late 1990s, humanitarian intervention was generally regarded as permissible in law, provided it was authorized by the UN Security Council. In the case of Kosovo this was not possible because Russia (supporting Serbia) would have vetoed a resolution. What then? NATO intervened without a UN mandate, exceptionally justifying this by reference to the overwhelming need to avoid a humanitarian catastrophe. This decision divided international legal opinion and raised serious questions about the role of the UN itself. The debate that followed was intense, some arguing that UN authorization was essential, others that it was not, given the humanitarian dimension. Perhaps the most balanced view, literally, was that the intervention was strictly unlawful but justified nevertheless.

This debate prompted the Canadian government to initiate an international commission (the International Commission on Intervention and State Sovereignty, or ICISS) with a commitment to report on a practical way forward for dealing with humanitarian crises in the event that the Permanent Members of the Security Council could not agree on the need for military intervention. The ICISS's report, entitled *Responsibility to Protect*, was submitted to UN Secretary General, Kofi Annan, in December 2001. It was staffed in New York and was one of the documents provided by the Secretary General to a High Level Panel on Threats, Challenges and Change charged with making wide-ranging recommendations on UN reform. That Panel reported in 2004 with a document (*A More Secure World: Our Shared Responsibility*) submitted directly to the Secretary General in advance of the 2005 UN Summit. Kofi Annan's hope in commissioning this report was to set in train reform of the UN, making it more responsive to the global demands the UN would face in the twenty-first century. He followed this up with a report of his own, in March 2005 (*In Larger Freedom: Towards Development, Security and Human Rights for All*), that was forwarded to all member states with the aim that it would provide the basis for a formal UN reform agenda for the UN Summit later that year.

▎ BOX 7.7 HUMANITARIAN INTERVENTION AND UN REFORM

1999: Kosovo Intervention by NATO without UN Security Council mandate
2001: Report of the International Commission on Intervention and State Sovereignty, *Responsibility to Protect*
2004: Secretary General's High Level Panel report, *A More Secure World: Our Shared Responsibility*
2005: Secretary General's report to Member States, *In Larger Freedom: Towards Development, Security and Human Rights for All*
2005: UN Summit – no further progress

In the end, Annan's hope for serious moves forward with UN reform foundered as a result of US opposition and his own much weakened position as Secretary General (caused by his impending retirement and the negative effects of his handling of the so-called 'Oil for Food' scandal, which rocked the UN in the later months of his Secretary Generalship).

The UN reform agenda was wide ranging, including not only security issues but also follow-on work related to the Millennium Development Goals. In the end, little emerged that served to clarify the legal position in relation to humanitarian intervention. Indeed, the legal situation today is not noticeably different from that which prevailed immediately following the NATO intervention over Kosovo. A useful and timely test case has been the increasingly serious humanitarian crisis in the Darfur region of Sudan. This crisis has been similar to that over Kosovo in one important and pertinent respect. General international concern and demands for UN action have been unsuccessful in applying pressure on the Security Council for the simple reason that China, a Permanent Member with veto power, has been unwilling to support a UN mandated Chapter VII intervention because of its own interest in obtaining oil from Sudan. Unlike Kosovo in 1999, when the broader regional security situation allowed for a NATO intervention, no military force has been forthcoming that might have acted without Chinese support or acquiescence. Clearly, NATO was acting in the national interests of its member states over Kosovo. National interests have not gelled in the same way over Darfur. In addition, US and British pre-occupations with both Afghanistan and the invasion, occupation and post-conflict reconstruction of Iraq have worked against those two key states acting in the relatively remote region of north east Africa. The result has been a totally ineffective international reaction to the humanitarian catastrophe unfolding there. In the summer of 2007, the UN was charged with working to provide an intervention force following the Security Council's agreement on an intervention force enshrined in Resolution 1769. This force is, however, only deploying with the consent of the Sudanese government and is endowed with none of the Chapter VII enforcement powers many consider essential for effective action.

The international law relating to humanitarian intervention is, therefore, still in an unsatisfactory state of development. Clearly, intervention authorized under Chapter VII of the UN Charter would be lawful. But in the absence of such a mandate, it is far from clear (as it also was in the case of Kosovo) whether a coalition of states could lawfully intervene. Some argue that an unauthorized intervention would be lawful on grounds related to the international community's 'responsibility to protect'. The fact that the UN Security Council is unable to deliver a mandate reflecting that responsibility does not absolve individual member states of their obligations. Others point to the words of the UN Charter and to the principles associated with non-intervention and the ban on resort to force without UN approval. Arguably, if the scale of humanitarian catastrophe in Sudan has failed to move the law forward, it is unlikely that any similar crisis will do so in the foreseeable future. We can only wait and see – and hope that circumstances do not conspire to allow further genocides to go unchecked in the meantime.

CONCLUSION

We started this chapter by making reference to Natural and Positive Law influences on international law. The previous section on humanitarian intervention demonstrates effectively how these two contrasting influences remain important in assessing the current nature of the law. The key question is to do with whether states have obligations imposed upon them through some form of higher law or whether they are only obliged to comply with that with which they have agreed to be bound. But it would be too simple to leave it at that. While the relationship between the UN Charter and human rights law, for example, can be related to the Natural Law influence, responsible Positivists would argue that a concern for human rights is reflected in the current law for the simple reason that states have agreed that it should be. Nevertheless, the division of opinion about the NATO intervention over Kosovo retains the character of a Natural Law/Positive Law distinction. Those assessing where the law is, need to be aware of the different emphases that these two contrasting schools apply and what effect they have on the interpretation of legitimacy when it comes to intervention. If one accepts and feels comfortable with the suggestion that the UN Charter reflects closely Just War doctrine, as this author does, then it is very likely that the shift towards a greater concern for humanitarianism and away from the theoretical sanctity of sovereign political boundaries will be seen as a welcome development in the law. Positivists are more inclined to stress the over-riding importance of treaty based agreements between states. So, for example, a strict compliance with the UN Charter would render humanitarian action impossible to justify in the face of a Security Council veto – no matter what the humanitarian consequences of inaction.

It is a feature familiar to international relations scholars that the Realist – and by inference, the Positivist – will stress the need for order in the international system. In contrast, the Liberal Internationalist – and by inference, the adherent of a Natural Law approach – will often stress the desirability of justice. Order and justice are not invariably compatible conditions, not least because the former is a matter of fact while the latter is a matter of opinion. The law, it must be admitted, is a product of the contrasting influences of these two positions. This is something we should never forget, not least because to argue one position effectively it is necessary to understand from where one's opponent in the debate is coming.

Ultimately, and formally, legal disagreements can be resolved by reference to the ICJ. The Court has tended, unsurprisingly, to follow the trend towards the Natural Law approach in more recent years, interpreting situations by reference to ideas as much as to strict application of treaty law. Unfortunately, the ICJ does not provide a definitive answer in all cases, for the simple reason that not all instances of legal dispute are put before the Court for judgement. The Court has never, for example, addressed the substance of the legality of NATO's intervention over Kosovo, despite Serbia's attempt to persuade it to do so. The invasion of Iraq is also never likely to be tested in this way. While one is inclined to assume that if it were tested the US and British positions would find it difficult to prevail, it is presumptuous to assume absolutely that the judgement would contain nothing from which those two states could take comfort.

There are a great many controversies within the field of international law relating to the use of force. This chapter has concentrated on the key issues of contemporary concern and has, indeed, been forced by reason of space to deal only cursorily with those. The list of contemporary issues will inevitably change as time goes by; but so too will the law. It is by no means fixed and is in a constant state of development. While the defensive response to terrorism by Israel in 1968 was deemed unlawful, President Clinton's reaction in very similar vein in 1998 was not. In this way, developments in law tend to reflect the needs of the international system – and so they should as state practice is the most vital component of customary law. Preventive war may even now not be unlawful in all circumstances but, if diplomatic approaches to proliferation fail to achieve results that are vital for the security of international society as a whole, the law may indeed require change, much as the US National Security Strategy has hinted. The instinctive reaction of many, including this author, to such suggestions is to be understandably wary. But if the law on the use of force were to fall entirely out of step with international politics and strategic reality it would have no practical utility at all.

UN REPORTS

The three reports related to UN reform and humanitarian intervention mentioned in the text are as follows:

ICISS, (2001) *Responsibility to Protect*, International Development Research Centre, Ottawa.

United Nations, *A More Secure World: Our Shared Responsibility* (Report of the Secretary General's High-Level Panel on Threats, Challenges and Change), available on the United Nations website.

United Nations, *In Larger Freedom: Towards Development, Security and Human Rights for All* (Report of the Secretary General), available on the United Nations website.

FURTHER READING

Bellamy, A. (2006) *Just Wars: From Cicero to Iraq*, Polity, Cambridge.

Dinstein, Y. (2005) *War, Aggression and Self Defence* (4th edn), Cambridge University Press, Cambridge and New York.

Gazzini, T. (2005) *The Changing Rules on the Use of Force in International Law*, Manchester University Press, Manchester.

Grey, C. (2004) *International Law and the Use of Force* (2nd edn), Oxford University Press, Oxford and New York.

Higgins, R. (1995) *Problems and Process: International Law and How to Use It*, Oxford University Press, Oxford and New York.

Wheeler, N. (2000) *Saving Strangers: Humanitarian Intervention in International Society*, Oxford University Press, Oxford and New York.

CHAPTER 8

Terrorism
David Brown

This chapter aims to explore some of the key debates and arguments surrounding the concept of terrorism. Terrorism has long featured as an integral part of the international security environment but has taken special prominence as such since 9/11. This chapter will first consider the concept of terrorism, starting with the perennial issue of definitions and how the concept has changed, and culminating in a brief examination of the nature and threat posed by Al Qaeda. Having established the main contours of the terrorist threat, the remainder of the chapter will deal with some of the potential responses utilized by the international community. This chapter will focus on two types of international response to terrorism. First, the so-called soft-line response that aims to identify and then rectify the alleged root causes of terrorism. Second, the contribution that the Armed Forces can make in combating terrorism will be examined.

THE DEFINITION DEBATE

The first point to note when exploring the concept of terrorism is the absence of any agreed international definition. Not for the want of trying, the international community – as represented by the United Nations – has been unable, during the course of numerous debates and twelve international conventions thus far, to articulate the concept in an internationally agreed political definition. So far, the UN has managed to define and criminalize aspects of terrorist behaviour, such as hijacking or the taking of hostages, but has not been able to agree on a definition that encapsulates the nature of the act of terrorism itself.

However elusive a single definition of terrorism may seem there has been a convergence around a number of key themes. A 1992 study of the available options conducted by Alex Schmid revealed surprising levels of agreement with approximately 80 per cent of the definitions highlighting the use or threat of violence, with 65 per cent emphasizing the political nature of the action and 51 per cent including some reference to the idea of fear (Schmid 1992).

The UK's 1974 Prevention of Terrorism Act incorporates three primary areas of agreement from Schmid's study and defines terrorism as: 'the use of violence for political ends, (including) any use of violence for the purpose of putting the public or any section of the public in fear'. The political aspect of any definition is arguably the most important for distinguishing terrorism from other forms of violence. For example, while a series of muggings may create fear in a wider community, such crime cannot be included within the definition of terrorism because of the lack of any political message to the community that is suffering the muggings. Equally, an act of violence for its own sake cannot be considered terrorism; rather, terrorism is unique insomuch as the targets of terrorism are usually part of a specific political agenda.

As with most political definitions, the 1974 Prevention of Terrorism Act (PTA) cannot fully encapsulate all aspects of terrorism, but reveals a specific caveat that needs to be addressed if such a definition is to more accurately reflect the concept of terrorism. Specifically, can a state can be guilty of an act of terrorism? The concept of state terror has a lengthy historical lineage; in fact, the word terrorism derives from the *Reign of Terror* enacted by Robespierre and his Jacobin allies in the aftermath of the 1789 French Revolution and consequently the link between state and terror seemed to make perfect sense. In a contemporary context, the idea of state terrorism remains ambiguous. For example, the 2003 invasion of Iraq (branded illegal by the then UN Secretary-General Kofi Annan) used violence for political ends and to initiate regime change. Additionally, the use of the Shock and Awe military campaign sent a wider message to the Iraqi populace and could be construed as using violence to put 'the public or any section of the public in fear'. However, whether or not the Iraq War of 2003 could be called an act of state terrorism is a hugely contested issue, with most definitions relying on a political agenda, not a universal agreement.

Given the potential for overlap, the actions of agents of a state (such as an army) must be distinguished from the action of a non-state terrorist group. State sovereignty means that a state can legitimately sanction the use of force or violence in its own territory. However, a strict interpretation of the PTA definition of terrorism – which makes no reference to the legitimacy of the source of the violent behaviour – does not allow any differentiation between the actions of an army and the actions of a terrorist group. As a result, it may be more accurate to restrict the application of the definition of terrorism to non-state actors. Therefore, a more usable definition would be: 'the use of violence for political ends, (including) any use of violence for the purpose of putting the public or any section of the public in fear by an illegitimate non-state actor'.

It could be argued that excluding state actors from definitions of terrorism allows states free reign to use violence and terror against citizens. However, such is not the case and there already exists a set of internationally agreed laws and conventions that criminalize acts of excessive or illegal violence by agents of the state. This was a clear point made by the 2004 Report of the Secretary-General's High Level Panel on Threats,

BOX 8.1 THE TERRORISM DEFINITION DEBATE

- No agreed definition
- Convergence: use or threat of violence/political nature of action/fear
- Non-state actors

Challenges and Change, in its examination of the main threats to international security and the contribution that the UN could make in challenging such threats. Noting that there already were a number of routes by which the state could be prosecuted, including provisions criminalizing genocide and the Laws of Armed Conflict (LOAC), the report concluded that there was no need to use an already contested term such as 'terrorism' to describe state behaviour. States have been – and will continue to be – brought to account for war crimes and therefore there seems little problem in restricting the use of the term terrorism to the sphere of non-state actors.

To date, a variety of factors have contributed to the lack of a single, internationally recognized definition of terrorism. First, it needs to be borne in mind that individual states have experienced a specific and individual variant of terrorism. Ensuring all such experiences were encapsulated into a single definition has proven to be a tremendously difficult task (especially considering the growth of the international community from the 51 original member states of the UN to the current 192 member states.) Second, terrorism remains a pejorative term with undoubtedly negative connotations that can be used to undermine opponents by casting doubt on the legitimacy of their actions. The term is associated with unacceptable violence and to be labelled a terrorist has severe and restrictive consequences in the international system. A single definition of terrorism would also have to contend with the notion that *one man's terrorist is another man's freedom fighter*. Such issues constitute the heart of the definition debate, and were most obviously evident in Yasser Arafat's claim to defend the cause of national self-determination – including his own Palestinian Liberation Organization – by suggesting that certain political causes were noble enough to justify non-state violence. Arafat's position was not upheld by the UN High Level Panel, but remains the main obstacle to an international definition of terrorism.

BOX 8.2 DIFFICULTIES OF DEFINITION

- States?
- Different variants
- Pejorative term
- 'One man's terrorist is another man's freedom fighter'

▍ TYPOLOGIES OF TERRORISM

It is also necessary to consider how terrorism is manifested. There are three major categories: nationalist/separatist, left- and right-wing terrorism, and religiously inspired terror. As well as giving some indication as to the range of potential threats facing the international community – and therefore the context in which Al Qaeda operates – such categorization also provides a useful chronology of terrorist development.

Nationalist/separatist

Nationalist or separatist terror describes where terrorism is used to achieve national self-determination or separation. For example, the long-term goal of the Provisional Irish Republican Army (PIRA) in Northern Ireland is to achieve reunification with the Irish Republic, whereas Euskadi ta Askatasuna (ETA) ultimately wants to detach the Basque region from Spanish control. Typically, if nationalist/separatist groups maintain some minority community support they become very difficult to completely eradicate.

Left and right wing

Both left- and right-wing terror groups believe that terror is a means to achieve some radical re-ordering of state structures or international institutions. The majority of politically motivated revolutionary groups in the 1970s and 1980s came from the left wing, using violence to try to undermine what they believed to be corrupt Western capitalist structures. Examples include the Italian Red Brigades and Action Directe in France. However, left-wing groups declined in importance following the end of the Cold War, save for a brief revival in 2004 when the Proletarian Nuclei for Communism (NPC) claimed responsibility for planting an explosive device near to where Tony Blair was staying in Sardinia.

Right-wing groups gained greater prominence in the late 1980s and early 1990s. Prompted, on occasion, as a reaction to increased left-wing violence (as was the case in Italy), right-wing groups were fuelled by the perception that government agencies were not doing enough to protect their national territories from foreign intervention. Right-wing groups operate under a typically racist and anti-Semitic ideology with two main targets. The primary targets were notably immigrants, asylum seekers and Jews. As a secondary targeting strategy, state agencies with responsibility for such matters were also considered as legitimate targets. As a result, although less durable than their left-wing counterparts, right-wing groups tended to be more violent and less constrained in their targeting.

Religious

Religious groups operate under the ideology that it is their mission to uphold the forces of good against the forces of evil. Inspired by their own interpretation of key religious texts and believing themselves to be the repositories of truth, religious terror groups have dominated the international political scene since the end of the Cold War, with religious groups such as Hamas, Hizballah, Islamic Jihad and Al Qaeda becoming household names. While religious groups also possess a discernible political programme – the political wing of Hamas, for example, has carried out a great deal of charitable work on the ground, providing welfare services that would (and, indeed, should) be the responsibility of government – their primary motivation remains the advancement of a particular religious view. This arguably affects not only their political viewpoint – (with a preference for religiously pure governments which has led some to question, in the case of Islam, whether it is able to co-exist with democratic structures) – but also their cultural outlook.

BOX 8.3 TYPOLOGIES OF TERRORISM

- *Nationalist/separatist*: PIRA, ETA
- *Left and right wing*: Italian Red Brigades, Action Directe, NPC
- *Religious*: Hamas, Hizballah, Islamic Jihad, Al Qaeda

WHAT IS AL QAEDA?

Considered to be a new threat on the international stage, substantive scholarship has been dedicated to understanding the development of the Al Qaeda terrorist network, with a plethora of literature charting the group's ideological foundations, its structure, the role of Osama Bin Laden and its major operations throughout the 1990s and into the post-September 11 era. This section will highlight some of Al Qaeda's main features, will consider how accurate it is to label Al Qaeda a new organization, and will assess the challenge posed by Al Qaeda to the wider international system.

Ideology

It is wrong to suggest that Al Qaeda has no political objectives. It is also wrong to suggest that Al Qaeda has no specific targets in mind when planning its operations. Al Qaeda shares some ideological elements with more traditional groups, such as an anti-Western stance (similar to traditional left-wing groups) and an anti-Semitic agenda (similar to right-wing groups). Al Qaeda also shares some ideological elements with nationalist/separatist groups because of the group's territorial claims to certain regions. Al Qaeda's programme many not be new, but the scale of operations is unlike any other terrorist group to date. Effectively, Al Qaeda has a transnational political agenda. According to Osama Bin Laden (and quoted during a speech by US President Bush, 2006) Al Qaeda seeks to impose a very specific version of Islamic rule on 'every land that was a home for Islam . . . The whole world is an open field for us'. Al Qaeda's programme is organized in stages, with the initial focus specifically being on Iraq and the wider Middle East. The long-term goal of the Al Qaeda group is to expel the US from the Middle East and establish an Islamic authority as a base for the renewed Caliphate. Furthermore, Al Qaeda plan to extend the wave of jihad to the remaining secular authorities before preparing for a final clash with Israel. As a result of this larger-scale political objective the targeting base for violence is similarly large. Bin Laden has declared that Jews, crusaders, and all who permit and contribute to the continuance of the US (such as supporters and tax-payers) are legitimate Al Qaeda targets. Such an agenda makes Al Qaeda potentially the most violent terrorist group in history, and fits with the general trend of the 1990s when there were fewer recorded terrorist incidents, but more fatalities. Brian Jenkins' assessment that traditional terrorist groups would rather have a lot of people watching, than a lot of people dead does not fit the Al Qaeda profile. Al Qaeda have managed to do both – 9/11 killed over three thousand people and generated huge and ongoing media attention.

Structure and organization

The post-9/11 world has seen the emergence of franchise terrorism, wherein groups share the ideological aims of the original Al Qaeda movement but act as independent units within a wider network. The three-tier strategy replaces the traditional central unit, borne out of the Afghan Mujahideen. The first tier encompasses the traditional unit of individuals or groups directly connected to core Al Qaeda. The second tier shares a loose but direct affiliation with the core unit and the final tier are inspired by, but have no direct affiliation with the core unit, such as the London suicide bombers of 7 July 2005. Furthermore, self-starter terrorist actions may become ever more prominent in the future and such changes will certainly make Al Qaeda more difficult to combat. Al Qaeda's global reach is exemplified by its extensive range of attack locations that include the US, Southeast Asia, Europe and Africa, with a recent focus on the Middle East. Equally, the strategy of using so-called clean skins – those with no background in radical or militant activity – to carry out attacks will only increase the difficulties in tracking and preventing future terrorist operations.

Recruitment

Changes to Al Qaeda's organizational structure have been mirrored by changes in its recruitment techniques. In the absence of the traditional Afghan training camps Al Qaeda has developed new recruitment strategies. The Internet has become a vital tool of virtual-jihad, allowing technical knowledge and experiences to be shared without face-to-face contact. Furthermore, Al Qaeda has never been dependent on top-down recruitment: 'there has never been a recruitment program in Al Qaeda. They have not needed one' (Banks 2005: 677). Although traditional recruiters still play a limited role – such as Abu Hamza at London's Finsbury Park mosque who was responsible for recruiting individuals such as shoe bomber Richard Reid – there has never been a shortage of willing recruits to Al Qaeda. Indeed, Sageman concludes that the main recruitment factor for Al Qaeda is kinship links where groups of friends participate together (as was the case with Mohammed Atta's Hamburg cell, part of the driving force behind the 9/11 attacks). Resultantly, it is very difficult for states to break the link between radicalization and recruitment.

Weapons of mass destruction

Al Qaeda is further differentiated from other terrorist groups by their use of Weapons of Mass Destruction (WMD). Although not the only group to consider WMD tactics – (the Liberation Tigers of Tamil Eelam (LTTE) in Sri Lanka have attempted to use chlorine gas, and the Aum cult in Japan have used sarin gas) – Al Qaeda have established themselves as WMD credible, with records showing that Bin Laden met with a Sudanese military official in 1993 to negotiate the sale of weapons-grade uranium. Al Qaeda's ambitions to be WMD capable continue to the present day with Bin Laden attempting to recruit nuclear scientists to Al Qaeda as recently as 2006. Al Qaeda's nuclear ambitions pose a significant and unique challenge to the international system.

BOX 8.4 AL QAEDA

- *Ideology*: Anti-Western, anti-Semitic, territorial, Islamic
- *Structural organization*: Franchise terrorism, three tiers, global reach
- *Recruitment*: Afghan/Pakistan border, Internet, willing recruits, kinship

COUNTER-TERRORISM: THE RANGE OF RESPONSES

Counter-terrorism relies on variety of strategies and mechanisms in an effort to predict and prevent terrorism. Increased aviation security, investigations into terrorist financing, the abilities to investigate, arrest, extradite and prosecute terrorist suspects, prevention of WMD proliferation, improved community relations and counter-terrorist propaganda are but a few of the strategies currently employed as counter-terrorism tactics. This chapter will present a snapshot of the counter-terrorism instruments available to the international community and elaborate on two wider themes, the first being an analysis of the so-called soft approach to counter-terrorism which aims to tackle the root causes of terrorism. Secondly, the contribution made by the military to combating international terrorism – specifically the adoption of the war model as a counter-terrorism strategy – will be discussed.

The softer option?

The soft approach to counter-terrorism seeks to eliminate the root causes of terrorism and to provide alternative means of expression to those who might otherwise employ terrorist tactics. By clearly identifying and tackling the likely root causes of terrorism and being prepared (if the situation requires it) to directly or indirectly negotiate a peaceful route to security and stability, the soft approach to counter-terrorism seeks to alleviate the problem of political violence. However, accurate identification of the root causes of terrorism and the political and practical obstacles involved in adopting a negotiating strategy remain problematic.

Commonly identified root causes of terrorism include poverty and political repression. In the case of the former, relative inequalities in income, social welfare and standards of living serve as instigators of radical and violent action, with terrorism regarded as an only option for those seeking a more just and equitable distribution of resources. However, studies across a range of terrorist groups have demonstrated that those who participate in terrorism generally do not originate from the under-educated lower classes. Participants in left-wing terrorist groups were most often disillusioned middle-class students who felt a moral responsibility to act on behalf of their less fortunate brethren. Participants in religious terrorism similarly do not specifically originate from economically poor backgrounds, and while three of the four 2005 London bombers grew up in a poor area of Leeds, there is 'little to distinguish it from many poorer areas of Britain's other big cities' (Home Office Report 2006: 13). Therefore poverty alone cannot be considered as the primary trigger for terrorist action and it remains that case that concentrated and consistent international efforts to eradicate poverty and improve levels of international education will only have a marginal impact on terrorist activity.

The strategy of regime change, or the imposition of a liberal democratic government, has been one of the most controversial and defining elements of the Bush Presidency. Based on the principle that democracies are better equipped to combat terrorism, the Bush administration has long advocated promotion of stable democratic models across the Middle East, and resorted to the use of military force in Afghanistan and Iraq to ensure regime change. The strategy of regime change has been advocated for a number of reasons. First, the presence of genuine mechanisms for consultation and participation within a state that would allow citizens the right to air and address concerns would arguably undercut both the need for violent action and the underlying legitimacy of such action, should it arise. Unlike alternative regimes, 'democracy offers an ownership stake in society' and therefore allows peaceful alternatives to political violence (US National Strategy for Combating Terrorism 2006: 10). Additionally, democracies are theoretically more responsive to citizens' concerns, such as relative poverty or perceived discrimination, and are better placed to tackle potential causes of discontent. Second, liberal democracies have, at their core, the principle of negotiation and bargaining and consequently democracies are considered to be very effective participants in the international community. Finally, there exists the assumption that democracies are likely to mirror and adopt Western principles and methods and are therefore more likely to ally themselves with Western political objectives, such as the War on Terror.

However, 'the data available [does] not show a strong relationship between democracy and an absence of or a reduction in terrorism. Terrorism appears to stem from factors much more specific than regime type' (Gause 2005: 62). In fact, terrorist activity is equally likely to flourish in a democratic system as in a repressive model. While repressive regimes may deny political participation and therefore instigate more violent responses to perceived problems, a repressive regime will similarly be less concerned about the methods used to combat terrorism.

The relationship between democracy and terrorism is also not a one-way street. Some critics would argue that in fighting the War on Terror certain states have been becoming *less* liberal and *less* democratic than they once were. For example, the War on Terror has seen the establishment of a range of control orders that arguably restricts freedom of speech. The presence of the US military detention camp at Guantanamo Bay in Cuba continues to raise questions concerning the democratic viability of indefinite detention without trial. Additionally, the use of torture (however redefined by the US government) as a weapon of war raises very real concerns about the limits of democratic values. It could be argued that the threat of terrorism is having a greater impact on the nature of democracy, rather than the other way round. Additionally, such measures undermine the political and moral image of states such as the US and UK and consequently make it much more difficult to win over the hearts and minds of more moderate elements. Equally, the use of armed force to impose democracy in another state can lead to a violent backlash, as is evident in both Iraq and the UK. Rather than decreasing terrorist activity, it has been suggested that the strategy of imposing democracy has merely succeeded in increasing the nature of the terrorist threat.

Finally, two points need to be made regarding the relationship between militant Islam and democracy. For militant Islamist terrorists, the freedoms that underpin a genuine liberal democracy are both to be rejected, as part of their wider criticism of the corrupt and decadent West, and exploited, in order to more easily prepare and plan their activities. Furthermore, the assumption that greater global democracy will result in an increase in Western allies is a strongly contested assertion. Indeed, certain results indicate that 'democratisation policy will lead to Islamist domination of Arab politics' (Gause 2005: 76). Examples from both Iraq (where the Supreme Council for Islamic Revolution in Iraq (SCIRI) and the Dawa Party now dominate the government) and the Palestinian Authority (where Hamas won a surprise electoral victory in 2006) reinforce such thinking.

Even if a clear and accepted link could be established between tackling the root causes of terrorism and a reduction in terrorist activity, there remain questions as to the acceptability of state negotiation with terrorists. Some scholars remain steadfastly opposed to the idea of negotiating; indeed Dershowitz explicitly opposes the idea on the grounds that negotiation with terrorists would merely serve to legitimize the terrorist group and encourage other groups to take up arms in order to further their cause. Dershowitz refers to the case of Palestinian terrorism as an example of how negotiation does not discourage further terrorist activity, but instead rewards terrorist activity and creates some form of contagion effect whereby other groups take part in copycat activities (Dershowitz 2002: 53–88). However, this was more of an issue for traditional terrorist groups with their more limited aims and objectives and it should be remembered that during the Northern Ireland peace process the UK government was only prepared to negotiate with Sinn Fein, the political representatives of the Republican movement, and not the PIRA directly.

Combating Al Qaeda terrorism presents a complicated plethora of issues to the international community. First, there is no agreement between Western states concerning the motivations behind Al Qaeda activity. The suggestion that Western foreign policies in general, or the policies of the US in particular, have motivated greater radicalization on the part of sections of the Muslim community remains a contested issue. Prime Minister Tony Blair was consistently of the view that it was the symbolic idea of Western values, as opposed to any specific policy, that enrages militant Islamists and consequently there are minimal policy changes that can be made to counter Islamist terrorism. Critics have argued, however, that Blair's position stems from a strategy to disconnect the 2003 Iraq War from any potential rise in terrorist activity. The alternative view is that 'US national security is threatened by the Islamists because of what America does in the Muslim world, not because of its beliefs or lifestyles' (Scheuer 2006: 21) and that, consequently, there are considerable policy changes that the US and its allies could enforce to alleviate terrorism. Such changes might include a retraction of perceived historical slurs and resultant anti-Islamic propaganda, or the development of a more consistent foreign policy that tackles WMD proliferation in *all* WMD suspect states, including North Korea and Israel.

A second problem to combating Al Qaeda terrorism lies with Al Qaeda's exceptionally broad goals – to extend a specific type of Islamist government across the wider Middle East and the destruction of Israel – making it difficult to even contemplate negotiating a political settlement (as was demonstrated in the EU states' immediate rejection of a ceasefire in return for their withdrawal from Iraq). Al Qaeda's goal of recreating an Islamic empire may seem too absolutist to negotiate, but the dream of an Islamic empire may not be any more unrealistic than any of the instances where Western states have historically imposed a national identity on a reluctant population (such as transforming West Germany into a Marxist workers' republic after the Second World War). The difference is that 'Al Qaeda's ideology does not constitute the majority twenty-first-century Western thinking and thus remains difficult to rationalise' (Neumann 2007: 129). Furthermore, even in the event of negotiating with Al Qaeda, the fragmented and international nature of the group means that 'it is unclear whether the organisation's local commanders would honour it' (Neumann 2007: 136).

BOX 8.5 SOFTER OPTIONS

- Tackling perceived root causes, plus negotiation
- Tackling poverty and inequalities (but many are middle class)
- Nature of political repression (by more liberal democratic model, but there is no evidence of a strong relationship)

THE MILITARY AND COUNTER-TERRORISM

The War on Terror has seen the prominent use of military intervention as a counter-terrorism tactic. As already noted, however, counter-terrorism strategies cannot necessarily be implemented in isolation and the poorly prepared and badly executed post-invasion phase of the Iraq operation has proven to have had a negative impact in terms of combating Al Qaeda recruitment and radicalization in both Iraq and other states.

The 2002 New Chapter doctrine details the UK's military response to 9/11 and is a useful tool for examining how the military can contribute to counter-terrorism. It outlines five principal counter-terrorist strategies: prevention, deterrence, coercion, disruption and destruction. The strategy of prevention calls for the use of the military to tackle conditions that breed terrorism, such as failing governments. The strategy of deterrence calls for the use of military strength to demonstrate credibility and resolve so as to displace terrorist activity. The strategies of coercion, disruption and destruction focus primarily on combating state sponsors of terrorism, although disruption could also include military action against terrorist training camps.

The strategy of focusing military strength against state sponsors of terrorism forms a significant part of the Bush Doctrine. Similarly, the Blair government endorsed the strategy of combating terrorism through the eradication of the international terrorism/rogue states/WMD nexus. However, the use of military force against the sponsors and facilitators of terrorism presents a number of problems. First, it presupposes a connection that is very hard to verify with hard evidence, as was evident with the Bush administration proving a direct between the Saddam Hussein's regime and Al Qaeda. Additionally, it seems illogical to assume that a rogue state such as Iraq would hand over any of its WMD capability to a terrorist group that it had no control over. The failure of the Iraq War coalition to convincingly demonstrate a link between the Iraqi state, Al Qaeda and WMD has severely undermined the credibility of this approach. As was made clear in the New Chapter, 'there is yet no sign of states deliberately providing chemical, biological, radiological or nuclear (CBRN) materials to terrorists' (Ministry of Defence 2002).

Second, questions remain as to the viability of targeting state sponsors of terrorism without any clear potential targets for military intervention. In 2006, the US State Department's annual review of terrorist trends highlighted five states as potential targets for future military interventions – Cuba, Iran, North Korea, Syria and the Sudan. Yet, Badey points out that, 'Iran appears to be the only state currently on the State Department's list whose involvement in terrorism is not subject to qualifications' (Badey 2006: 310). It could be argued that Cuba, the perennial bogeyman of US foreign policy, is included for reasons other than terrorist activity. Indeed, the State Department's report merely notes that 'Cuba did not protest the use of Guantanamo Bay base to house enemy combatants' as justification for labelling Cuba a state sponsor of terrorism. In the case of North Korea, the US State Department (2005) notes that 'North Korea is not known to have sponsored any terrorist acts since 1987' (US State Department 2005: report renamed as *Country Reports on Terrorism*). Furthermore, the New Chapter accepts the position that state sponsored terrorism is in decline. Although Al Qaeda was reliant on Afghanistan for the provision of training grounds, the group retains a high level of autonomy and financial independence and has yet to be unquestionably linked to any particular state sponsor.

Perhaps the most active and feasible role for the military in terms of combating terror lies with homeland defence. The military, however, have traditionally only played a supporting role to civilian authorities and reports suggest that strategies such as the 2003 decision to place Armoured Personnel Carriers at London's Heathrow result in heightened concern, not reassurance, to the civilian population. Indeed, the New Chapter's deterrence role focuses on overseas terrorism based on the belief that it is better to go to the crisis, than have the crisis come to you. However, history has proven that states must fight terrorism where it exists, not where they choose, with 9/11 and the 2005 London bombings demonstrating that Islamist terrorism does not only exist abroad.

Despite arguments to the contrary, there does exist a role for the military to play in combating terrorism. However, thus far it can be argued that military action has been focused at the wrong times, in the wrong places, and that it may be more productive for the military to focus on terror prevention roles such as providing military assistance to failing states before situations escalate to the point that they require long-term military commitment from the UK or US. Bringing stability to failing or failed states would not only serve to deny potential terrorists a home, but would also potentially encourage another state to become a partner in the War on Terror. In place of the long-term military intervention model that has proven to be both domestically and internationally controversial, military counter-terrorism could be conducted as part of a wider Security Sector Reform programme that assists failing states to improve both their military capabilities and their law enforcement capabilities.

BOX 8.6 MILITARY OPTIONS

- Prevent
- Deter
- Coerce
- Disrupt
- Destroy

CONCLUSION

This chapter has highlighted the main issues concerning the continuing threat posed by international terrorism. While traditional terrorist groups may have declined in prominence and been eclipsed in terms of size and operational capability by their religious counterparts, a revival in traditional terrorism can never be ruled out. Unable, thus far, to fully define the nature of the terrorism threat, states have found it equally difficult to articulate a coherent and successful counter-terrorist response. As a result, the 'war on terror' is likely to be with us for some time to come.

REFERENCES

Badey, T.J. (2006) 'US Counter-terrorism: Change in Approach, Continuity in Policy', *Contemporary Security Policy* 27(2): 310.

Banks, W.C. (2005) 'Alternative Views of the Terrorist Threat', *International Studies Review*, 7(4): 677.

Bjorgo, Tore (1995) *Terror from the Extreme Right*, London: Frank Cass.

Bjorgo, Tore (ed.) (2005) *Root Causes of Terrorism: Myths, Reality and the Way Forward*, London: Routledge.

Blair, Tony (2007) 'A Battle for Global Values', *Foreign Affairs* (Jan.–Feb.): 79–80.

Dershowitz, A. (2002) *Why Terrorism Works: Understanding the Threat, Responding to the Challenge*, London: Yale University Press 53–88.

Gause, F.G. (2005) 'Can Democracy Stop Terrorism?', *Foreign Affairs* Sep./Oct.: 62.

Intelligence and Security Committee (2006) *Report into the London Terrorist Attacks on 7 July 2005*, London: HMSO, P. 27.

Ministry of Defence (2002) *The Strategic Defence Review: A New Chapter: Supporting Evidence and Analysis*, London: HMSO, 3.

Neumann, P. (2007) 'Negotiating with Terrorists', *Foreign Affairs* Jan./Feb.: 129.

Sageman, M. (2004) *Understanding Terror Networks*, Philadelphia: University of Pennsylvania Press.

Scheuer, M. (2006) 'Courting Catastrophe: America Five Years After 9/11', *The National Interest*, Sep./Oct.: 21.

Schmid, A.P. (1992) 'The Response Problem as a Definition Problem', *Terrorism and Political Violence*, 4(4): 7–14.

United Nations (2004) *A More Secure World: Our Shared Responsibility: Report of the High Level Panel on Threats, Challenges and Change*, New York: United Nations, section VI.

US State Department (2005) *Country Reports on Terrorism*, Washington, DC: Office of the Coordinator for Counter terrorism, 2001–4.

US White House (2006) *National Strategy for Combating Terrorism*, Washington, DC: The White House.

FURTHER READING

Alexander, Y. and Swetnam, M. 2001) *Usama Bin Laden's Al Qaeda: Profile of a Terrorist Network*, New York: Transnational Publishers.

Benjamin, D. and Simon, S. (2005) *The Next Attack: The Globalisation of Jihad*, London: Hodder and Stoughton.

Booth, K. and Dunne, T. (2002) *Worlds in Collision: Terror and the Future of Global Order*, Basingstoke: Macmillan.

Burke, J. (2007) *On the Road to Kandahar: Travels Through Conflict in the Islamic World*, New York: Thomas Dunne Books.

Corbin, J. (2002) *The Base: In Search of Al Qaeda, the Terror Network that Shook the World*, London: Simon and Schuster.

Freedman, L. (2002) *Super Terrorism: Policy Responses*, Oxford: Blackwell Publishing.

Gunaratna, R. (2002) *Inside Al Qaeda: Global Network of Terror*, London: Hurst and Company.

Laqueur, W. (2001) *The New Terrorism: Fanaticism and the Arms of Mass Destruction*, London: Phoenix Press.

Wilkinson, P. (2006) *Terrorism Versus Democracy: The Liberal State Response*, London: Frank Cass.

Woodward, B. (2002) *Bush at War*, London: Simon and Schuster.

Woodward, B. (2004) *Plan of Attack: The Road to War*, London: Simon and Schuster.

Woodward, B. (2006) *State of Denial*, London: Simon and Schuster.

Wright, L. (2006) *The Looming Tower: Al Qaeda's Road to 9/11*, London: Allen Lane.

▌USEFUL WEBSITES

UK Foreign and Commonwealth Office, www.fco.gov.uk
UK Home Office, www.homeoffice.gov.uk
International Institute for Counter Terrorism, www.ict.org.il
UK Military Intelligence 'MI5', www.mi5.gov.uk
UK Ministry of Defence, www.mod.uk
National Commission on Terrorist Attacks on the US, www.9-11commission.gov
Northern Ireland Office, www.nio.gov.uk
RAND, www.rand.org/research_areas/terrorism
September 11 Studies, www.academicinfo.net/usa911
Statewatch, www.statewatch.org
US Department of Defense, www.defenselink.mil
US Department of Homeland Security, www.dhs.gov
US State Department, www.state.gov

CHAPTER 9

International Regimes and Organizations

David Galbreath

International relations encompasses the study of conflict and cooperation and international institutions are one of the most important mechanisms through which conflict and cooperation occur. Indeed, many would argue that international institutions have become important actors in international relations in their own right, transcending the sum of their parts. One only needs to look around today to see international institutions at work. For example, the United Nations (UN) is present throughout the world, from Afghanistan to Zambia, providing peacekeeping, food aid, water projects, health services and protection of children's rights, to name only a few tasks. International institutions help govern our life. The World Trade Organization (WTO) and Organization for Economic Cooperation and Development (OECD) help govern our trade and economic cooperation. Institutions like the European Union (EU) and Mercusur in Latin America help bring regions together. The North Atlantic Treaty Organization (NATO) and the African Union (AU) provide for regional security. Institutions like the Council of Europe and Organization for Security and Cooperation in Europe (OSCE) promote democracy and human rights. Most of these institutions in fact have multiple functions that are strategic, political, economic and cultural. These inter-governmental organizations often rely heavily on the work of international non-governmental organizations or INGOs such as the International Red Cross (IRC), Médecins Sans Frontières (Doctors without Borders), Amnesty International and Oxfam. Together, all of these institutions create a web of cooperation and collaboration that forms the foundation of international relations.

This chapter aims to explain the evolution and development of international institutions and to chart their contemporary relevance in international relations. Why

BOX 9.1 IGO AND INGO DEFINITIONS

- IGO requires: A basis of a formal instrument of agreement between governments; three or more states; a permanent secretariat (IGO: Intergovernmental Organization)
- INGO requires: At least three states with international aims; voting rights and funding from at least three states; permanent HQ and secretariat, evidence of activity (INGO: International Nongovernmental Organization)

do states find it necessary to cooperate? Where did the idea of international institutions originate? When was the first international organization created? What do international institutions do? Why do we have so many international institutions in the world today? What impact do international organizations have on international relations in general, and on individuals specifically? Such questions allow the reader to engage critically with the concept of international organizations and will inform the majority of this chapter.

COOPERATION AND INSTITUTIONS

Any examination of international institutions should begin with a discussion defining cooperation and institutions. Individually, it is clear what both of these terms mean but their relationship in terms of international relations is significantly more complex. Cooperation 'requires that the actions of separate individuals or institutions – which are not in pre-existent harmony – be brought into conformity with one another through a process of policy coordination' (Keohane 1984: 51). In other words, cooperation requires each party of the relationship to change their behaviour in relation to the behaviour of other parties. Importantly, it also distinguishes co-operation from harmony. States may cooperate to prevail in military and political conflict. Rich states may cooperate to keep themselves rich and poor states poor. 'International cooperation does *not necessarily* depend on altruism, idealism, personal honour, common purposes, internalised norms, or a shared belief in a set of values embedded in a culture' (Keohane 1988: 380, emphasis added). However, many states do cooperate because they share interests, ideals, norms, values and belief systems. A cooperative relationship demands that there be some level of trust between two or more parties. Not only are international institutions predicated on these shared understandings, but international institutions also offer an arena through which parties can witness the behaviour of other states.

Nevertheless, cooperation can occur outside of international institutions with a large proportion of cooperation between states occurring through bi-lateral relationships that are not dictated by institutions. However it remains that international institutions facilitate the greatest amount of cooperation. We can define international institutions as 'international social institutions characterized by behavioural patterns based on international norms and rules, which prescribe behavioural roles in recurring situations that

◼ BOX 9.2 COOPERATION REQUIREMENTS

- Separate states bought into conformity
- Trust
- Transparency

lead to a convergence of reciprocal expectations' (Rittberger and Zangl 2006: 6). We can also identify two types of international institutions: international inter-governmental organizations and international regimes. The first set of international institutions is ordinarily what we refer to when discussing international organizations such as the UN, EU and OSCE. These institutions have a range of issue-areas that they address. On the other hand, Stephen Krasner has defined regimes as 'principles, norms, rules and decision-making procedures around which actor expectations converge in a given issue-area' (Krasner 1982: 185). In other words, international regimes are issue-specific. Overall, international regimes aim to coordinate communication about a specific issue, such as trade, whaling, air quality, and nuclear proliferation. International organizations differ from international regimes because they can engage in 'goal-directed activities' such as raising and spending money, policy-making, and making flexible choices (Keohane 1988: 384, fn. 2). In both cases international institutions provide for formalized cooperation in international relations and form a specific and complex area of study for students of international relations.

Why does cooperation occur in international relations? In politics, people come together to cooperate towards common and collective goals – common goals being goals that all can share and collective goals being those that can only be achieved if parties work together. At the domestic level political communities work in cooperation to provide common public services such as roads, telecommunications, disaster relief, and education. The average member of the population does not work specifically in any of these areas but instead pays the state (through taxation) to carry these services out on their behalf. The state and its institutions work together to meet the common needs of the population.

As the world becomes metaphorically smaller, states and their citizens are forming international institutions. Just as citizens act together within a state for common and collective goals, states come together in international institutions for common goals such as in 1815 with the creation of the Rhine River Commission. Today, the Rhine runs through Switzerland, Liechtenstein, Austria, Germany, France and the Netherlands. Historically, the Rhine was an important trade route for Western Europe so that during the 1815 Congress of Vienna states came together for the common goal of ensuring freedom of navigation on the river. Eventually, the commission developed into a regulatory and policing body and as early as the 1860s the commission developed provisions for regulating hazardous materials and water pollution. The Rhine River Commission (also known as the Central Commission for Navigation on the Rhine or CCNR) is important because affected states could come together to agree common rules and regulations for navigation along the Rhine. The commission is also important for being the first international organization and it still exists to this day.

Like citizens of a state, member states of an international institution are constrained by their membership. Before considering why states act together to form international institutions, it is important to first understand some underlying assumptions about international relations. The first assumption is that states desire ultimate sovereignty and control over their own geographical area, and, secondly, that states strive to maximize their sovereignty. These assumptions present us with something of a conundrum: if states desire to maximize their sovereignty, why would they agree to become members of an organization that by its very existence will constrain their sovereignty? The simple answer is that states are willing to sacrifice a bit of sovereignty to gain common and collective goals. For example, acquiring clean air is a common and collective good. Having clean air is common because everyone can use it, and collective because having clear air requires cooperation between all parties who would seek to benefit by having it. In other words, it only takes one bad polluter to make the air bad for the rest of us and therefore we must work together to avoid the collective bad of air pollution.

International institutions are ordinarily suited to address common and collective goals towards dealing with borderless problems such as water pollution, acid rain, malaria, HIV-AIDS, nuclear reactor disasters, terrorism, organized crime and the global economy. Furthermore, these problems require a huge amount of resources simply to address, much less to eliminate. The majority of states do not have the resources to combat such problems and consequently seek out other similar states to pool their resources akin to traditional military alliances where states act in unison to defeat, attack or prevent another state or group of states from acting contrary to their interests. The development of international institutions such as NATO and the OSCE is a contemporary development of traditional alliance politics.

BOX 9.3 THE COOPERATION DILEMMA

International institutions occur when states wish to maximize sovereignty but are willing to sacrifice in order to gain common and collective goods, as they realize that these goods are beyond their own individual capacities and that they need to pool resources

The development of international institutions can be surmised in two debates. The first debate concerns the importance of international institutions in the international system and whether international organizations are actors in their own right or simply a subject of their constituent parts (member states). The realist agenda argues that states are the key actors in international relations and international institutions represent the interests of their member states, especially those which have the most power. Realists argue that states are unlikely to invest in formal institutions to the extent that they cede power to that organization. Anarchy impedes international cooperation and thus reduces the importance of international institutions in international relations. The liberal agenda argues that international institutions can be important actors in international relations because states have a rational and strategic interest in investing in long-term cooperation and international institutions. Liberals argue that cooperation and interdependence produce grounds for stable, trusting relationships between states. Once created and imbued with powers, international institutions then affect their constituent member states. While both realists and liberals accept the anarchical state of the international system, there are core differences in their interpretation of cooperation.

BOX 9.4 REALIST *VERSUS* LIBERAL ASSUMPTIONS

- *Realist*: States are key actors; institutions represent interests; states do not wish to cede power
- *Liberal*: Institutions can be important actors; states have rational and strategic interests in long-term cooperation and interdependence; institutions can affect state behaviour

The second debate covers the reasons why states create and join international institutions. There are two theoretical sides to this debate: rationalism and constructivism. Rationalism assumes that actors will seek the strategy (or strategies) that benefits themselves. In the study of international institutions, the rationalist approach argues that cooperation can be mutually beneficial and that states come together in international institutions to reduce the transaction costs of such cooperation. International institutions also reduce the uncertainty of cooperation by providing information and stabilizing expectations. The rationalists argue that international institutions develop where are mutual expectations of benefits from cooperation. Where the costs of cooperation are too great (e.g. too many restrictions, favourable conditions for others), it is unlikely that international institutions will emerge. Alternatively, constructivism argues that actors' decisions are determined by their own values and perceptions of the world around them. The constructivist (also referred to as reflective) approach concentrates on the importance of social interactions and international institutions. Constructivists argue that actors are not only acting in their own rational self-interest, but are also acting as a response to shared values and norms (e.g. economic, political culture). This approach does not look for a constellation of shared interests but rather a constellation of shared norms to explain the development of international institutions. Thus, while states may have a shared interest in a given issue-area, an international institution only forms once states have a shared understanding of the problem. The recent debates over carbon emission are a good illustration of the difficulties of cooperation in general and institutions specifically. All of the major greenhouse gas-producing countries accept that carbon emission is a problem leading to environmental damage. Nevertheless, global cooperation is extremely underdeveloped, even within an established organization like the EU.

The post-Cold War international system has witnessed a renewed interest in international institutions. Specifically, the second debate has been largely played out in terms of regional integration, primarily focusing on the development of the EU. Andrew Moravcsik (1997) emphasizes the role of interests and preferences in the development of the EU, while others such as Jeffrey Checkel (2001), Karin Fierke and Antje Wiener (1999) focus on the importance of norms and values in further integration and

▌BOX 9.5 RATIONALISM AND CONSTRUCTIVISM

- *Rationalism*: States will benefit themselves; cooperation is beneficial; cooperation reduces transaction costs and uncertainty
- *Constructivism*: Actors respond to shared values and norms

enlargement. However, these two approaches are not poles apart. Many authors, these included, have recognized interests and norms as connected (Schimmelfennig 2001). Rationalists have begun to look at the importance of social communication while constructivists have begun to focus on decision-making. As we look at specific international institutions more closely, we will see that both interests and norms are important in our study since they characterize the very institutions that form the basis of the study.

▌INTERNATIONAL INSTITUTIONS AND THEIR FUNCTIONS

International cooperation has been evident throughout history but international institutions only emerged in the early nineteenth century. The impetus for the first international institution was the European Napoleonic Wars of 1804–1815 and the defeat of Napoleon Bonaparte at Waterloo in March 1815, after which the victorious powers came together to organize a post-conflict Europe known as the Congress of Vienna (from September 1814 to June 1815). Borders were re-drawn, political leaders were removed or created, and colonies were confirmed or forfeited. While this was not so much a Congress as a place for informal discussions between powers, it was a concerted effort to seek cooperation and consensus across a great number of actors. The Congress of Vienna led to much longer lasting institutionalized forms of cooperation, including the previously discussed Rhine River Commission. The Congress also resulted in a condemnation of slavery, confirming the move towards the end of the trans-Atlantic slave trade.

By the early part of the twentieth century Europe was once again at war. The First World War (1914–18) had many causes, one of which was the breakdown of an informal, non-institutionalized arrangement between the great powers in Europe, orchestrated by Germany's Otto van Bismarck. Following the end of the war the victorious powers in Europe came together in the Paris Peace Conference (January 1918 to January 1919) to dictate the terms of peace. The conference established the League of Nations in January 1919 as an attempt to prevent another great war. Prior to the creation of the League, there had been two peace conferences in The Hague in 1899 and 1907 which are largely considered to be the forerunners to an institutionalized attempt at peace (Scott 1973). The League had its first meeting in 1920 in London but was moved to Geneva later that year. The organization was devoted to conflict prevention through disarmament and diplomatic negotiation.

The structure of the League consisted of a Secretariat, a Council, and an Assembly; a structure that has maintained itself repeatedly in the formation of international institutions. The Secretariat worked as a civil service or bureaucracy and the Council had the authority to deal with any problem challenging international peace. Similar to the UN Security Council, the Council of the League of Nations initially had four permanent members – the United Kingdom, Italy, France and Japan – although it was originally intended to also have the United States as a fifth member. The Council also had a series of non-permanent members as determined by the Assembly. The Assembly met once a year, every September, to discuss the non-permanent membership of the Council and to discuss and decide on mechanisms to deal with any problems in the international community. Over time, the Assembly created seven other bodies – including the International Labour Organization (ILO), the Permanent Court of International Justice, and the World Health Organization (WHO) – all of which would eventually become part of the League's successor organization, the United Nations.

BOX 9.6 INSTITUTIONS OF THE LEAGUE OF NATIONS AND THE UN

League of Nations

- *Secretariat*: Led by Secretary General
- *Council*: Initially four permanent seats (France, Italy, Japan, United Kingdom)
- *Assembly*: Representatives of all member states (42 founding members)

United Nations

- *Secretariat*: Led by Secretary General
- *Security Council*: Five permanent seats (China, France, Russian Federation, UK, USA) and ten non-permanent members
- *General Assembly*: Representatives of all member-states (192 member-states at time of writing)
- *Economic and Social Council*: 54 seats allocated by region and voted for by the General Assembly
- *International Court of Justice*: 15 judges voted for by the General Assembly and Security Council
- *Trusteeship Council (suspended in 1994)*: Five permanent members of the Security Council

The League of Nations is most remembered for its failure to prevent the Second World War. However, the League of Nations had a beneficial influence on many areas of potential conflict that has largely gone unnoticed except by scholars of international institutions. Several cases are worth mentioning. After the First World War, Austria and Hungary were committed by the Treaty of Versailles (passed by the first act of the League of Nations in 1920) to pay substantial reparations to the victors of the war, the financial stress of which was forcing both states into bankruptcy. However, the League stepped into the crisis by arranging financial loans and thus preventing economic melt-down. Secondly, the League intervened in the dispute between the newly established states of Yugoslavia and Albania. After the war, Yugoslav troops still held Albanian territory but the League was instrumental in organizing a withdrawal of Yugoslav troops by 1921. (Ironically, however, the United Nations would find itself in the same region approximately eighty years later for very similar reasons.) Finally, the League resolved a conflict between the new states of Turkey and the UK-mandated Iraq regarding the city of Mosul. Formerly a part of the Ottoman Empire, Mosul was claimed by both the empire's successor state, Turkey, and by the British to become part of the new Iraq. The League sided with the British and Iraqis claiming protection of the Kurdish autonomy and by 1926 all parties agreed to the settlement. (However, the Kurdish struggle for a Kurdish state in Turkey and northern Iraq still haunts the region to this day.) In these events and many more, the League of Nations illustrated an ability to mediate between opposing forces and utilized observer missions, peacekeepers and diplomatic bargaining to encourage compliance – the same mechanisms used by many contemporary international institutions and especially the United Nations.

Although aimed at conflict prevention, the League of Nations could not stop the rise of a belligerent Germany, Italy and Japan. The failure of the League to act in the case of Japan's invasion of Chinese Manchuria in 1933 or the German invasion of Poland and Czechoslovakia in 1939 spelled the end of the organization. The organization also suffered as a result of the West's general disinterest in the League. The United States Senate never ratified the Treaty of Versailles (which would have brought the United States into the League) and the UK and France demonstrated a continued preference to work outside the confines of the organization. Eventually the onset of the Second World War ended all interest and faith in the League of Nations, although it officially continued to exist until 1946. Where the Napoleonic Wars and the First World War begot the Congress of Vienna and League of Nations respectively, the Second World War produced the United Nations, which in its turn would face even greater challenges to international peace and security.

Nearing the end of the Second World War the soon-to-be allied victors met at the Dumbarton Oaks Conference in Washington, DC, to establish a new international institution. From April to June 1945, fifty states met in San Francisco at the United Nations International Conference to discuss the Dumbarton Oaks recommendations, the result of which was the establishment of the United Nations and the creation of the UN Charter. The charter sets out four core aims: prevention of inter-state conflict, ensuring human rights, establishing international law and encouraging development. Such aims are similar to those of the League of Nations but the UN was empowered by its charter to be a much stronger actor and has consequently been able to be far more active than the League of Nations.

In many ways the structure of the UN mirrored that of the League: a secretariat, a council and an assembly, as well as a plethora of other councils and commissions. Importantly, the core institutions of the UN were located in New York. The United Nations is composed of six principal organs: the Secretariat, the General Assembly, the Security Council, the Economic and Social Council, the International Court of Justice and the Trusteeship Council. The Secretariat is the bureaucratic heart of the UN with almost 9,000 employees from 170 member states and headed by Secretary-General Ban Ki-Moon since 2007. The Secretary-General is not only the director of the UN Secretariat and the UN in general but is also chair of the UN Security Council. The General Assembly has representatives from each of the 192 member states and has the authority to pass resolutions affecting UN policies. There are also several bodies established under the General Assembly, including the Human Rights Council (see Mertus 2005). The

Security Council is the most visible organ in the United Nations for two reasons (Luck 2006). First, international politics is often played out in the Security Council, as seen in the lead-up to the 2003 US-led invasion of Iraq. Second, the Security Council is the only body that can give the UN the mandate to intervene in a military dispute and to permit UN peacekeepers.

The Economic and Social Council (ECOSOC) looks at the international aspects of economic and social issues. The council has 42 seats voted for by the General Assembly and allocated by geographic region. Through this forum, ECOSOC is able to make policy recommendations to other parts of the UN. ECOSOC coordinates several high-profile, autonomous specialized agencies, including the WHO, the UN Educational, Scientific and Cultural Organization (UNESCO) and the ILO. The International Court of Justice (not to be confused with the International Criminal Court) has 15 judges that need to be approved by both the General Assembly and the Security Council. The ICJ's role is to settle any legal disputes brought to it by member states and to issue legal advisory opinions when requested by other UN agencies. The first case brought to the ICJ was the *Corfu Channel Case (United Kingdom v. Albania)* submitted on 22 May 1947. At the time of writing, there have been 136 cases brought to the ICJ's attention. Finally, the UN Trusteeship Council was established to oversee decolonization and the establishment of state institutions. Following the independence of Palau (southern Pacific Ocean) in 1994, the Trusteeship voted to suspend operations. The Trusteeship Council can be recalled by a majority vote in the Security Council or General Assembly, or by its five permanent members (China, France, Russian Federation, UK and USA).

BOX 9.7 EXPANDED FUNCTIONS OF THE UN

- Avoidance of war
- Promotion of order and stability
- Maintaining international peace and security
- Functional cooperation
- Disarmament
- Socio-economic improvements
- Establishment of international law
- Encouraging human rights
- Encouraging development

The UN also has a huge network of other agencies and commissions, such as the International Monetary Fund (IMF), the World Bank, and the Universal Postal Union. These other agencies and commissions are collectively referred to as the UN System. Overall, there was a significant expansion of responsibilities and infrastructure from the League of Nations to the United Nations. The UN is the largest international institution in the world and has the ability to intervene in armed conflict, enforce resolutions through political, economic or military means, and even to dissolve states and validate new ones.

The Cold War played a major role in shaping the development of the UN – on one hand, the permanent seats on the Security Council helped keep the Cold War from becoming a hot war, on the other hand, the permanent seats allowed five nations to have a veto over UN actions rendering the UN less effective and less responsive in many cases. The UN is ever changing, although some would argue that it is not changing fast enough. Reform in the UN is difficult because many member states have an interest in maintaining the current structure, specifically the structure of the Security Council. While many parts of the UN are evolving, the Security Council remains rooted in the same structure as was established in 1945, much to the frustration of those who seek to see a more contemporary and representative Security Council.

Regional institutions

There are many global international institutions, but many would argue that regional institutions are of equal and arguably more immediate relevance to individual lives. As Box 9.8 illustrates, every geographic region in the world has established a regional institution, although there continue to be many states that remain outside regional institutions. The box also shows that Europe is particularly heavily laden with regional institutions, in many cases with overlapping functions. Other regions, such as Asia and Africa, have fewer and weaker regional institutions. This section looks at prominent regional organizations and considers why some regions are better organized than others.

Since the Second World War Europe has seen a significant growth in the number of institutions as well as a proliferation of their functions. The EU is Europe's most visible regional institution and it has the widest remit in terms of functions. The road to the EU began with the establishment of the European Coal and Steel Community (ECSC)

BOX 9.8 PROMINENT REGIONAL INSTITUTIONS

Region	Organization
Africa	African Union (formerly OAU)
	Southern African Development Community
Asia	Association of Southeast Asian Nations
Europe	Council of Europe
	European Union
	North Atlantic Treaty Organization*
	Organization for Security and Cooperation in Europe (OSCE) (formerly CSCE)
	Western European Union
North America	North American Free Trade Agreement
	Organization of American States
South America	Andean Community
	Mercosur
	Union of South American Nations

Note: *Trans-Atlantic regional institutions

in 1951, The founding members of this were West Germany, France, Italy, Belgium, the Netherlands and Luxemburg. On the basis of the ECSC, the same countries came together in the European Economic Community (later to be renamed the European Community in 1992) and the European Atomic Energy Community (EURATOM) in 1957 (Treaties of Rome). For a generation there were four major institutions in the Communities – the Council of Ministers, the Commission, the Assembly (Parliament) and the European Court of Justice. There are now five with the addition of the Court of Auditors. In 1992, the Treaty of Maastricht was signed, creating the European Union which then came into effect in November 1993.

The EU that we have today is unlike any other international institution, having assumed the role of governance with involvement in most areas of public policy, from consumer safety to foreign policy. Importantly, however, the EU remains closely linked to its member states, particularly France and Germany. The current pillar system, created in 1992, established a procedure for decision-making in different issue-areas and represents the breadth of issues dealt with by the EU. The first pillar corresponds to the original purposes of the European Economic Community: the movement of people, money and trade. The second pillar deals with Common Foreign and Security Policy (CFSP) and European Security and Defence Policy (ESDP). The third pillar deals with regional police issues, such as organized crime, corruption and terrorism.

BOX 9.9 THE EUROPEAN UNION

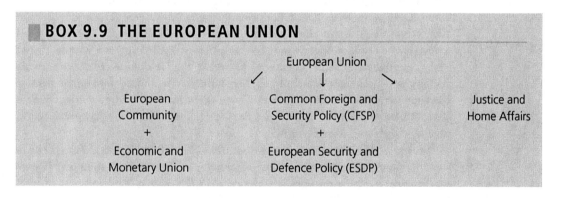

The EU is an ever evolving and developing organization and has undergone a variety of major changes since its inception. Firstly, the EU is in the process of negotiating a European Constitution that would increase the state-like status of the EU but which has so far failed to galvanize the necessary support from the member states. Current negotiations to revive the Constitutional Treaty primarily focus on issues related to proposed changes which would see the pillar structure replaced by increased decision-making power for the member states at the EU capital. Secondly, the EU expanded to include 12 new members in 2004 and 2007 and consequently experienced a significant change in political culture.

Predecessor organizations to the EU primarily focused on improving finance and trade. The emergence of policy issues such as human rights, democracy and social protection on the EU agenda is a relatively recent occurrence. However, the Council of Europe – founded in 1950 by Belgium, Denmark, France, Ireland, Italy, Luxembourg, the Netherlands, Norway, Sweden and the UK and not to be confused with the EU's

European Council – was created in 1950 to address such issues. Where the European Communities were aimed at rebuilding Europe, the Council of Europe was aimed at ensuring that war and genocide did not recur based on the principles of the European Convention for Human Rights. The Council has a Parliamentary Assembly (drawn from national parliaments), a Committee of Ministers who represent each state, a Commissioner for Human Rights and the European Court of Human Rights (not to be confused with the EU's European Court of Justice). Following the end of the Cold War the Council of Europe also expanded to take in more states to the East, including the Russian Federation in 1996. Although the EU has become an increasingly substantial actor with these issues, the Council of Europe still remains an important voice for human rights and democracy.

The final two prominent European institutions are NATO and the OSCE. NATO's founding in 1949 was in response to perceived Soviet plans to expand into Western Europe (see Lindley-French 2006) and saw many Western European states (with the notable exceptions of Ireland and Spain), the US and Canada come together in a collective defence organization in response to the Soviet threat. Following the formation of NATO, the Soviet Union and its allies came together in the so-called Warsaw Pact to form a counter-collective defence organization. NATO's stronghold on defence politics was maintained throughout the duration of the Cold War but was later complemented by the creation of the Conference on Security and Cooperation in Europe, or CSCE, during the period of détente (Galbreath 2007) in 1961 when the Western allies and the Soviets were on diplomatic speaking terms following the brink of nuclear war. The countries of NATO and the Warsaw Pact as well as neutral states came together to formulate the Helsinki Final Act to increase stability and cooperation in Europe. The Final Act is divided into three areas of cooperation: political-military, economic and environmental, and the human dimension. While the period of détente did not last for long, the CSCE has continued to function albeit with limited impact.

The end of the Cold War changed both NATO and the CSCE although not in ways that many observers would have expected. NATO remains a collective defence organization but now operates out-of-area as in the cases of Afghanistan and, to a limited extent, in the Darfur region of Sudan. The CSCE changed from the Conference to the Organization in 1994 the same time as it developed a secretariat, council, and assembly. In addition, the now OSCE developed mechanisms of conflict prevention such as the Conflict Prevention Centre and the High Commissioner on National Minorities. Both NATO and the OSCE would expand to the East, with the former including several former Soviet republics (the Baltic States) and the latter encompassing the entire former Soviet region.

An examination of the EU, Council of Europe, NATO and the OSCE reveals two specific points. The first is that Europe, unlike any other region, has become highly institutionalized. The second point is that the increasing enlargement and integration of the EU is encroaching more and more on the development and enlargement of alternative organizations. Already another European institution, the Western European Union, has been subsumed by the EU. The EU now has security and defence mechanisms and focuses intensely on issues such as human rights and democracy as well as the original issues of finance and trade. Additionally, all EU member states maintain membership of one or more additional institutions. For instance, the UK is a member (or participating state in the case of the OSCE) of all four institutions and consequently questions are increasingly being asked concerning how such significant functional and membership overlaps can be maintained in Europe.

No other region maintains the complex institutional fabric of Europe, but nevertheless, every region has institutions. North America is partially integrated into the European institutions, with US and Canadian membership of NATO and the OSCE, and is additionally a member of the North American Free Trade Agreement (NAFTA). NAFTA was created in 1994 by the governments of Canada, the US and Mexico following a 1988 free-trade agreement between the US and Canada (see Duina 2006). NAFTA aims to reduce trade barriers (whilst protecting intellectual copyright) between the three states, but does not reflect the structure of several of the other institutions that we have seen so far in this chapter. Instead, it is a multilateral treaty governed jointly by the three states. What makes NAFTA more than a trade agreement and, rather, a regional institution worth examining here is the subsidiary bodies of the North American Agreement on Environmental Cooperation (NAAEC) and the North American Agreement on Labour Cooperation (NAALC). Negotiators of the original NAFTA articulated two potential problems with its creation – firstly, that environmentally destructive companies would simply leave Canada and the US and move to Mexico and, secondly, that labour standards would suffer – and consequently the NAAEC and the NAALC were created. Both these organs have councils of ministers as well as tri-national secretariats to support them. Other forms of cooperation exist in North America but do so outside the confines of a regional institution, perhaps as a result of the limited number of potential member states (as opposed to Europe).

South American and Asian regional cooperation has been similar to the North American experience. Both regions have developed major economic institutions: Mercosur (Southern Common Market) and ASEAN respectively. Mercosur, which maintains a Committee of Permanent Representatives in Montevideo, Uraguay, was born out of the economic relations between Argentina and Brazil in the 1980s (see Manzetti 1993; Carranza 2003). In 1991, Argentina, Brazil, Paraguay and Uruguay came together to negotiate a common market, resulting in the Treaty of Asunción that was later developed into a regional institution by the 1994 Treaty of Ouro Preto. Mercosur suffered from the general economic slump in South America and was hit especially hard by the Argentine economic collapse of 2001. However, Mercosur enlarged to include Venezuela in 2006 and is now negotiating to join with the Andean Community (another trade bloc) to form the Union of South American Nations.

ASEAN was founded as an anti-communist organization by Indonesia, Malaysia, the Philippines, Singapore and Thailand in 1967 and has since expanded and evolved to include six more countries including Vietnam, Cambodia, Laos, Myanmar, the Philippines and Singapore. East Timor currently has candidate-state status in the organization. ASEAN has expanded from its anti-communist roots and now focuses on being a larger economic and security community, such as the EU and the early CSCE respectively (Narine 1998). ASEAN also works to expand the cultural exchange between member states in a function similar to the Council of Europe. The largest problem facing ASEAN is Myanmar's (formerly Burma's) membership which has prevented ASEAN/EU trade talks. Unlike the OSCE, ASEAN does not factor domestic politics into its negotiations.

Africa's relationship with regional institutions is less visible. A pan-African institution has gone through several phases from the Organization of African States to the Organization of African Unity and today's African Union is a descendant of these past institutions (Magliveras and Naldi 2002). The African Union was established in 2002, following a campaign to resurrect an African regional organization by the Libyan government. At the time of writing, every African state – except Morocco – is a member of the African Union. The African Union largely adopted principal organs akin to those of the EU when the Constitutive Act of the African Union (2001) established an executive council, a commission, a body of permanent representatives and an assembly. Any comparisons to the EU, however, should consider that the African Union still very much remains an inter-governmental institution, unlike its European counterpart. The African Union's biggest challenge to date has been the ongoing military crisis in the Darfur region in Sudan. Begrudgingly, the Sudanese government has allowed African Union peacekeepers into the Darfur region, but only in low numbers and the African Union has not had the resources to bring peace to the Darfur region, much less limit the violence. Additionally, African Union peacekeepers have been frequent targets of the violence. The Darfur crisis not withstanding, the African Union has made great strides towards creating cooperation in the region.

CONCLUSION

International relations have increasingly become organized around international institutions, as is evident with the global presence of the UN and the regional presence of the EU, ASEAN and the African Union. In some cases, member states have bequeathed their institutions with functions that challenge the primacy of the state but this phenomenon largely seems limited to Europe. In other regional institutions, member states still maintain considerable control over their own politics. Nevertheless, by the very act of entering into an international institution, member states have agreed to be bound by certain constraints as a result of common rules and procedures, even when these rules and procedures appear to be a redundant function. Most importantly, international institutions are about serving states, and also about serving the citizens of those member states. International institutions have come to affect us in our everyday life, from the food we eat and the products we buy, to the cars we drive and rights we have.

REFERENCES AND FURTHER READING

Carranza, M. E. (2003) 'Can Mercosur Survive? Domestic and International Constraints on Mercosur', *Latin American Politics and Society* 45: 67–103.

Checkel, J. T. (2001) 'Why Comply? Social Learning and European identity change', *International Organization* 55: 553–88.

Duina, F. (2006) 'Varieties of Regional Integration: The EU, NAFTA and Mercosur', *Journal of European Integration* 28: 247–75.

Fierke, K., and Wiener, A. (1999) 'Constructing Institutional Interests: EU and NATO Enlargement', *Journal of European Public Policy* 6: 721–42.

Galbreath, D. J. (2007) *The Organization for Security and Cooperation in Europe.* London: Routledge.

Gordenker, L. (2005) *The UN Secretary-General and Secretariat.* London: Routledge.

Grieco, J. M. (1988) 'Anarchy and the Limits of Cooperation: A Realist Critique of the Newest Liberal Institutionalism', *International Organization* 42: 485–507.

Keohane, R. O. (1984) *After Hegemony: Cooperation and Discord in the World Political Economy.* Princeton, NJ: Princeton University Press.

Keohane, R. O. (1988) 'International Institutions: Two Approaches', *International Studies Quarterly* 32: 379–96.

Keohane, R. O. and Nye, J. S. (1974) 'Transgovernmental Relations and International Organizations', *World Politics* 27: 39–62.

Krasner, S. D. (1982) 'Structural Causes and Regime Consequences: Regimes as Intervening Variables', *International Organization* 36: 1–21.

Lindley-French, J. (2006) *The North Atlantic Treaty Organization: The Enduring Alliance.* London: Routledge.

Luck, E. C. (2006) *The UN Security Council: Practice & Promise.* London: Routledge.

Magliveras, K. D. and Naldi, G. J. (2002) 'The African Union: A New Dawn for Africa?', *International and Comparative Law Quarterly* 51: 415–425.

Manzetti, L. (1993) 'The Political Economy of Mercosur', *Journal of Interamerican Studies and World Affairs* 35: 101–41.

Mertus, J. (2005) *United Nations and Human Rights.* London: Routledge.

Moravcsik, A. (1997) 'Taking Preferences Seriously: A Liberal Theory of International Politics', *International Organization* 51: 513–53.

Narine, S. (1998) 'ASEAN and the Management of Regional Security', *Pacific Affairs* 71: 195–214.

Peterson, M. J. (2005) *The United Nations General Assembly.* London: Routledge.

Rittberger, V. and Zangl, B. (2006) *International Organization: Polity, Politics and Policies.* Basingstoke: Palgrave.

Ruchay, D. (1995) 'Living with water: Rhine River basin management', *Water Science and Technology* 31: 27–32.

Schimmelfennig, F. (2001) 'The Community Trap: Liberal Norms, Rhetorical Action, and the Eastern Enlargement of the European Union', *International Organization* 55: 47–80.

Scott, G. (1973) *The Rise and Fall of the League of Nations.* London: Hutchinson.

Stein, A. A. (1990) *Why Nations Cooperate: Circumstances and Choice in International Relations.* Ithaca, New York: Cornell University Press.

CHAPTER 10

Globalization and Development

Ben Thirkell-White

During the 1990s, literature on the international political economy was dominated by the idea of globalization. Dramatic decreases in transport costs and the rise of fast and cheap telecommunications technology have made geography less relevant and facilitated massive increases in global trade and new forms of multinational production. Whether or not such developments are good or bad is a topic of ongoing political debate. Some argue that an expanding global economy provides new opportunities for the developing world to integrate into global markets and to achieve rapid rises in living standards – pointing to ongoing global growth and a reduction in absolute poverty. Others argue that the expanding global economy has instead increased global exploitation and inequalities, and further marginalized the developing world.

International politics has played a key role in converting new technological opportunities such as travel and communications (globalization in a narrow sense), into new forms of economic regulation and business practices (globalization in its broad sense). Stronger governments have had more choice than weaker governments concerning their response to global pressures for more international and less regulated economic activities. Even the weakest government, however, has had some room for manoeuvre. Additionally, there has been considerable variation between responses from the developed and developing worlds. This chapter introduces the predominant means of thinking about globalization, from the historical experience of the developing world to provide the tools required for assessing the viable options developing countries currently face under globalization.

GLOBALIZATION

Three approaches to globalization

There exist three broad theoretical approaches to thinking about globalization. Generally, however, no single approach is usually adopted, but, rather, a combination or mixture of the three is used.

First, there exists the extreme liberal, or neoliberal, view. Liberal thought values individual freedom and tends to be optimistic about the potential for mutual gains in human interaction, including under globalization. Most liberals are enthusiastic about the economics of the free market. In the international realm, such thinking is most obvious in liberal views concerning free trade (though many liberals would take a slightly more ambiguous view than the neoliberal one set out here).

Liberals argue that trade benefits everyone because it helps people concentrate on what they are best at (the formal version of this argument is the theory of 'comparative advantage'). For example, Britain sells tweed jackets and country sportswear to French aristocrats who pay for it by selling wine to the British. Less obviously, even a country that is not the best in the world at making anything can benefit from free trade because it allows them to devote their resources to whatever it is that they are relatively good at and buy in everything else. Imagine a person deciding whether to spend an hour growing rice to feed their family or to spend an hour working in a textile factory. If the person earns more working in the factory, they can spend some of their wages on buying the rice that they would have produced and still have money left over for other things. Comparative advantage (a state's most efficient production) varies from state to state (for example, Argentina may be better at beef farming than textiles). Allowing free trade sends price signals that encourage people to work at what they are best at, a strategy that benefits everyone over the long term. Globalization has helped to reduce transport and transaction costs so the potential gains from specialization are increased. Globalization has also increased competition giving people incentives to keep becoming more efficient.

Liberals argue that multinational production works in a similar way. Many products are now made in more than one state. For example, a car could be designed in Germany, the car's silicon chips made in South Korea and the assembly of larger electronic components done in Malaysia, mechanical parts made in Mexico, the main car assembly done in Eastern Europe and the marketing, distribution and retail responsibilities going back to Germany. Multinational production capitalizes on the resources and skills available in different places, making cars cheaper. It also brings new jobs and technology to different countries and makes profits for the car company that can be re-invested in making ever better cars. Globalization makes production more efficient, thus allowing a greater distribution of wealth around the world as new production processes are introduced to developing countries. Ongoing global economic growth, coupled with the fact that the best performers tend to be particularly open to globalized forms of production (such as India and China for example), suggests that the spread of wealth is inherently linked to globalization.

However, writers in the Marxist tradition perceive globalization as a highly negative phenomenon. As with liberalism, there is no single Marxist viewpoint, but instead degrees of Marxist variation. Indeed, much anti-globalization writing is not compatible with classical Marxist thought. Fundamental to all, however, is a considerable scepticism concerning the liberal emphasis on mutual gains from economic interaction. Marxists concentrate less on efficiency gains (though many accept these may take place) and focus more on how changing production provides new kinds of economic power that can be used to extort profits from those that are weaker.

Marxists argue that globalization has given new power to people that own businesses ('capital' in Marxist terminology). When workers in Europe or the US ask for higher wages employers can easily threaten to move production somewhere cheaper, arguing that growing competition produced by free trade will drive them out of business. Immigration rules and relative poverty mean that workers can't threaten to move in the same way. Furthermore, governments need business, and business's tax revenues to provide their citizens with expected services. State citizens also expect to be provided with good job prospects and rising incomes, or governments will lose power. Multinational business can manipulate these needs (and perhaps, sometimes, use straight bribery) to press governments to pursue business-friendly policy: keeping down corporate tax, wages and environmental or health and safety regulations. If policy is less attractive, business can threaten to move somewhere else, thus creating difficult choices for government about the balance between the need to keep business in place and the desire to tax and regulate it in the interests of the electorate. For the developing world, 'doing what you are best at' in trade may mean providing sweatshop labour so that consumers in Europe can have cheaper trainers or electronic goods. Economic efficiency can mean maximum exploitation of workers, rather than technological innovation. Globalization, then, can be said to increase the exploitation of workers everywhere – and rising global inequalities will testify to such a fact.

Marxist and liberal approaches assume the globalization of production as a fact, and concentrate on the effects that globalization has on people's welfare. However, there exists a third approach, an agency-centred approach that does not rule out liberal or Marxist perspectives but shifts attention to concentrate on how government policy can shape the consequences of globalization. It asks where globalization came from, who wanted it, who didn't want it, and how the people that did want it got their way.

It is necessary to understand that advances in transport and communications technology do not always lead to greater trade or business relocation. The internationalization of economic activity in Europe first took off in the fifteenth and sixteenth centuries, with the development of new shipping technology that led to Spanish colonization of Latin America. However, the Chinese had developed better and more sophisticated technology much earlier but did not choose to use it to promote economic expansion. Similarly, the nineteenth century proved to be an era of increased international commerce, triggered by the industrial revolution but, in the 1930s, this economic expansion was reversed as political turmoil created the Great Depression. The contemporary phase of globalization only started to return global economic activity to nineteenth-century levels in the late 1970s.

Technological development does not necessarily lead to global production because governments can control how technology is used. The classic instrument for restraining trade is to impose taxes on imported goods (called tariffs) so that foreign products are artificially expensive and can't compete with domestic goods. All countries have tariffs on goods, although some taxes are more protectionist than others. Similarly there exist restrictions on foreign investment or the movement of capital. In being able to choose how much liberalization to allow, governments are responding to a variety of factors and politics.

Liberals argue that governments should want to promote free trade to make everyone wealthier. Technological change makes the benefits especially large and therefore increases incentives to liberalize trade, particularly as companies will pressure for opening so they can profit from outsourcing production. However, governments are not interested only in the procurement of cheap goods for their citizens – from a security perspective, it may be more prudent to produce weapons, and perhaps food, domestically. From a political perspective, foreign competition can bankrupt domestic businesses (which may benefit consumers with better value, more efficient goods, but disadvantages domestic companies whose employees face redundancy). Security and domestic opposition may give governments political reasons for restricting trade (in addition to the danger that capital mobility can grant problematic power to economic interests, pushing the government to lower taxes or reduce regulation, as we saw from the Marxist perspective).

The liberal model oversimplifies real world politics and presents an overly optimistic picture of the international economy. Indeed, international economic opening goes hand in hand with international economic volatility: consider the ramifications if domestic companies are put out of business because foreign products are temporarily cheaper, rather than fundamentally better, or because export prices are temporarily low. Buying products from overseas can also create vulnerabilities: consider if foreign suppliers acquired a monopoly (or form a cartel, a group of producers that, instead of competing with each other, fix prices) and then use it to inflate international prices or even refuse to sell at all. In the 1970s the oil producing countries joined together to form a cartel called OPEC (Organization of Petroleum Exporting Countries) that twice dramatically raised oil prices, with far-reaching consequences for the global economy. Finally, arguments about specialization are very short-term. The model of comparative advantage considers states' current best production with no consideration for companies that are currently inefficient but may be learning new skills that will eventually make them more profitable. If such companies are immediately exposed to competition, they may go bust before the necessary learning can take place. For instance, developing countries may initially be bad at industrial production and make more money from producing agricultural products and trading for manufactures but they will always remain poor unless they can learn more sophisticated and efficient forms of production. To frame the argument in Marxist terms, a monopoly over technical knowledge and managerial techniques creates power that can be used for exploitation.

If governments were completely free to make their own choices, they would presumably try to weigh up the efficiency and prosperity gains from globalization against the economic vulnerabilities and potential political opposition that may come from economic liberalization (removing tariffs and restrictions on investment and capital flows). An agency-centred approach emphasizes the space to make this kind of choice, but writers from the other two perspectives would argue that governments are actually left with little choice. Liberals argue that technology may not force change on its own but it helps so many people to see the potential benefits of liberalization that it creates political momentum for liberalization. Marxists, on the other hand, argue that technological developments give new power to multinational businesses that then use that power to press for liberalization, consequently creating a cycle of increasing globalization.

An agency-centred approach sees these claims as over-simplifications. Although it is possible to discern broad global shifts in international economic policy-making, there has also been considerable variation in continuity, suggesting that a level of choice persists. Recent writing on Europe emphasizes variation in welfare state policy between states suggesting that there is ongoing argument and debate concerning trade-offs. Different political interests line up behind the different positions to create pressure for a variety of responses. However, simultaneous changes in international economic ideas and domestic politics have also created international political pressure for change. Our primary interest is the political economy of the developing world, but developing countries have often been forced to respond to changes created elsewhere.

■ BOX 10.1 THREE VIEWS OF GLOBALIZATION

Neoliberal

- Economic relationships mutually beneficial
- Globalization and trade increase specialization, efficiency and therefore wealth
- Developing world benefits as new economic activity moves there
- Globalization driven by people seeing the benefits

Marxist/antiglobalization

- Economic relationships are exploitative power relationships
- Globalization increases the power of mobile capital over workers and of rich countries over poor countries
- Workers impoverished everywhere. Developing world increasingly exploited
- Globalization driven by power

Agency-centred approach

- Economic relationships can be good or bad depending on political regulation
- Globalization is strongly shaped by political decisions and changing forms of regulation
- Globalization provides opportunities and constraints for developing countries, the politics of different regulatory responses are therefore important.
- Globalization is driven by complex political processes at various different levels

A short history of globalization from a western perspective

The nineteenth century was an era of unsurpassed economic expansion, partly driven by the invention of steamships and the railways, partly by political systems that were dominated by the middle classes and provided few opportunities for poorer workers until the First World War, however, when the existent system was thrown into turmoil: workers were permitted to vote and demanded more government protection against the volatilities of the global economy whilst international economic dislocations (caused by the war) continued. Governments tried to lower their exchange rates to gain advantages in global trade and to turn inwards, raising tariffs, but since everyone was playing the same game to do so closed off potential benefits for trade and made existing difficulties worse. The world economy drifted into the Great Depression, which involved slow economic growth and high unemployment across much of the world. Many argue that the Depression was an important cause of the rise of fascism, communism and the Second World War. In the 1940s, international institutions were established to try and strike a balance between nineteenth-century internationalism (globalization if you like) and the Depression era's collapse of international economic exchange. This middle way involved a reasonable degree of free trade, some opportunities for overseas investment and fairly tight government controls over international financial flows. The institutions involved were the IMF (International Monetary Fund), World Bank and GATT (General Agreement on Tariffs and Trade), which later became the WTO (World Trade Organization).

The post-Second World War compromise of welfare states and moderately liberal international economic policies was quite successful until the early 1970s. However, the post-war financial system had been tied to the US dollar and disputes between the Europeans and Americans over US government spending on Vietnam (amongst other things) led to the collapse of these arrangements. Shortly afterwards OPEC initiated the first oil shock: oil exporters did very well out of this, making a great deal of money that they wished to invest in international markets and oil importers were short of money because of high oil prices and happy to borrow, kick-starting financial globalization as banks sought to move money from one group to the other. However, borrowing in response to rising oil prices also created inflation, which undermined production and created tense labour relationships as unions tried to keep their wages rising in line with prices. By the late 1970s, the economic situation in the West was considered very bad indeed, and US and UK political parties (Reagan's Republicans and Thatcher's Conservatives) came to power with promises to curb inflation with high interest rates, to discourage borrowing (which included cutting spending on public services) and liberalize economic management nationally and internationally, to boost economic growth.

Liberalization only creates new opportunities if other countries liberalize too. The global change in intellectual consensus in the early 1980s, and domestic political change in a number of European countries, fed into a different political consensus within international economic institutions. The balance of power shifted in a direction of more liberal international economic regulation, particularly an expansion in WTO rules to require countries to reduce their tariffs (a policy recommended by neoliberals). Many countries wanted change but those that didn't found themselves under pressure from a new pro-liberalization political majority and a new intellectual consensus that made it very difficult to defend protective regulation. The new political balance created growing liberalization that, in turn, created new opportunities for business to use internationalizing technologies and management techniques. Business then became a powerful political lobby for further liberalization and globalization can be attributed to a combination of technological and political change.

The story of globalization is more complex than the overwhelming attractiveness of multinational production (for liberals) or the power of transnational capital (for Marxists). The 'neoliberal turn' was also a reaction to a perceived economic crisis, which was not purely driven by changing technology, and the neoliberal approach to globalization was never universally accepted. Economic liberalization has also created political challenges and something of a political backlash. Over time, electorates in the UK have certainly reacted against the excesses of Thatcherism, particularly in terms of the quality of public services. On the other hand internationalized economic policy has proven harder to unwind, particularly when it has been embedded in the policies of international economic institutions.

Globalization, then, can be seen to be the product of a complex process involving changes in economic ideas and shifting political coalitions at national and international levels, as well as new technologies that have brought the world closer together. Globalization has always been controversial and the balance of power between pro- and anti-globalization forces has varied over time. That balance has partly depended on shifting political interests (as more people developed a stake in globalization during the early 1980s, political support increased) and on changing ideas about how much liberalization is best for the national interest. Different states have taken different views over time but have also experienced pressure to conform to inter-national preferences. Similar dynamics are discernible in the developing world but, generally, developing states have been less able to shape international consensus and have had to choose how to adapt strategically to the global economic environment.

GLOBALIZATION AND DEVELOPMENT

The rise of globalization has had a significant impact on the developing world, but the contrast between the era of globalization and pre-globalization is less acute than it is in Europe. Developing states were created as political units as a result of earlier phases of economic expansion and have always struggled to forge an independent path in the face of foreign economic (and political) influence. In a sense, developing states are products of globalization, created through interactions between colonial powers and local populations.

Development theory and practice from 1945 to 1979

How colonization created the developing world as we currently know it is a hotly contested issue and there is powerful political debate concerning what might have happened to these states if they had not been colonized (leaving aside obvious moral questions regarding whether colonizing states had any right to political authority over their colonies). Ideological justification for colonialism was based on the false idea that Europeans were colonizing an empty space. In some parts of Asia, Latin America and Africa, there existed political organization and production on a fairly large scale. Even where human occupation was less settled, areas of apparently so-called empty land had supported human societies (albeit very different ones to those in Europe) for many centuries.

Colonial powers generally justified their presence on the basis of trusteeship, or as part of a so-called civilizing mission to introduce more sophisticated forms of political organization and economic production. Colonialism certainly transformed the developing world but evidence suggests that it was primarily an economic enterprise designed to profit from the developing world. New state forms were introduced but they were dominated by foreigners and provided little opportunity for local accountability or for local people to gain experience of government (though this varied between different colonial powers). New economic activity was designed to promote the export of primary commodities from the colonies which would then import European manufactures. Such 'development' provided railways, new technology, new infrastructure and techniques of political management, but it mostly benefited the colonizers. When developing states won independence at the end of the Second World War, they were left with significant challenges. Populations had radically lower standards of living than those in the West, production tended to be concentrated in a narrow range of primary commodities (agriculture and minerals) and countries were dependent on other states for imports of everything else. Infrastructure in developing states also served to promote this outward orientation with railways often running from mines or agricultural areas to the coast, rather than to the capital or neighbouring countries. Formerly colonized states often had little experience of government and experienced something of a power vacuum making it difficult to establish stable authority, particularly where national borders had been drawn with a ruler to suit colonial administrators.

A combination of guilt, altruism and Cold War geopolitical interests (trying to 'save' the developing world for capitalism) encouraged an international search for solutions to these problems, even after independence. Governments of developing countries have been involved in attempting to secure domestic authority and have engaged with international institutions and foreign powers in an attempt to shape global economic rules and foreign aid to their own purposes. This process has involved power struggles at multiple levels. It is possible to distinguish two broad theoretical approaches that guided thinking about development and shaped actual policy in the post-war period, before the current phase of globalization took hold.

The mainstream view, called modernization theory, concentrates on encouraging developing states to compete more successfully in the international economic system. According to this view, colonialism began the process of preparedness, but there is still much for developing countries to learn. Modernization theory drew on the historical experience of the European Industrial Revolution and suggested replication in the developing world. Political change was required to introduce political systems that were partially democratic but also capable of restraining short-term popular demands in the interests of long-term investment in industrial growth. Development experts felt governments should actively mobilize capital for industrial investment. In some cases capital was then provided cheaply to industrialists to start private sector growth. In fundamental industries, like power generation, cement or steel production, governments invested in state-owned plants. Finally, there needed to be wide-scale changes in culture and populations needed to become less conservative and more entrepreneurial. Traditional familial and community ties needed to be replaced by a merit based appointment system and developing states needed to engineer the creation of capitalism. This perspective was a developing world form of liberalism very different from the extreme neoliberalism of globalization advocates.

The alternative view, called dependency theory, is broadly Marxist in its hostility to globalization. Dependency theorists argue that the history and contemporary realities of the international capitalist system have created and sustained the problems experienced by developing states. Developing states were not trying to create capitalism from nothing but were instead being incorporated into a pre-existing capitalist system in ways that made normal industrialization extremely difficult, no matter how hard they tried to do what the modernization theorists suggested. Radical theorist Gunder Frank coined the term 'development of underdevelopment', and argues that problems in developing states have been actively created by their relationships with the developed world. Various kinds of monopolies have enabled foreign countries to extort profits from the developing world that should have been re-invested at home to promote further industrialization. Money, or perhaps more accurately value, was flowing from the periphery to the core of the capitalist system.

In the colonial period exploitation was particularly blatant with people forced to work to produce primary commodities for minimal wages either as slaves or through the destruction of their traditional livelihoods and/or the need to pay punitive taxes to colonial governments. Colonies' products were then sold for vast profits to European traders (with trading monopolies) or artificially cheaply to western manufacturers who made their profits later in the production process. In either circumstance, the profits of labour were not staying where the work was done and did not enrich the local population.

Since decolonization, naked imperialism had been replaced by more subtle forms of exploitation. Instead of government control and legally enforced monopolies, the developed world maintains a monopoly of capital and technology. New industries can only be established via foreign borrowing and paying fees to license technology. New industries in the developing world have to compete against established business in the West and are handicapped by the need to repay licence fees and borrowings. Less obviously, the monopoly of manufacturing production in the West meant the developing world had to produce more and more primary commodities to pay for the same amount of imports of final goods, or tools and machines to set up their own industry.

Development could no longer take place normally on the historical model of the West. Instead there appeared economic dualism, uneven development and the creation of a comprador bourgeoisie. Developing states tended to have an indigenously owned primary goods production sector and a more advanced foreign owned sector. The foreign sector was often disconnected from the domestic economy (economic dualism). A select few of the domestic population profited from this system as landlords of large farms or in their ability to support foreign enterprise (the comprador bourgeoisie). Populations often did not have ambition to become an independent, national capitalist class that would eliminate foreign control; their interests were better served by collaborating with foreigners, consuming foreign luxury goods and ensuring that foreign interests found it easy to continue doing business in their countries. Domestic economics and politics were shaped in ways that prevented national self-determination and economic betterment.

In practice, both modernization and dependency thinking impacted the politics of international development. The developed world tried to use aid to promote the adoption of western institutions and technology, along with ongoing participation in the international trade regime (this participation was regulated with some acknowledgement of governments' role in development but it did not yet constitute neoliberalism). Developing states tried to encourage the flow of western resources but wanted to prevent interference into how resources were used, arguing that they had a right to self-governed development. Many aimed to produce an industrialized economy but in a way that was strongly regulated and often contained elements of socialism. They also tended to argue that the global trading system was fundamentally unfair, with particular emphasis on the unstable and declining prices of primary commodities, and argued for interference in commodity markets to promote greater stability and fairness under the banner of campaigns for a New International Economic Order. Domestic policy tended to involve tightly managed trade with high levels of protection for emerging industry.

The New International Economic Order (NIEO) movement was sustained by economic strength as much as by the power of ideas and came closest to achieving some of its ends in the late 1970s. OPEC was, in some ways, its crowning achievement (though it benefited some developing states far more than others). Oil-exporting countries were benefiting from windfall wealth gains and oil importing-countries found it unusually easy to borrow on the international financial markets. Lower income countries that couldn't borrow on the private markets were given fairly lenient treatment by the IMF, which considered the first oil shock as a temporary problem. However, the West's neoliberal turn rapidly undermined developing states' power. Attempts to curb inflation in the West involved a sharp rise in interest rates that was rapidly reflected internationally. This had a devastating impact on borrower countries who found themselves with much larger interest bills to pay than they had expected and were unable to borrow new money to buy time so that they could pay those bills. The developed world was also in recession, reducing potential developing country export earnings and the result was a widespread debt crisis. Indebted countries needed to borrow more money than ever before from the IMF and World Bank. However, the IMF and the World Bank likewise came under the influence of the new neoliberal economic orthodoxy and pushed developing countries to adopt it, in return for unprecedentedly large loans. This was the beginning of the current phase of globalization in the developing world.

Development and globalization since 1980

The new economic orthodoxy, echoing emerging practice in the West, suggested that government attempts to kick-start development had been highly wasteful and had tended to crowd out private-sector entrepreneurs. The solution to the debt crisis was for governments to spend less, sell off assets that would be better run by the private sector (often including pubic utilities like power generation, water and communications), and reduce government control over economic activity. The new orthodoxy was sceptical of active government efforts at industrialization, which had been acceptable to earlier modernization theorists, let alone international attempts to regulate the economy of the kind proposed by dependency theorists and the NIEO programme.

In Africa, agricultural marketing boards (which had exercised a monopoly over trade in agricultural products, fixing low-level prices paid to producers) were targeted. These boards were supposed to stabilize prices for farmers, keep food prices down for urban consumers and secure export profits, but prices were often set too low in order to keep food costs down for urban consumers (which helped to keep wages down) or produce profits for government trading companies. Low prices reduced production as a result of the fewer incentives to improve efficiency. Such schemes were also highly vulnerable to corruption. In Latin America, the targets were often large consumer goods industries, created in the 1960s to assemble goods that had previously been imported (such as cars). The production plants were not as efficient as their global rivals and were only staying in business because they were protected against foreign imports by heavy tariffs. This was always going to be the case to begin with, while new industries were setting up, but they were supposed to become more efficient over time. Politicians should theoretically have reduced tariffs over time to force ongoing improvements but were either incapable of doing their jobs or were influenced by the politically powerful interests that owned the new factories.

The neoliberal message was that such abuses, along with inefficiencies, could be removed by a more free-market policy stance. Governments should cut red tape (which discourages innovation, distorts market incentives and creates opportunities for corruption) and should allow free trade (which would increase competition and reduce the costs of inputs to the production process). The attempt to foster national industry had failed, producing expensive and inefficient businesses so governments should place fewer restrictions on foreign investment allowing foreign companies to introduce expertise and capital. The reduction in government spending and sale of state assets would gain revenues to pay off debt. At the same time the new policies would produce faster growth over the long term, preventing debt problems returning.

Those who consider globalization a good force for the developing world argue that such policies were not simply being imposed by the international institutions, but were also being increasingly accepted by developing state governments. Globalization was making capital more mobile, meaning more investors were willing to set up production in the developing world. A fully economically integrated world would be one in which the differentiation between developed and developing countries ceased to exist.

Although the neoliberal vision is somewhat utopian, many developing states felt that the policies of the 1960s and 1970s had failed and it was consequently worth trying something like the new orthodoxy. Others may have felt that their chronic debt and shortage of investment capital, alongside pressure from the international institutions and the increasingly competitive world environment, meant that they had little choice but to adopt some of the new agenda. Development policy moved in a new direction as a result of shifting power structures and changes in economic ideas. However, this shift was always unpopular with left-wing politicians, academics and political activists. Critics argued the neoliberal approach was too optimistic about global markets. In the background is a false view of (international) economics as a mutually beneficial activity that makes everyone better off. In particular, there is a lot of evidence that those who trade in manufactured goods gain more by trade than those who trade in primary commodities (even if everyone does gain). The neoliberal view fails to meet the arguments economic nationalists and more radical dependency theorists make about the difficulties of late industrialization. Second, markets tend to produce inequality within and between countries. Pressure to reduce the role of the state undermined what welfare provision there had been in developing states. Foreign companies want to use developing state labour because they can get it cheap, making large profits that don't stay in the developing world, transferring very little technology and undermining working-class jobs at home. Hence the neoliberal revolution was an exercise of developed state power, designed to open up developing markets for economic exploitation. Claims about private sector efficiency and mutual benefits were simply ideology. Policy change was imposed through pressure from the international institutions and multinational companies.

In practice, the results of the neoliberal turn were not good, even in terms of growth which was poor for most of the 1980s. It is possible to identify three broad sets of responses to the neoliberal experience which approximately overlap with the three approaches to globalization introduced at the beginning of the chapter: orthodox liberal responses, particularly the current stance of the IMF and World Bank, a set of Marxist-inspired radical responses and a set of strategic political possibilities.

BOX 10.2 PERSPECTIVES ON DEVELOPMENT

Modernization theory

- Development is relatively easy – adapt to the global economic system as it is
- Countries should reproduce the cultural, political and economic transformations that took place in the West
- The state has a key role to play and failure to develop is probably countries' fault

Dependency theory

- The global economic system prevents development, sucking resources from periphery to core, failure to develop is due to external conditions
- Global system creates dualist economies, limits investment and creates political systems that serve outsiders
- The solution is either 'delinking' from the global economy or global economic transformation

Neoliberalism

- Development is about adapting to the global economic system as it is
- That requires letting markets work their magic, everything else will follow
- The solution is to roll back the state and globalize the economy

The mainstream response and a post-Washington consensus

In retrospect even the Bretton Woods institutions acknowledge that 1980s neoliberalism paid too little attention to the role of governments in promoting development. By the mid-1990s, official development policy was shifting towards a so-called post-Washington consensus that paid more attention to reforming state institutions as well as simply letting markets work. The World Bank's 1989 review of structural adjustment in

Africa pointed out the ways in which bad governance had derailed what were otherwise good policies. At the same time, political pressure led to a growing focus on poverty. The IFIs started to raise more questions with governments about where expenditure cuts were being made, criticising cuts in welfare to allow military spending.

These changes can be regarded as modest concessions to the left-wing critics. There is an acceptance that globalization and liberalization on their own will not create development, and that something needs to be done to 'make globalization work for the poor'. However, the more fundamental criticisms by dependency theorists in the 1970s, aired by contemporary anti-globalization critics, have not really been addressed. Engagement with international markets through relatively free trade, liberal investment regimes and open access for foreign capital and multinationals continue to be at the heart of the orthodox project. In this vision, the state is there to support engagement with the world market, not to shape it, let alone insulate countries from it. The new agenda is largely one of facilitating the operation of international markets by giving the poor the skills they require to benefit (or 'making the poor work for globalization' as one critic has put it). Indeed, there are striking similarities with the modernization theory approaches of the 1960s, albeit with more emphasis on the international economy and less on the role of the state in mobilizing the development process.

BOX 10.3 RESPONSES TO GLOBALIZATION IN THE DEVELOPING WORLD

Mainstream 'post-Washington consensus'

- Still in favour of markets and globalization fundamentally good
- But actively need to help the poor, through safety nets, training and education
- More attention to the state and democratization (back towards modernization theory?)

Marxist and anti-globalization responses

Left-wing critics still argue that the post-Washington concensus approach will fail because the international economy is an arena of power-struggle not mutual gains. Foreign investors want to exploit developing state labour, not transfer skills and promote industrialization and are unlikely to invest in their host states and certainly won't spend the money required for welfare provision. Their presence prevents local actors from gaining the economic power to resist their interests. Even if the post-Washington consensus could be implemented (and many argue it is too naïve about the political power structures), it would do nothing to resolve the more fundamental international conflicts of interest. Stated bluntly, it is a grossly inadequate response to the morally unacceptable poverty and hunger that continues to haunt the developing world. The question for left-wing anti-globalization activists, though, is what if anything can be done about the structures of power that developing states confront?

The dependency theorists of the 1970s advocated turning away from the global economy and pursuing an indigenous path to (socialist) development. Implicitly, the argument was that engagement with the global economy from colonization through neo-colonialism had actively harmed developing countries by siphoning resources away from the periphery to the core. If states had been left to act alone, the profits of industrialization would have been re-invested locally and states could have developed normally. However, this view represents a misreading of Western development, where relationships with outside states were a key part of stimulating production and industrialization. Indeed, Marxist theorists of imperialism (like Lenin) have argued that capitalism was sustained through these unequal relationships with the periphery.

In any case, the delinking strategy lost favour even with the left when states that tried to pursue an autarchic path to development (like North Korea) or had it forced upon them (like Cuba) also struggled to develop. Autarchic development is only really sustainable on the basis of a conception of so-called green development, often found in NGO publications, wherein small-scale local communities assisted to achieve self-reliance. This is an appealing vision to environmentalists and romantics in the West (and the developing world) because it avoids the disruption of traditional cultures and forms of reciprocity that accompany the transition to industrial capitalism. It can also represent a significant advance on the conditions that the poorest communities in the world currently enjoy. However, in the long term, it doesn't seem to offer the potential for material gains that many people seek because it doesn't allow people to benefit from the specialization of production achieved through larger-scale production and trade (not necessarily fast cars and designer furniture, but even the costs of health care to increase life expectancy are difficult to secure on the basis of this kind of economy). Additionally, questions arise concerning how it can be acceptable to promote this kind of life in the developing world when people in the West would not consider it acceptable.

A third possibility is to hope for a radical transformation of politics worldwide. In some ways this is the classic Marxist vision in which the transformation of the world to a capitalist mode of production paves the way for a global socialist revolution. The problem here is that this is likely to be a long time coming (and according to some dependency views, may never come at all).

BOX 10.4 LEFT-WING RESPONSES

- Post-Washington consensus is more of the same. Fails to address global economic exploitation. Small concessions made since 1980s will do little for the poor
- 'De-linking' is no longer seen as a viable strategy – except in a (non-Marxist) 'green' variant that emphasises low consumption, sustainable, village-based development
- Hope for a politics that can fundamentally alter global economic system

Strategic options and political agency

The third alternative is to acknowledge some of the potential benefits of globalization but to work to shape those benefits through forms of national and international regulation. The most promising stories here come from the development of some Asian countries. In 1945 Korea had a similar GDP to Kenya but by 1996 Korea had joined the OECD, arguably making it no longer a developing country. Korean growth was achieved through a strategic engagement with the global economy and the Korean government operated a system of managed competition wherein it offered companies some protection and assistance in introducing new technologies but also required them to meet performance targets (usually export targets) in return. Protection was gradually removed once companies had acquired new skills and only offered for ever more sophisticated forms of production. Korea made sure it built up domestic capacity before exposing companies to foreign competition. A less demanding and slightly less success-ful strategy was adopted by Malaysia, which devoted less attention to building up domestic companies and more to encouraging foreign companies to choose Malaysia as a location for their plants. Malaysia, then, sought to benefit from the growth of trans-national production that constitutes such a large part of globalization. Again, though, Malaysia engaged strategically with the international economy, encouraging only desir-able foreign investment (rather than sweat shop production competing with existing domestic companies).

Such examples might be taken to suggest that developing countries could develop if they ended corruption and bettered economic management (perhaps akin to the more regulatory social liberalism of the post-war period). However, it is important to recog-nize that Korea inherited a very special set of circumstances, being relatively quick off the mark in the development process and having experienced some industrialization during pre-War Japanese colonization. It was also on the front line in the Cold War, receiving a lot of foreign aid and very favourable access to world markets in an effort to keep it 'safe from communism'. Different states are all in different strategic positions when it comes to globalization. Malaysia was perhaps less unique in that respect but it benefited from a relatively well educated workforce and proximity to Japan, which was a pioneer in setting up the kinds of transnational production chains that leading Malaysian firms formed a part of. It is also important to recognize that Korean and Malaysian development was far from perfect. Atul Kohli has described the Korean state as 'quasi-facist' – such a concerted industrialization project was only possible for a very authoritarian regime that violently suppressed opposition from organized labour, even if the result was prosperity over the longer term.

Additionally, although globalization may have made these paths to development easier in some ways (more transnational production and capital looking for a home, more open export markets), it may have closed them off in other ways. International economic regulation has closed off some of the techniques used by Korea and Malaysia. WTO rules, particularly Trade Related Investment Measures (TRIMs) prevent some of the tactics employed by the Korean and Malaysian development plans. The opening of export markets is also far from complete, particularly for goods produced by weaker developing states (such as part-processed agricultural products).

Globalization is a political process in which there is some room for manoeuvre. Successful development should not attempt to replicate experiences but should develop plausible strategies based on others' experiences. However, Marxists are right to point out that global power structures place real restraints on what is possible; achieving a better deal for developing countries will be as much a matter of political organization as finding technical solutions to development problems, and political organization may need to take place at national, regional and international levels. The Doha round of WTO negotiations has halted because developing states have refused to accept an unreasonable deal. The IMF is concerned that it is losing clients as states find alternative ways to secure themselves from debt. Equally, though, such strategies are largely driven by relatively well-off and powerful middle-income countries in Latin American and Asia. African countries are more marginalized and have less chance of benefiting from globalization and may consequently look to more radical solutions.

BOX 10.5 STRATEGIC RESPONSES

- Draw on 'success stories' to try to control/get the best from globalization
- Home-grown industrialization on the Korean model, but very difficult
- Trying to attract 'good' multinational investment
- Either probably requires ongoing struggles to re-open, or keep open options that the WTO is trying to close down
- It may also be difficult for Africa to repeat experience

CONCLUSIONS

This chapter has argued for an approach to globalization and development that pays more attention to the politics that shapes global economic regulation and the room to manoeuvre that continues to exist in the face of globalization. Far from considering the tired arguments about whether globalization is right or wrong, it is more interesting to consider what can now be done to make globalization work for the benefit of all populations. Of course, asking what is to be done only makes sense against an evaluation of liberal claims about the potential benefits of globalization and Marxist concerns about the power structures that support and sustain globalization. However, it also goes beyond those normative debates and focuses our attention on historical processes. Understanding the events that shape the international system is the first step towards thinking clearly about plausible avenues for future political change.

This chapter has outlined some possible responses to the current situations of developing states and has tried to establish reasons to feel optimistic or pessimistic about them. However, there can be no easy answers and certainly no answers that apply to the whole of the developing world. In that sense, thinking in terms of 'globalization and development' might be a mistake, as to do so suggests quick fix global solutions, when what is actually required is long-term political action at a number of different levels, applied differently to different states.

FURTHER READING

Chang, H. (2002) *Kicking Away the Ladder: Policies and Institutions for Economic Development in Historical Perspective*, London: Anthem Press.

Frank, A. (1996) Capitalism and Underdevelopment in Latin American History, New York: Monthly Review Press.

Gore, C. (2000) 'The rise and fall of the Washington consensus as a paradigm for developing countries', *World Development*, 28 (5): 789–804.

Held, D., McGrew, A., Goldblatt, D. and Perraton, J. (1999) *Global Transformations: Politics, Economics, Culture*, Cambridge: Polity.

Hoogvelt, A. (2001) *Globalization and the Post-colonial World: The New Political Economy of Development*, Baltimore: Johns Hopkins University Press.

Kohli, A. (2004) *State-Directed Development: Political Power and Industrialization in the Global Periphery*, Cambridge: Cambridge University Press.

Martinussen, J. (1997) *Society, State and Development: A Guide to Competing Theories of Development*, London: HSRC Press.

Payne, A. (2005) *The Global Politics of Unequal Development*, Houndmills: Palgrave.

Rodrik, D., *Industrial Policy for the Twenty-first Century* (unpublished paper available at http://ksghome.harvard.edu/~drodrik/UNIDOSep.pdf).

Stiglitz, J. (2003) *Globalization and its Discontents*, London: Penguin.

Yun, C. (2003) 'International production networks and the role of the state: Lessons from East Asian developmental experience', *European Journal of Development Research*, 15 (1).

CHAPTER 11

The Environment
Antje Brown and Gabriela Kütting

The environment in international and global politics is gradually becoming one of the most pressing issues of the early twenty-first century. It has been recognized that many, if not all, problems of environmental degradation are transboundary in nature and therefore need an international solution. National policy measures essentially cannot cope with international environmental problems because the source of pollution or the impact of pollution may not be within a particular state's jurisdiction.

Traditionally, international environmental problems have been addressed at international environmental conferences where treaties are designed that commit the signatories to controlling the problem in question. Since the 1970s the number of international environmental agreements (IEAs) has risen to reach record numbers. There is a loose assumption that this is a good thing and that this rise has resulted in a commensurable improvement in environmental protection. But is this actually the case? In fact, many would argue that there is little positive correlation at all. What are the connections between environmental diplomacy and environmental protection and how can environmental protection be achieved?

IEAs are international legal instruments adopted by a large number of states and intergovernmental organizations with the primary purpose of preventing, and managing, negative human impacts on natural resources. IEAs can take the form of a single instrument or a series of interlinked documents such as conventions, followed by protocols and amendments. For example, The Framework Convention on Climate Change (FCCC) and the Kyoto Protocol are part of the same framework.

IEAs cover a broad range of policy areas, from biodiversity to regulating human-made greenhouse gas emissions into the atmosphere, and the control of chemicals

BOX 11.1 PROMINENT IEAs AND PROTOCOLS

- Framework Convention on Climate Change (1992)
- Basel Convention on Hazardous Wastes and their Disposal (1989)
- Biodiversity Convention (1992)
- Stockholm Convention on Persistent Organic Pollutants (2001)
- Kyoto Protocol on Climate Change (1997)
- Montreal Protocol on the Ozone Layer (1987)
- Cartagena Protocol on Biosafety (2000)

and hazardous wastes. The implementation of IEAs is a complex process, involving coercion of a wide range of actors into accepting environmental goals and subsequently implementing the necessary behavioural changes. To these ends, IEAs adopt a series of constitutional measures: a Conference of Parties (COP) to act as a decision-making body on behalf of the policy; a secretariat to support the COP and administer the policy, and various other executive and subsidiary bodies to advise and report on the policy on a non-mandatory basis.

Institutional arrangements such as international (or multilateral as they are also called) environmental agreements reflect negotiated compromises at the policy level and are the sum total of what is politically feasible to achieve. However, these compromises also tell a story about priorities in policy-making which reflect the interests of the most powerful actors in this policy process or indeed other overlapping policy processes. These priorities can be manifested in economic terms, in social terms, in agenda-setting in general and in evaluations or definitions of the environmental problem in question.

As the case studies presented in this chapter will show, there is very often a lack of connection between the political compromises that shape an international agreement on the environment and the ecological demands of a particular environmental problem. There is also often a level of abstraction to policy remedies that do not account for social inequalities between states but also between social groups in states and how they are affected by an environmental problem and how the economic and social cost of a solution affects them. It is felt by many analysts and activists of global environmental politics that the state-centric form of agreement-making marginalizes the environment and many of the world's citizens. They see the actors in global environmental politics as a triangular set of relations rather than as an issue of the state that regulates everything with other actors subordinate to the state. So a triangular vision would see the state, economic actors and civil society actors all vying to influence environmental outcomes. It cannot be denied that since the 1980s non-state actors have experienced a significant rise in influence on the international scene. States are still the only sovereign actors (the ones with the legal and military power to make decisions) but non-state actors have been integrated into all international decision-making processes and perform important stakeholder functions. Non-state actors may not be able to sign legal documents but they perform agenda-setting tasks, influence meetings, provide information, act as a voice of caution or reason, and also bring in new dimensions to any discussion. We now have an international and global field of politics in which there are international legal agreements on the environment between states, legal agreements signed by states and other actors (legally binding for the states) and agreements between non-state actors that are seen as equally influential as state-led arrangements (not legally binding, although very much in the spotlight).

Non-state actors are defined simply as actors not representing governments and can range from environmental non-governmental organizations (NGOs) to community advocacy groups, scientific think tanks and multinational corporations (MNCs). Since the 1970s, environmental policy has seen a dramatic intensification of non-state actor involvement and subsequently environmental policy-making and international regime building can no longer be described as a singularly government/state centric activity (it is currently estimated that 40,000 NGOs are operating in international regime building). Environmental policy-making represents a complex and ambiguous policy process whereby both state and non-state actors shape the content and implementation of IEAs. Additionally, the process of economic and media globalization has further blurred the line between actors.

The assumption is that with these trends we as a global society have the means to move away from abstract agreements driven by economic rationality and political compromise and hampered by the constraints of lengthy lead times to a more democratic form of decision-making that can focus more on the most pressing challenges of the twenty-first century. However, these trends do not resolve the fundamental problem of growing inequality among various social groups on this planet, nor do they address the debate between technological progress and consumption. The question remains whether the existing frameworks for dealing with environmental problems are adequate to rise to this seemingly insurmountable challenge.

CONSUMPTION

The environmental side of consumption is a major consideration for several reasons. First, the social and structural origins of environmental degradation can be found in the excessive consumption of the planet's resources. Second, the dominant neoliberal, or even liberal, approach in global management institutions is based on the assumption that the current standard of living enjoyed by the richest 20 per cent of the world population can be extended to encompass the whole globe. In terms of resource availability, this is clearly a myth and leads to serious questions concerning both the environment and equity. Third, consumption is not the last stage in the production chain; rather, the last stage is disposal of the product consumed. Waste is a serious environmental problem not just for local authorities but also has a global dimension which affects the earth's capacity to act as a sink.

The argument that excessive consumption leads to environmental degradation is not a new one and dates back to the late 1960s and early 1970s. In 1968 the Club of Rome (founded by Aurelio Peccei of Italy and Alexander King of Scotland) produced a report titled 'Limits to Growth' (1972) that was published in over thirty languages and became an international bestseller. Its key message was that economic growth could not continue indefinitely because of the limited availability of natural resources on earth and specifically mentioned oil as a finite resource. The Club of Rome still operates to this day and has not changed its key message of limited resources and their sensible management.

The early environmental movement in the 1970s questioned the ideology of consumerism in the period of unlimited expectations of the late 1960s and argued that the ideology of wanting more and more was fundamentally flawed and would lead to the ecological collapse of the planet. Rather, there should be an ideological shift to considering what people actually needed for a fulfilled life rather than what they wanted, i.e. a questioning of the ideology of unlimited economic growth and of an expected rise in the standard of living of those who had already achieved a high level. This movement coincided with the first oil crisis and the first United Nations Conference for the Human Environment in Stockholm in 1972. The idea that there are insufficient resources has often been discredited with the discovery of new oil fields and the introduction of more energy-efficient technologies which have pushed back the date for when oil will run out from a predicted twenty years (in the 1970s) to somewhere in the middle of the twenty-first century being the current estimate. Now the oil resources issue has acquired a new face with the increasing competition between India, China and the western world for energy resources. The debate has turned from resource availability to access, as recent negotiations between the EU and Russia on gas supplies have shown. It is interesting to note that the emphasis is on distribution and access to resources rather than availability and resource limits. While the concern about running out of resources and the need not want campaign have lost their immediate urgency and momentum, the problem of resource dependency (on other countries) as well as a constant search for alternatives (i.e. renewables) still remains.

A lot of alternative forms of creating energy have been created and existing resources are being recycled. Technological advancements make it possible to find replacements for materials when the need arises. However, all these measures do not change the fundamental truth that there is only a fixed amount of resources on this planet and although we are not in danger of running out just yet, these resources are being used up at an unsustainable rate by only a small part of the world population. What is more, it is not only a question of using up resources but also of degrading sinks, i.e. using ecosystems to deposit the wastes of the industrial production process.

The neoliberal economic order, like preceding economic orders, treats the natural environment as if there was an unlimited supply of natural resources. The goods and services provided by the planet are not costed, unlike capital goods and resources owned by a supplier, and therefore they are externalized by economists and taken for granted in economic valuations. To come back to the subject of consumption and environment, no inhabitant of this planet has not been exposed to some form of environmental degradation and suffered a decline in conditions of living because of it and is therefore aware of the limited capacity of the planet to cope with the rate of extraction of resources and depositing of waste. Therefore, the need for creating a careful balance between environmental and societal needs is abundantly clear and the link between an individual's pattern of consumption and environmental decline is obvious.

Lastly, there is not only a problem with uneven levels of consumption but also with the clearing up of excessive consumption. Consumer goods have a limited lifespan and then need to be disposed of by the consumer, in addition to the waste products that are unintended consequences of the production process. A veritable economy of waste has

▉ BOX 11.2 SUSTAINABLE DEVELOPMENT

- *Environmental protection*: How can further environmental degradation and pollution be prevented?
- *Policy integration*: How can social, economic and environmental needs be accommodated without being counter-productive?
- *Inter-generational responsibility*: How can future generations be ensured similar (if not better) environmental standards?
- *Equity*: How can the poor of the present generation be provided with a decent and fair quality of life?
- *Participation*: How can stakeholders of civil society be active in the process?

developed, especially in the field of toxic or nuclear waste. This trade in waste removes the unwanted by-products of excessive consumption away from the consumer and further alienates the consumer from the social and environmental impact of his/her actions. So, the consumer is detached from the social and structural origins of his/her patterns of behaviour. First, the manufacturing process of the product to be consumed is something the consumer is only vaguely aware of and, second, the waste removal is also something that is not immediately obvious to the consumer. Such alienation, for want of a better word, also disconnects the consumer from their social and environmental responsibilities.

▉ BOX 11.3 CHALLENGES TO SUSTAINABILITY

- Environmental degradation can be traced to excessive consumption of natural resources
- The current neoliberal economic climate accelerates this process
- Consumption also involves the use of natural resource sinks such as landfill sites and oceans
- Natural resources are not factored properly into economic calculations.
- Uneven consumption patterns suggests a global inequity and a global economy of waste
- Solutions are hampered by an inherent detachment/alienation between the consumer and the product

▉ EQUITY

The connection between equity and the environmental dimensions of international relations is rarely made as the environment in IR or in global political economy is generally treated from a strictly scientific perspective or as a purely regulatory matter. Thus, the environment is seen as a subject determined by cause-and-effect relationships and its effects on the running of international affairs need to be understood and managed. From the perspective of seeing the environment as subordinate to the international system, it is as good as impossible to perceive of environmental values as such. However, there are many questions relating to the status of the environment and how it relates to social status that are being addressed in other academic disciplines.

Traditionally, governments have monopolized the role of safeguarding natural resources, sinks and protecting their citizens from environmental harm. Nationally this happens through the rule of law. Internationally this has been effected through the role of international environmental agreements and through other more private forms of regulation. As governments are the appropriate legal channels through which such interests can be represented at the international level, there does not seem to be an ethical problem with this form of organization. However, under globalization there have been practical (but not de juro) changes in the role of governments at the international level. First, neoliberal practice suggests that market ideology and the market as a regulatory mechanism are the most efficient ways of dealing with social (including environmental) problems. Thus governments have begun to participate in a division of labour resulting in a changing role. States now increasingly become the custodian of neoliberal ideology and push for well functioning markets. This has become their prime responsibility/task and it is assumed that the other tasks traditionally carried out will be adjusted through the market mechanism. Thus the traditional roles of the state have in many ways been transferred to private hands by means of voluntary regulations, and also many tasks have been outsourced to private organizations such as companies, research institutes or civil society, presenting an organizational question as well as a moral issue.

Unlike environmental ethics, the subject of environmental equity has a more anthropocentric focus. It is about control over and access to environmental resources and a clean living environment as well as even distribution of resources. At the national level, research has shown quite clearly that it is especially people at the lower end of social strata who are more exposed to environmental degradation and accordingly suffer health and deprivation problems. One such reason for this phenomenon is that socially marginalized people often cannot afford to live in areas unaffected by pollution and often have to live near industrial estates with pollution problems. In addition, they are likely to be less able to overcome environmental restraints through the purchase of healthier goods or filtering devices. In many ways, these findings can be extrapolated to the global level.

Of the various types of environmental problems, the North's are typically associated with industrialization whilst those of the South are associated with the more immediate environment such as deforestation, desertification and polluted drinking water. Urban problems are associated with both North and South. Global problems are structural and affect both North and South, albeit in different ways. There is a definite income gap between those whose direct living environment is subject to immediate environmental problems and those whose homes are better equipped to overcome immediate environmental concerns. Indeed, it is no accident that slums or lower-income housing is often situated in the more polluted parts of town or closer to industrial estates. This has an effect on health but also on access to environmental 'goods'. Therefore there can be no misunderstanding about a close connection between income and environmental quality of life. In recent years, the relationship between income and environmental quality has received a lot of attention by researchers and practitioners. The empirical tool most commonly used to identify and illustrate a causal link between income per capita and pollution is the Kuznets curve. It demonstrates how various economic stages in a given country or region correlate with environmental standards. The Kuznets curve has been criticized for over-simplifying conditions and determinants. Nevertheless, recent studies have confirmed the link between income and the environment: economically poor areas tend to suffer more from poor environmental quality than others. People with low income are particularly affected by local pollution problems such as acid rain, soil and river pollution; they cannot afford high environmental standards and more importantly, they cannot afford moving away to other locations.

This argument can be extended to the international and the global in that wealthier states can increase their environmental quality by, for example, getting rid of their toxic waste or by outsourcing certain dangerous practices. Trade in waste is a reality and it is also well known that capital flight takes place to areas where there are less stringent environmental regulations (see Case Study 1). Thus there is a definite issue of environmental equity as not all citizens of the world have access to the same environmental rights and these discrepancies are used for profit in the organization of the global political economy. Although some inequity can be found in the environmental conditions of different geographical locations in the world, as they are obviously not the same, these are inequalities generated by the structural constraints of the global economic system. An inhabitant of a mountain village in the desolate ranges of the Bolivian Andes obviously has different food access than an inhabitant of the lower Pyrenees in France. This is not a question of environmental equity. However, both inhabitants' ability to be in control of their respective environment is an issue of environmental equity.

Another equity issue is the evolution of a global division of labour and the equity dimensions associated with this process. In this global division of labour some regions have clearly been relegated to an agricultural role in the global economy whilst others have the role of cheap labour supplier. Such roles are not of choice but are dictated by intrinsic global economic connections. Thus environmental access and equity in terms of consumer goods availability are pre-programmed with no realistic way out of this equity deficit. Again, this is a structural constraint of the global political economy and one that has existed throughout history in various forms of colonialism. The difference today, however, is that through the privatization of control, interest in the continued well-being of a particular agricultural area or other economic region is not part of the political set-up any more. Once one region is depleted in environmental or social terms, another region will take its place.

Thus, the levels of problematic international environmental equity can be discerned. First, there is the agenda-setting power of the various states of the world when it comes to environmental degradation. Second, there is a monopoly on positions of power in the world economy. Third, there is the issue of purchasing power and consumption.

The agenda-setting power of various actors in the international system is a fundamental environmental equity issue and is also a structural issue. In the field of global governance, it is particularly obvious in the phrasing of the climate change debate. There exists a rift between different countries which can be superficially described as a rift between developed and developing countries although this distinction is simplistic and does not take account of the various energy-producing roles and the way different states will be affected by global warming. However, it can be argued that the debate has been framed by developed countries who want this issue to be treated as a contemporary and future problem. Many developing countries see climate change as a historical problem and want past emissions to be incorporated into possible emission reduction strategies – an idea that is not seriously discussed in diplomatic channels. However, at the same time developed countries are quite serious that future emissions should be taken into consideration. The debate is clearly framed to ensure that 'today' is the baseline from which discussions on equity start and anything that happened before today is not part of the debate. This is an example of agenda-setting power as there is clearly a temporal dimension to the debate concerned with today and the future. With temporality an issue, it seems illogical that it is not applied in both directions, i.e. past and future. However, this would dramatically alter the commitment and power dimension of the negotiations. Therefore equity takes on a very subjective meaning determined by the social and power relations of the interplay between developed and developing countries. Although the climate change example is a particularly dramatic case, it is by no means atypical. Thus agenda-setting power is a major determinant in environmental equity relations.

Agenda-setting power is an indirect, structural type of power but equity concerns are by no means limited to structural power. Equity problems can also be found in direct power relations between North and South or between any social groupings. Although coercion by violent means is a relatively rare phenomenon in the international system given the number of actors in it, the number of violent conflicts with an environmental or resource dimension is rising. Since the 1970s researchers have sought to establish a causal link between environmental resources and security problems. This link works in two distinct ways. First, it applies to cases of resource scarcity such as water shortage and their impact on the stability and security of a country or a region. Second, environmental security refers to effects that military/security activities have on the natural environment. Examples include the bombing of oil fields and gas pipelines and the storing and decommissioning of nuclear submarines. Many articles have been written, for instance by Thomas Homer-Dixon, on various aspects of environmental security. Practitioners, too, have recognized and acknowledged the link between the environment and security. For instance, NATO conducted a separate study on environmental security and the USA created the post of Deputy Under Secretary of Defense for Environmental Security. The UN, too, is well aware of the dilemmas that particularly developing countries face; partly as a result of climate change they suffer increasingly from the natural resource 'curse' and the inability to tackle it. Often regions affected by environmental resource scarcity lack the capacity to solve the problems or adapt to them. In some cases resource pressures can be resolved through immediate projects and international cooperation. But in many other cases, the countries or regions concerned develop security problems, which can only be resolved with the help of the international community. It is therefore not surprising that the UN put access to clean drinking water at the top of the Johannesburg Summit agenda in 2002 and declared 22 March 2007 as World Water Day in an effort to highlight the issue.

Additionally there exists financial and political coercion – a historical phenomenon that has become especially obvious understood through colonialism and modern forms of colonialism. Despite the fact that in political terms most states are independent and sovereign, their economic position in the global political economy (derived from historical social relations) suggests a different story. Power can also be exercised by a refusal to participate, as demonstrated by the withdrawal of the United States from the climate change negotiations. Furthermore, the exercise of direct power through global economic institutions determines how environmental resources and sinks are used. We will now demonstrate how these issues apply to particular issue areas with two case studies, one on waste and one on climate change.

CASE STUDY ONE: TRADE IN (HAZARDOUS) WASTE

The disposal and processing of waste not only signifies our neoliberal economic order and consumption society, but demonstrates an ever-increasing and complex equity problem. From a purely environmental point of view, the processing and disposal of domestic waste such as plastic containers, bottles and increasingly 'e-waste' (such as old electronic equipment) presents the primary environmental concern. A large part of such waste is highly toxic and needs to be processed carefully to ensure minimal damage to the environment and human health. The problem of waste becomes an equity issue when resources and space become limited. These pressures lead to more stringent legislation in developed countries, which in turn puts pressure on manufacturers and waste processing companies to dispose of the waste in the most economic and efficient manner. This means that an ever-increasing share of the North's waste is shipped to developing countries where waste can be disposed of cheaply. Some of the main exporters of waste are also arguably the 'greenest' when it comes to environmental regulation: Germany, the Netherlands, USA and the UK.

To illustrate the problem, around 70 per cent of toxic plastic waste that is produced by predominantly industrialized countries in the North finds its way – often illegally – to China. The UK alone exports approximately 2 million tonnes of waste every year for 'processing' where waste is recycled, dumped in landfill sites or simply burned. The large-scale impacts of this waste import into China include river, soil and air pollution but also serious health problems for local residents as well as (migrant) workers who earn £1.50 per day. Health problems include respiratory illnesses and skin conditions. Despite existing IEAs (see below) and a continued effort in tackling waste trade by the UN and NGOs, the problem will continue (and indeed worsen) as long as the issues of consumption and equity are not tackled by all concerned.

The evolution of a policy

The process of regime-building started in the mid-1980s with the UN preparing a set of 'Cairo guidelines' on the management and disposal of hazardous wastes. These guidelines were not legally binding but called for a more transparent notification, consent and verification system between exporters and importers. While well intended, these guidelines were considered insufficient by African countries as they did not tackle the ongoing illegal trade, nor did they oblige non-signatories to adopt the same standards. African nations were joined by environmental NGOs and the European Parliament in their campaign for a better regime.

In 1987 the UNEP working group started with the preparation of a global convention. However, while African representatives wanted a total ban and export-state liability in event of illegal trafficking, waste exporters from the North wanted permission to trade waste freely as long as prior notification and consent by the importer were given.

After an elaborate process of negotiation and compromise, the Basel Convention on the Control of Transboundary Movements of Hazardous Wastes and their Disposal was adopted in 1989. During the process the USA had formed a 'veto coalition' with other exporters, which ensured that the free market (yet monitored) export/import option was adopted. The Organization of African Unity (OAU) had suggested a waste export ban to countries that lacked the same facilities and technologies as developed countries, as well as regular inspections of disposal sites by UN inspectors. However, these proposals were rejected due to the OAU failing to reach a consensus with other waste export critics.

The Basel Convention itself covered waste that is explosive, flammable, poisonous, infectious, corrosive, toxic or ecotoxic. It prohibited the export of hazardous waste to countries that banned the import of such waste as well as non-parties to the Convention (Article 4). It allowed for export to countries whose facilities for storage/disposal were less advanced than those of exporting countries as long as the importing countries could provide detailed information on waste movements and written consent. Critics complained about the minimal effect the new Convention would have on trading practices as it was open to interpretation.

Due to ongoing pressure, the veto coalition began to crumble. This coincided with the (then) European Community's trade negotiations with ACP (African, Caribbean, Pacific) partners, which included the issue of waste export. With newly gained confidence and support from the OAU, 12 African states signed their own Bamako Convention, which called for a ban of hazardous trade imports into their countries. Although the number of participants was small, it was a symbolic gesture to the rest of the world. The pressure continued with over 100 countries agreeing in 1994 to a ban on hazardous waste imports. This initiative was supported by one of the largest and most influential NGOs, Greenpeace, which had just published a report of 1,000 cases of illegal toxic waste exports. Already, waste exporters signalled that they were about to change tactics. For instance, the US Government (under Bill Clinton) adjusted its policy on waste exports to developing countries over a five-year transition period. However, the new policy still included a number of exceptions such as the export of scrap metal, glass, textiles and paper. Although these types of waste were not strictly speaking toxic, they nevertheless continued to pose environmental problems for importers.

At the following Geneva meeting of Basel Convention COP (Conference of the Parties), more pressure was put on exporters to ban the trade in waste. This time so-called recyclables were included into the equation. Experience had shown that these items were not recycled as intended but were simply dumped in developing countries. This time the waste critics were more united. The meeting produced a more committed and inclusive Ban Amendment, which was adopted in 1995. Three years later, in 1998, another 'improvement' on the international regime was adopted: the COP specified hazardous and non-hazardous wastes more clearly, thereby closing more interpretation loopholes. In 1999, a protocol on liability and compensation was adopted.

In 2002, the COP adopted a Strategic Plan for the Implementation of the Basel Declaration to 2010. The parties also discussed the coordination of the Basel Convention with other Conventions for greater effectiveness; in particular the Stockholm Convention on persistent organic pollutants (i.e. chemicals that are highly toxic, persistent, bio-accumulate and can travel long distances) and the Rotterdam Convention which covers an informed consent system for certain hazardous chemicals and pesticides in international trade.

More recently, in November 2006, the COP met again to discuss one paramount waste problem: e-waste. The meeting was intended to tackle the 20 to 50 million tonnes of electronic waste produced worldwide every year and final negotiations were still in progress at the time of writing. Other focal points included the prevention of illegal waste trade, the introduction of (voluntary) partnerships with industry and a more innovative policy on 'integrated life-cycle' production.

The UN policy on waste is supported by 13 Basel Convention Regional Centres (providing technical assistance) and a Technical Cooperation Trust Fund. Outside the UN framework, there are also environmental NGOs that specialize in waste issues, such as BAN (Basel Action Network), which monitors and, if necessary, names and shames non-compliant exporters and importers. However, whether or not all the measures described above can outweigh the pressures stemming from an ever-more competitive and globalized neoliberal economy is highly debatable. The problem of waste trade from rich to poor countries will continue in years to come.

CASE STUDY TWO: CLIMATE CHANGE

The atmosphere is not just the air that we breathe; a healthy atmosphere is also essential for our biosphere and our survival in general. For most of the earth's history, the earth's atmosphere was quite successful in regulating itself and maintaining equilibrium. But recent decades of interference with the environment and particularly our burning of fossil fuels appear to have challenged this equilibrium. It has to be noted that the problem of global warming is not entirely human made. However, the majority of the research community and international actors would now agree that the problem of climate change has been accelerated by our excessive consumption patterns and particularly the use of natural resources as energy providers and pollution sinks. As a result, global temperatures have risen, affecting rising sea levels and desertification. Long-term impacts will also include severe changes in food supplies, the spread of new diseases and population migration, which in turn could lead to security problems especially in less developed regions.

While the UN identified climate change as a common concern of humankind that required urgent attention, the international community has so far failed to bind all polluters into an effective and coherent global commons framework and it is impossible to enclose our atmosphere and exclude or punish offenders for exploiting this public good. Climate change also strikes at the heart of our consumption culture and our neoliberal economic order. Greenhouse gases have been emitted for centuries by developed nations and are a feature of our economic order. They are unlikely to be cut to sustainable levels unless our global competitive economy is changed fundamentally. Furthermore, climate change highlights (and contributes towards) the inequity problem that dominates relations between the North and South. While the North has great difficulties in tackling greenhouse gas emissions, the developing South is expected to leapfrog into adopting emission control measures. These measures, however, could have a dampening effect on the economic and social development efforts of whole regions. Finding an IEA that meets the needs of all and incorporates sustainable development as defined by the Brundtland Commission in 1987 is the most pressing and challenging task the international community has faced to date.

The evolution of a policy

The issue of climate change started as a scientific one in the 1970s. It took a decade for the subject to reach international policy-makers: in 1988 the UN set up an intergovernmental panel on climate change (IPCC), which considered the issue compelling enough to develop into a Framework Convention on Climate Change (FCCC). The FCCC was ready for signature by the time the UN convened the Rio Earth Summit in 1992 and was duly adopted.

Right from the beginning, the FCCC caused controversy. While the then European Community was prepared to set specific CO_2 targets at 1990 level by 2000 (while allowing for internal variations), the US was reluctant to commit to specific targets. In addition, developing nations demanded to continue with their economic and social development while calling for the North to admit responsibility for the problem and provide funding and technology for those countries in the South that were willing to adopt climate change policies.

The final version of FCCC entered into force in March 1994. It recognized global warming as a 'man made' anthropocentric problem. Its objective was to 'stabilize greenhouse gas concentrations at a level that would prevent dangerous anthropogenic interference with the climate system'. Further, the FCCC included periodic reviews of scientific evidence, methods and objectives and made reference to the precautionary principle. The document made a distinction between developed and developing nations and their varying responsibilities and commitments on climate change. Developing countries were not forced to adopt CO_2 limits, in fact they were allowed to increase their emissions. Developed countries, on the other hand, were expected to take the lead and commit to an overall emission level. However, it was left to each individual state to specify its own target.

After several COP meetings and ad hoc negotiations, the FCCC was followed up with the Kyoto Protocol of 1997. The Protocol sought to bind signatories more effectively into a common framework with more quantifiable emission targets (with a global target of 5.2 per cent reduction of greenhouse gas emissions in relation to 1990 baselines by 2012) and other 'complementary' measures such as energy efficiency and carbon trading initiatives and so-called carbon sinks. The latter option involved the planting of trees and was intended to compensate for a country's overall contribution to climate change.

Interestingly, the EU (belonging to the 'big bubble' group of negotiators) pressed for quantifiable targets, while the USA preferred the policy tools of carbon sinks and carbon trading. In the end, however, the USA (and partners such as Australia) refused to fully adopt the Protocol. Reasons for this decision included simple domestic economic calculations but also the argument that the exclusion of developing countries and particularly the growing economies of China and India from emission targets would put the USA at a competitive disadvantage.

The Protocol entered into force in February 2005 thanks to Russia whose ratification pushed the Protocol over the required participation threshold of countries emitting 51 per cent of greenhouse gases. However, this still leaves the problem of not binding non-signatories into a common framework, particularly the USA, which is the biggest polluter on the planet.

Despite recent admissions by US President George W. Bush that 'America is addicted to oil' and continued pressures from international actors, the USA is unlikely to join the Kyoto Protocol or sign its successor. In view of the Protocol's expiry date in 2012, international actors are currently debating options such as a more stringent framework (already termed Kyoto Plus) or a less stringent framework (called by many Kyoto Lite). The latter would focus entirely on voluntary commitments and rely on technological progress. One of the current 'lite' suggestions on the table is the disposal of greenhouse gases under the deep-sea bed, a suggestion that is not only scientifically challenging but also begs the question whether future generations will have to deal with this 'waste' at some point in future.

Regardless of what option will ultimately be adopted as a successor to the Kyoto Protocol, the question remains whether any of them will tackle the climate change problem. The fact remains that even within the EU (which has been an adamant supporter of the current Kyoto Protocol and Kyoto Plus) greenhouse gas levels are not controlled effectively to ensure sustainability. Already, the Commission is pointing out that targets are not being met by member states. Furthermore, the EU-wide emissions trading scheme (ETS) has not worked as previously intended. EU member states were supposed to introduce a tight trading scheme system that would internalize environmental costs and encourage clean production and consumption. Instead, member states' practices can be described as 'business as usual'. For instance, in Italy (third largest CO_2 producer in the EU) ETS permits are issued that allow for emissions 11 per cent higher than emissions from the year 2000, which is a far cry from the original target of an 8 per cent reduction at 1990 levels. This rather generous issuing of permits has the impact that the actual value of these permits decreases, rendering the scheme ineffective. On a wider economic scale, the EU will continue to compete on the global economic market. Both North and South will continue in their striving to achieve economic growth and prosperity without properly internalizing the environmental costs that their actions will cause. The above international measures may prevent some of the greenhouse gas emissions. But the overall problem of climate change will continue to dominate headlines and peoples' lives as long as fundamental changes to consumption and equity patterns are not made.

CONCLUSION

This chapter has moved beyond the traditional analysis of IEAs and environmental regime-building and has highlighted the need for studying the underlying and fundamental issues of consumption and equity. Unless these issues are tackled by international actors, we will continue to see a deterioration of our environmental resources. Consumption involves the excessive and unsustainable use of resources and subsequently the processing or disposal of waste. This process has been accelerated by our current neoliberal economic world order, and while efforts have been made to counteract this development, the overall negative impacts on our natural environment have not been internalized properly. Furthermore, there is an increasing equity gap between rich and poor consumers as well as a dangerous detachment from the consequences of our consumption culture.

Second, equity concerns the often-neglected connection between societal equity and environmental quality. This lack of equity is an ongoing problem and will undoubtedly intensify under our current economic system. The latter not only determines how we organize and govern our resources and societies, it also dictates the way we allocate responsibilities on environmental regulation. Currently, the North enjoys a dominant agenda-setting position on environmental regulation, while the South is expected to accept (and implement) international environmental standards.

These key arguments are manifest in the case studies on waste and climate change. In the case of waste our global economic system has shifted the burden of waste from the North to poorer parts of the world, i.e. developing nations in the South. Despite the development of an IEA which looked promising at times, the problem of waste will remain as long as there is an equity gap and as long as there is an economic incentive to conduct environmental dumping. In the case of climate change, the human-made problem of greenhouse gas emissions can be traced back to early industrialization in the North. In order to tackle the problem there must be major concessions in terms of economic output and redistribution. However, despite elaborate debates and negotiations the international community is far from reaching decisive concerted action. Both cases have demonstrated that environmental policy intentions and IEAs may exist on paper, but when it comes to proper action international actors have failed to live up to expectations.

This chapter has demonstrated that you can study international relations and environmental regime-building ad nauseam. However, as long as you do not consider the real issue of environmental protection as well as the fundamental issues of consumption and equity from a critical perspective, your findings are going to be limited. The environment issue highlights like no other the inherent limitations and weaknesses of the current international political and economic system.

FURTHER READING

Anheimer, H., Glasius, M. and Kaldor, M. (2001) *Global Civil Society*, Oxford University Press, Oxford.

Bryner, G. (2001) *Gaia's Wager: Environmental Movements and the Challenge of Sustainability*, Rowman & Littlefield, New York.

Clapp, J. (2001) *Toxic Exports, the Transfer of Hazardous Wastes From Rich to Poor Countries*, Cornell University Press, Ithaca, NY.

Conca, K. (2001) 'Consumption and environment in a global economy', *Global Environmental Politics* 1(3), 53–71.

Conca, K., Princen, T. and Maniates, M. (2001) 'Confronting consumption', *Global Environmental Politics* 1(3), 1–10.

Connelly, J. and Smith, J. (2002) *Politics and the Environment: From Theory to Practice*, Routledge, London.

Daly, H. (1996) *Beyond Growth: The Economics of Sustainable Development*, Beacon Press, Boston.

Haas, P. M., Keohane, R.O. and Levy, M.A. (eds) (1995) *Institutions for the Earth*, MIT Press, Cambridge, MA.

Homer-Dixon, T. (2000) *The Ingenuity Gap*, Toronto, Vintage Canada.

Keck, M. and Sikkink, K. (1998) *Activists beyond Borders*, Cornell University Press, Ithaca, NY.

Keohane, R.O and Levy, M.A. (eds) (1996) *Institutions for Environmental Aid*, MIT Press, Cambridge, MA.

Kütting, G. (2004/2006) *Globalization and Environment: Greening Global Political Economy*, SUNY Press, New York.

Lipschutz, R. (2003) *Global Environmental Politics: Power, Perspectives, Politics*, Washington, DC, CQ Press.

Lipschutz, R. and Conca, K. (eds) (1993) *The State and Social Power in Global Environmental Politics*, Columbia University Press, New York.

Lipschutz, R. and Mayer, J. (1996) *Global Civil Society and Global Environmental Governance*, SUNY Press, New York.

O'Brien, R., Goetz, A.M., Scholte, J.A. and Williams, M. (2000) *Contesting Global Governance: Multilateral Economic Institutions and Global Social Movements*, Cambridge University Press, Cambridge.

Paterson, M. (1999) 'Globalisation, ecology and resistance', *New Political Economy* 4(1), 129–145.

Princen, T. (2001) 'Consumption and its externalities: where economy meets ecology', *Global Environmental Politics* 1(3), 11–30.

Princen, T. and Finger, M. (1994) *Environmental NGOs in World Politics*, Routledge, London.

Stevis, D. (2000) 'Whose ecological justice?', *Strategies* 13(1), 63–76.

Stevis, D. and Assetto, V. (eds) (2001) *The International Political Economy of the Environment*, 12th International Political Economy Yearbook, Lynne Rienner, Boulder, CO.

Wapner, P. (2002) 'The sovereignty of nature? Environmental protection in a postmodern age', *International Studies Quarterly* 46(2), 167–187.

USEFUL WEBSITES

United Nations Environment Programme, www.unep.org

Intergovernmental Panel on Climate Change, www.ipcc.ch

International Environmental Justice database, http://web1.msue.msu.edu/msue/imp/
modej/modejc.html

CHAPTER 12

Governing the Global Commons
Mark F. Imber

DEFINING THE GLOBAL COMMONS

The global commons is the collective name given to a variety of remote and inaccessible territories and to the earth's complex ecological systems. These are essential to human survival but have for centuries remained almost wholly outside the jurisdiction of states. There are five global commons: the high seas, the deep ocean floor, outer space, the uninhabited continent of Antarctica and the climate system. The combination of extreme geographical isolation and previous limits of human exploration meant that for centuries these territories were beyond the reach of the international legal and political system. Rather than being subject to territorial claims by states and so subject to the rule of sovereignty, they were literally *res nullius* (not subject to law). Parts of Antarctica were claimed at the turn of the last century by some exploring powers but such claims were essentially non-effective and Antarctica remains an uninhabited wilderness.

Since 1945 accelerating scientific, economic, military and environmental changes have exposed the dangers inherent in continuing to rely upon the *res nullius* principle; benign neglect outside the rule of law has proven to be an inadequate standard by which to govern the commons. Military and economic competition has created pressures to expropriate or claim sovereignty over parts of the commons. Additionally, new frontiers of exploration on the ocean floor and in space and the growing awareness of environmental harm to the global commons have propelled the question of ownership and management further up the agenda. Newly identified global commons such as the stratospheric ozone layer and the global climate system are of particular concern because no single state can own them, but all states are responsible for their over-exploitation and all states are vulnerable to their existence. This so-called *tragedy of the commons* poses the question: How can 192 territorial, sovereign states rise to the challenge of governing those parts of the planet beyond sovereign control? This is the dilemma, challenge and opportunity discussed in this chapter.

SOVEREIGNTY, COMMON HERITAGE OR PRIVATIZATION?

Efforts to establish governance over territories previously regarded as *res nullius* have used three very different approaches to defining title and rule over the commons. First, attempts have been made to simply extend existing sovereign borders to include new territories (under the assumption that something previously owned by no one can logically pass to the ownership of one or to another, or may be traded between them). For example, the traditional limit of a three-mile territorial sea was transformed in the 1980s into a legal claim to a 200-mile exclusive economic zone for every coastal state. Second, there emerged in the 1970s an interest in advancing the principle of common heritage by placing the global commons under the rule of all UN members, who would in turn act as custodians or trustees of the natural environment. This principle was pioneered as a means of preserving the economic potential of the deep seabed for the common good by a system of UN licensing and revenue sharing. Such a system is most successful in application to those commons that are physically impossible to place under sovereign rule such as the climate system and the ozone layer. Third, in the 1990s there emerged a third model of commons ownership wherein market forces are used as an incentive for the preservation of the environment. Major charities and non-governmental organizations have explored this route and tropical forests have been purchased for conservation and Third World debts were paid off in return for conservation pledges.

METHODS: CONVENTIONS, CONVENTION PROTOCOLS AND MARKETS

The governance of the global commons is addressed through multilateral diplomacy; that is, international negotiations involving three or more countries. Sometimes these negotiations are global, and limited to a single task or function, such as preserving the ozone layer. Four of the five global commons are governed by treaties that emerged from negotiations conducted within the universal membership of the UN. These were The Outer Space Treaty of 1967, the Law of the Sea Convention (UNCLOS) of 1982, The Vienna Convention on Substances Harmful to the Ozone Layer of 1985, and the Framework Convention on Climate Change (FCCC) of 1992. The Antarctic is governed by the Antarctic Treaty (AT) of 1959 that was negotiated between a limited group of countries with a historic record of exploration of the continent and those with conventional territorial claims to parts of Antarctica. Other negotiations affecting the global commons may be purely regional, such as the European Union's standard setting and legislation on air pollution, and its regional creation of a carbon-trading market.

Multilateral diplomacy is usually conducted with the purpose of adopting a legally binding treaty or convention to govern the commons in question. All five global commons are governed by such a multilateral treaty, but as will be shown, the form of these treaties and the incentives for countries to sign them have evolved over decades of sometimes frustratingly slow progress. The Outer Space Treaty and the Law of the Sea Convention are both traditional treaties that define every obligation and benefit arising from signature. Latterly, and partly in response to the conflicts of interest and delays in negotiation associated with the Law of the Sea process 1970–1982, a so-called convention-protocol approach was adopted in the 1980s for the ozone layer and climate negotiations. In this approach the Convention is worded in very general terms with few specific obligations, to encourage a large number of signatures and to sustain the momentum of bargaining by deliberately avoiding points of dispute. However, these conventions include a commitment to continue negotiation towards more precise and binding targets. In both cases the Montreal and Kyoto Protocols (which create precise targets and time limits for compliance) are much better known to the public than the original Conventions from which they derive.

Another trend in negotiations has been the gradual introduction of market forces and market pricing into the protection of the commons. The most obvious and complex example of this is the incentives built in to the Kyoto Protocol in 1997, including the creation of an emissions trading system wherein states that comply with their Kyoto targets can sell on their unused carbon dioxide quotas, for cash, to countries that are going to exceed their own targets. The emissions trading system rewards countries which comply and creates very real costs and choices for countries which do not, all within an agreed ceiling of emissions. Although controversial in attempting to put a price on the 'priceless' global commons, the lesson of the twentieth century is that the global commons have been abused precisely because they are literally priceless.

BOX 12.1 THE MANAGERIAL PROBLEM

- The five global commons are the high seas, the deep ocean floor, outer space, the uninhabited continent of Antarctica and the climate system
- The management of the global commons is subject to disputed claims
- A wide variety of instruments ranging from global and regional treaties to market forces and the voluntary NGO sector have been used to manage the global commons

CHARACTERISTICS OF THE GLOBAL COMMONS

The global commons are as old as the planet earth and pre-date both human existence and human political organization. The global commons are, however, new territories in the sense that political rule and sovereignty have historically been limited to habitable land territory and maritime zones.

A series of twentieth-century technological breakthroughs first raised the possibility of human access, use and potential conflict over the use of the global commons. Events such as the first aircraft flight in 1903 or the first human exploration to the South Pole in 1911 raised questions concerning who had jurisdiction over the skies, or the Antarctic. The advent of space exploration – rocket launched satellites from 1957, manned space flight from 1961 and the first moon landing in 1969 – all raised similar questions concerning the jurisdiction of outer space. Later developments such as sonar equipped deep-sea fishing, offshore oil exploration, and the first scientific evidence of damage to the stratospheric ozone layer all raised the same questions: Who owns the commons? Who has title and legal rights of use? And who, if anyone, has a duty of care towards these territories?

Military rivalry over access to the global commons has, ironically, produced several vitally important treaties to prevent their militarization. A high level of political and legal protection has been sought for the commons in response to their potential use as areas of military confrontation and arms-racing (as was evident during the Cold War). Some of the mid-nineteenth century's most enduring international environmental agreements developed out of Cold War-era arms control agreements between the USA and the USSR. For example, the Outer Space Treaty prohibits placing nuclear weapons in earth orbit or on the moon or other planets and the Seabed Treaty prohibits placing nuclear weapons on the seabed. During the late 1950s the testing of nuclear weapons above ground – in the USA, Australia and on Pacific islands – raised levels of airborne nuclear fallout to dangerous levels. However, the Partial Test Ban Treaty (PTBT) of 1962 prohibits over-ground nuclear testing and thus protects both the atmosphere (a global common) and human health. All parties to the PTBT must now conduct nuclear tests underground, with some signatories electing to conduct all nuclear testing far, far away from home soil. Therefore some far-sighted Cold War military arms control agreements actually did much to pioneer the idea of a duty of care towards the global commons, so beginning a shift in attitudes from *res nullius* towards the idea of the common heritage of humankind, the legal principle that has become dominant in attempts to manage the oceans, the atmosphere, the ozone layer and climate in more recent years.

The ecological vulnerability of the global commons is another factor in the international communities' responsibility to protect them. The full extent of the sustainability and or vulnerability of the global commons remains under investigation, but evidence to date would suggest that our record of stewardship of the commons has been quite reckless. Climate change, ozone layer depletion, the accumulation of persistent levels of pollution by heavy metals, pesticides and oestrogens, soil erosion, the depletion of sustainable fish stocks and the rate of extinction of other species are all having a very real impact on the earth's ecosystem. All states can impact negatively on the environment, but no single state can fully protect the commons, and thus forms of multilateral cooperation are needed to secure the global commons.

A final incentive to the management of the global commons is that they hold enormous economic potential, which in itself raises increased pressure to ensure their responsible and sustainable management. More profoundly, if the global commons are truly a common commodity, then there exists the argument that any economic benefits of their development are likewise a common commodity, and could be used to finance global development and environmental protection. The 1980s witnessed bitter disputes – still not fully resolved – between the US administration and the UN majority membership over proposals to extend a UN licensing and taxing role to deep-seabed mining and oil recovery. The falling prices for land-produced copper and other metals and minerals, combined with technical limits to recover oil from beyond the 200-mile exclusive economic zones now legally claimed by coastal states, has postponed interest in testing or activating the UNCLOS provisions for the common heritage of humankind on the seabed.

BOX 12.2 PRESSURES ON THE GLOBAL COMMONS

- Potential military rivalry and conflict over access to and denial of access to the commons
- Environmental vulnerability
- Economic potential, investment stability and competition

THE FIVE GLOBAL COMMONS COMPARED

Antarctica

The Antarctic Treaty – negotiated in 1959 and entered into law in 1961 – represented a breakthrough in extending the idea of managing one of the last uninhabited and unexplored regions of the world on a non-competitive, peaceful and science-led basis. The negotiations were initiated by states with territorial claims to the territory, including the UK, France, Norway, Australia and New Zealand and other countries with a continuous record of exploration including the USA and the former USSR (now the Russian Federation).

The key provisions of the treaty, and its enduring lessons for the management of other global commons was to de-territorialize, de-militarize and promote scientific research, not commercial exploitation.

The signatories to the Antarctic Treaty have grown significantly since 1961 and now comprise 2 categories – 28 states with an established record of exploration are known as Consultative Parties and have voting rights, and 17 states without voting rights are known as Acceding States. The Consultative Parties meet annually and have adopted over 200 separate agreements on the administration of the Antarctic wilderness. Subsequent extensions of the Antarctic Treaty have included Conventions on the conservation of seals, or other flora and fauna, and one on marine-living resources. The parties have also agreed a moratorium on mining and oil exploration. (As a potential source of oil, the moratorium on mining and oil exploration represents a real concession to the idea of the global commons as a shared, but vulnerable commodity.)

Outer space

The Outer Space Treaty – otherwise known as the Treaty on Principles Governing the Activities of States in the Exploration and Use of Outer Space, Including the Moon and Other Celestial Bodies – was signed into law in 1967 and shares key characteristics with the Antarctic Treaty. Both the USA and USSR were keen to manage their Cold-War confrontation and prevent the escalation of hostilities into outer space. The fear of both sides was that nuclear weapons might be placed in earth orbit and on the moon giving an enormous and threatening advantage to the country able to achieve this first. The rational solution was for both to agree not to enter a military space race.

The treaty is remarkably clear and concise on its goals. Article I defines the territory as: 'outer space, including the moon and other celestial bodies . . . and shall be the province of all mankind'. Subsequent articles permit 'freedom of scientific investigation' (Article 2) and restrict space research for the purpose of 'international peace and security and promoting international cooperation and understanding'. (Article 3) The Treaty also specifically prohibits the emplacement of nuclear weapons in Earth orbit:

> States Parties to the Treaty undertake not to place in orbit around the Earth any objects carrying nuclear weapons or any other kinds of weapons of mass destruction, install such weapons on celestial bodies, or station such weapons in outer space in any other manner.
>
> The Moon and other celestial bodies shall be used by all States Parties to the Treaty exclusively for peaceful purposes. The establishment of military bases, installations and fortifications, the testing of any type of weapons and the conduct of military manoeuvres on celestial bodies shall be forbidden. The use of military personnel for scientific research or for any other peaceful purposes shall not be prohibited. The use of any equipment or facility necessary for peaceful exploration of the Moon and other celestial bodies shall also not be prohibited.
>
> (Treaty on Principles Governing the Activities of States in the Exploration and Use of Outer Space, Including the Moon and Other Celestial Bodies, Article IV, 1967)

One of the long-term consequences of the Outer Space Treaty was to limit the development of US plans for a 'strategic defence initiative' or 'Star Wars' weapons systems in space during the 1980s. The complexity of the plans advanced for the scheme were limited as a result of the treaty's prohibition of placing nuclear weapons in space. The 2007 revival of US–Chinese tensions over the potential use of non-nuclear anti-satellite weapons in space, and US–Russian tensions over anti-missile missile defence, will place renewed strain on this regime for the demilitarization of space.

The Law of the Sea

The negotiations that extended from 1970 until 1982 under the name of the United Nations Conference on the Law of the Sea addressed the third of the global commons, namely the two-thirds of the earth's surface that constitutes the oceans. Unlike the Antarctic and Outer Space treaties UNCLOS encountered numerous problems. Its long delayed and disputed outcome did more to extend national sovereignty as a dominant principle than to secure a measure of international administration for the oceans.

The most obvious reason for the much more protracted and disputed negotiation compared to the other global commons is that the oceans have been explored and used, competitively and in some small part controlled by national and international laws for centuries. Coastal states have claimed, and tried to exercise sovereignty over their so-called territorial waters for many centuries. The larger naval powers in every modern century have tried to extend, control and defend their empires by making strategic territorial claims that control access and trade through crucial straits and waterways. The British colonization of Gibraltar, Aden and Cyprus was not for their value as land territories but as naval bases. In short, parts of the oceans have been a feature of the Westphalian system of competition between sovereign states for centuries. However the 1970s saw a full-scale revision of the customary laws of the sea and an urgent consideration of the fate of the wider high seas and the unexplored seabed.

During the 1960s there developed a trend towards extending claims to ever-wider territorial seas and fishing zones that threatened to undermine the simple distinction between the nationally administered 3-mile territorial waters and the high seas (or international waters) which were as *res nullius* free to all. Extended claims were not made by the major powers but by South American states wishing to claim 200 mile waters and by some European fishing nations, such as Iceland and Norway, wanting to extend sovereignty over their traditional fishing-grounds covering a similar radius. Unless limited by some formal agreement there was a danger of such creeping extension of territorial claims having no practical limit, and in the absence of formal agreement to the contrary, coastal states could be tempted to maximize their claims and to create new maritime boundary disputes.

Furthermore considerable scientific speculation in the late 1960s centred on the possible recovery of significant quantities of metals and minerals from the deep ocean floor. The existence of nodules of manganese, copper and other land-mind metals created a further possibility of deep-ocean territorial disputes. Maltese Foreign Minister Arvid Pardo proposed in a 1968 speech to the UN that potential military and commercial rivalries would only be regulated by a comprehensive re-writing of the law of the sea which would consolidate existing legal good practice, limit claims to extended sovereignty and create a so-called 'common-heritage of mankind' status for the deep-ocean seabed. Pardo also proposed that UN licensing and taxation would spread the benefits of future seabed mining among the developing countries and also ensure environmental quality of the still largely unknown deep-seabed and high-seas fisheries.

The negotiation of the UNCLOS was a UN-level conference unlike any other, extending over 12 years and the source of considerable dispute between coastal states, geographically disadvantaged states (those with very limited coasts), and landlocked states. The coastal states not only wanted to enlarge their territorial waters, but also to create an Exclusive Economic Zone (EEZ) allowing them complete title and control over the fisheries and sea-bed, whilst allowing traditional 'high-seas'-style navigation rights to other states on the surface.

A second dispute concerned the proposed international administration of the common heritage of the seabed, to be licensed under UN control beyond the limits of the EEZ. The smaller, poorer and land-locked developing countries had an obvious interest in maximizing UN claims. The small minority of developed countries such as the USA and Japan who had already committed millions of dollars to research and investment in deep-sea mining technologies were hostile to an international, re-distribution of wealth being foisted on countries that had already undertaken the costs and risks of exploration.

Other interests concerned the preservation of international navigation rights through the numerous narrows and straits that would be designated as territorial waters under the extension of the old 3-mile limit into a new consensus on 12 miles. Vitally important international waterways such as the English Channel, the Straits of Hormuz in the Persian Gulf (through which all Iraqi, Saudi Arabian, Iranian and Emirates oil exports sailed) and the Straits of Malacca, Sunda and Bali (between the Indian and Pacific Oceans) all had to be brought into a codification of ancient customary laws on 'innocent passage' and a new doctrine of 'transit passage' to balance traditional freedoms of navigation with coastal states' legitimate new interests in extending their maritime safety, pollution controls, suppressing drug trafficking, smuggling, terrorist infiltration and other illegal activities.

The package-deal that eventually emerged in 1982 was a massive victory for the majority of coastal states, and a defeat for the Pardo-originated dream of a 'common-heritage of mankind'. The treaty as finalized extended national territorial waters from the historic 3-mile limit to a new 12-mile limit, and in addition created the entirely new 200-mile EEZ by which coastal states can now reserve all fishing rights, undersea drilling and mining rights to themselves, whilst still being obliged to permit the traditional freedom of the seas navigation rights to all states on the surface of the seas 'above' their EEZs. These zones now comprise approximately one-third of all the ocean area of the world. In the years since, as prices for land-mined metals such as copper, molybdenum and nickel have continued to fall no country has sought to activate the International Sea-bed Authority system for UN licences for mining, and no commercial oil drilling has ventured beyond the EEZ. This one-sixth of the world's surface has been taken from *res nullius* status into sovereign status. This is a larger extension of sovereignty than occurred at the European seizure of Africa in 1888. The US, which did not, and has not signed the treaty because of its opposition to these dormant mining rights, immediately enacted domestic legislation to claim the 200-mile EEZ now allowed.

BOX 12.3 THE LAW OF THE SEA OUTCOMES

- Created the largest gains for coastal states with new rights to a 12-mile territorial sea and 200-mile EEZ
- The common heritage of mankind rules were limited to the seabed beyond the 200-mile EEZ
- The 200-mile EEZ has protected some fisheries whilst raising pressure on high-seas stocks, especially migratory fish stocks

The ozone layer

The ozone layer exists in the upper atmosphere or stratosphere, at an altitude between 15 and 40 kilometres above the earth's surface, and filters the sun's most harmful ultra violet (UV) radiation to protect plant, animal and human life on earth. Among the proven risks associated with increased UV radiation are skin cancers, cataracts, a form of blindness, DNA damage and thus genetic mutation in later generations. The ozone layer comprises a particular isotope of oxygen O_3, rather than normal life-giving O_2.

The discovery that the ozone layer was under attack and losing its protective qualities and the subsequent solution to the crisis has been one of the great scientific detective stories since the 1970s. The chlorofluorocarbons (CFC) chemicals identified as the cause of the problem were, at the time of their invention and use after the Second World War, thought to be harmless. CFCs were valued because they were so chemically stable that they did not form reactions with other chemicals when mixed. Their use in industry boomed in applications as diverse as refrigeration, dry-cleaning fluid, industrial cleaners, and propellants for aerosol cans, as fire extinguishers and for creating plastic foam. In an effort to test and verify the non-reactive and indestructible qualities of CFCs, Mario Molina and Sherwood Rowland conducted an investigation into the fate of the millions of tonnes of CFCs released since the 1940s. Their 1974 article published in *Nature* produced a devastating proposition: that at very high altitudes in the stratosphere, sunlight broke down the CFC molecules to release chlorine which thereafter attacked the ozone layer, thus thinning this layer and reducing its ability to filter UV light. In illustration of how previous good management of the commons came to assist the plight of another, pioneering and rapid research conducted by the British Antarctic Survey confirmed Molina and Rowland's hypothesis by proving massive erosion of the ozone layer over Antarctica and its spread away from the poles. The discovery that CFCs were eroding the ozone layer set in motion a global rush to negotiate a treaty to outlaw the manufacture and use of CFCs and to halt further damage.

The rapid negotiation of a global treaty – the Vienna Convention of 1985 and the subsequent Montreal Protocol of 1987 – conducted during the height of the Cold War, superseded the *res nullius* status of the ozone layer with a vigorous assertion of a common heritage of humankind approach taking collective responsibility for the vital environmental good. The Montreal Protocol set a timeframe for the complete prohibition on the manufacture and use of CFCs, allowing poorer Third World countries an extra decade for compliance and creating a financial mechanism to compensate them for the additional costs of compliance, including the use of more expensive non-CFC substitute chemicals and for closing recently constructed production plants for the now illegal CFCs. Compared to climate change, the ozone layer negotiations were largely unique because of the conjunction of numerous favourable conditions.

Climate change, FCCC, Kyoto and after

The rise of climate change as a subject of multilateral negotiation can be traced directly to the late 1980s when a series of largely technical debates in the World Meteorological Organization was taken over by the UN process that planned the 1992 Earth Summit at Rio. This event, properly named the UN Conference on Environment and Development (UNCED), adopted the negotiation of a Framework Convention on Climate Change (FCCC) as the focal point of attempts to launch sustainable development as a comprehensive, global movement. The FCCC sought to link two goals – economic development and environmental quality – that had previously been considered separate or even competing aims.

The FCCC, as the name implies, was constructed as a means to secure agreement from the major developed states to a series of medium-range aspirations to limit carbon dioxide (CO_2) and other greenhouse gas emissions. The FCCC did not require the parties to fix legally binding, quantitative targets for emission reductions within a fixed time period. Neither did the FCCC require any commitment on the part of the large industrializing countries such as China, India and Brazil. Rather, it bound the developed parties to continue the negotiating process towards a later agreement. These negotiations took place in a series of annual Conferences of the Parties (COPs) held around the globe, the most well known of which was held at Kyoto in December 1997. By 1997, however, the original target of reducing emissions by the year 2000 to the level recorded in 1990 (the Rio target of '1990 by 2000') was clearly unobtainable and the deal that emerged from Kyoto can be summarized much more awkwardly as '1990 emissions – 5.2 per cent by 2012'. In practice the national targets allowed ranged from a permitted rise in emissions for Iceland, Australia and Norway and a variety of emissions cuts for other states (6 per cent for Canada and Japan, 7 per cent for the USA and 8 per cent for the EU). For politically crucial reasons, Russia and the Ukraine were set an easy target that required no emission reduction at all over the period.

Under Kyoto the reductions in emissions by developed countries were also spread over different end-years from 2008 through 2012. Although many EU members signalled their immediate acceptance of its terms the Kyoto Protocol did not take legal effect until 2005, when states representing 55 per cent of emissions ratified the treaty.

BOX 12.4 KYOTO REDUCTIONS IN GREENHOUSE GASES (%)

− 8	Switzerland, East Europe and EU total
− 7	USA
− 6	Canada, Japan, Hungary, Poland
0	Russia, Ukraine, New Zealand
+ 1	Norway (to allow gas-flaring, reduced hydro-electric output)
+ 8	Australia (to allow for methane released in mining)
+ 10	Iceland (to allow for geo-thermal emissions)

Even if the Kyoto Protocol were fully implemented by all potential members – including the USA that has yet to ratify – it would result only in trivial reductions by 2050. Rapid economic growth in the large developing countries that are exempt from the cuts will overturn the reductions set in the protocol for the developed member states. The significance of the agreement therefore rests in its ability to keep these parties in negotiation and to encourage India, China and Brazil to join the process. Kyoto uses a number of market mechanisms to encourage countries like the USA that were expected to have great difficulties both politically and technically in achieving reductions in CO_2 and other greenhouse gases in the timeframe allowed.

Such market mechanisms included the clean development mechanism wherein emission reductions achieved in developing countries with aid or investments from developed countries are credited to the state supplying the investment. Joint implementation refers to any two or more developed countries' targets jointly, such as in the EU where Germany and the UK will make deeper cuts to allow Spain, Portugal and Greece to emit more. Finally, emissions trading allows the cash purchase of unused targets between developed countries, such as the planned US purchase of unused Russian and Ukrainian targets (both the 1990 start date and the 0 per cent target for Russia and Ukraine were bargaining ploys to create a temptingly large surplus of unused emissions for the Americans to buy, easing US compliance problems and creating financial incentives for the Russians to sign).

The Kyoto Protocol required separate ratification by its parties as a legally binding annex to the FCCC. US President Clinton advocated ratification despite Senate opposition from 1997 to 2000 and President Bush indicated in March 2001 that he would not seek ratification. Russia then delayed ratification until 2002. All attempts to bring additional members into Kyoto appear fruitless. Serious negotiations on limiting CO_2 emissions are now focused on Kyoto's successor after 2012, with special emphasis being afforded to identifying ways to encourage participation by the USA, and also China, India and Brazil.

FUTURE NEGOTIATIONS ON THE GLOBAL COMMONS

To strike an optimistic note on an issue that is fashionably prone to pessimism and predictions of doom, the record of multilateral negotiations to legally protect the global commons is actually rather impressive. In the cases of Antarctica and Outer Space, comprehensive and enduring agreements have been reached that created and extended the principles of the common heritage of mankind, disarmament and environmental protection. In the case of the oceans, the response was slower and more mixed, but the extension of sovereign rule through expanded 12-mile territorial waters and 200-mile EEZ's has stabilized an otherwise unlimited competition to extend competing claims and has secured the national maritime resources of a majority of poor coastal states. The world's most voracious deep-water fishing fleets, those of Spain, Japan and South Korea must now respect the 200-mile zones or negotiate, by treaty, the right to fish within them with countries willing to negotiate. States with strong national conservation policies such as Canada have extended their national protection to fishing stocks that would have disappeared long ago as part of the high seas without the EEZ being established in law. The UNCLOS sea-bed mining revenue-sharing regime has not been activated, but in time it will and the legal regime in place will produce revenues for the UN to promote sustainable development as well as profit for the individual firms and countries that bear the cost and risk of exploration. The issue of the ozone layer has been a paradigm case of rapid multilateral action to secure a vulnerable and vital global common property. These four cases therefore stand in contrast to the most important and apparently unsuccessful case of negotiations to date, to secure the climate system from man-made harm.

When the neglect or active damage to the global commons can be translated into an urgent perception of a high level of threat to human welfare, this is more likely to create the basis for collective action than long-term threats of a low-level or uncertain nature.

For example, democratic politics in the USA, where re-election happens every four years, does not create a strong incentive to think and act in generational terms. Additionally, when scientific opinion is in agreement on the nature and seriousness of this threat, this is more likely to prompt political action than when leading scientific opinion is in disagreement. Furthermore, when political agreement can bring benefits to all parties, rather than gains to some and losses to others, this will also promote successful agreements. In the cases of the Montreal Protocol the financial incentives for compliance were important. Finally, when each party to an agreement can be reasonably assured that other parties will be subject to verification of their compliance, then agreements gain credibility and thus wider acceptance. A democratic opposition, an attentive public and press, and campaigning NGOs all keen to identify non-compliance all suggest that strong verification supports strong treaties.

Such positive conditions have been seen at work in the cases cited above and in several other more limited environmental agreements such as the protection of exotic species, under the Convention on International Trade in Endangered Species, (CITES) which administers the ban on the ivory trade, the European controls on acid rain, and a number of agreements made on nuclear accidents since Chernobyl.

BOX 12.5 ENCOURAGING THE PROTECTION OF THE COMMONS

- Urgent issues
- High levels of threat
- Scientific consensus on solution
- Win–win outcomes possible for all
- Verification/compliance credible

However, the reversal of the above factors may in turn undermine the incentives of states to achieve results:

- Inability to articulate urgency of threat
- Low-level threats
- Scientific doubt/dispute
- Some win–some lose results likely
- Verification/compliance unlikely

In numerous ways the obstacles to more rapid and comprehensive negotiations on climate change resemble the latter set of conditions. The timeframes, the level of threat, mixed scientific advice on climate, the uneven pattern of likely harm and difficulties of verification all test the willingness of current electorates to pay higher prices and taxes and to accept legal restraints on current lifestyles. Although the global impulse can be triggered by spectacular catastrophes such as the 2004 Asian tsunami, the hard evidence of large wealthy democracies voting for sustainable development policies across continents and across generations is very limited. Individual desires for vigorous diplomacy to protect the global commons and to implement policies of sustainable development do not always translate into collective decisions and binding agreements at the governmental and international level. Saving strangers and future generations are powerful rhetorical messages, but have yet to prove powerful enough to shift voting opinions. More extreme climate events may push electorates to change their perceptions of urgency and security risks, and more imaginative changes in taxation and incentives may create positive rewards for carbon-emission reduction. Greater scientific consensus on the detailed consequences and timeframes of climate change will further assist that process. The cases of Antarctica, the outer space treaty and ozone layer protection are there to illustrate, inform and inspire thinking that the global commons can be valued and saved from the persistent *res nullius* attitude that is currently hindering long-term positive action towards climate change.

FURTHER READING

Buck, S. (1998) *The Global Commons*, London: Earthscan.

Hardin, G. (1968) 'The tragedy of the commons', *Science*, 162: 1241–1248.

Held, D. and McGrew, A. (eds) (2002) *Governing Globalization*, Cambridge: Polity Press.

Kaul, I., Grunberg, I. and Stern, M. (eds) (1999) *Global Public Policy*, Oxford: Oxford University Press.

Rischard, J. F. (2002) *High Noon*, Oxford: Perseus.

Vogler, J. (1995) *The Global Commons: A Regime Analysis*, New York: J. Wiley and Sons.

Wilkinson, R. (ed.) (2005) *The Global Governance Reader*, Abingdon: Routledge.

World Commission on Environment and Development (1987) *Our Common Future*, Oxford: Oxford University Press.

USEFUL WEBSITES

The British Antarctic survey: www.antarctica.ac.uk/

Framework Convention on Climate Change: www.unfccc.int/2860.php

The secretariat of the treaties governing the ozone layer: www.ozone.unep.org

The international seabed authority: www.isa.org.jm

Full text of the outer-space treaty: www.state.gov/t/ac/trt/5181.htm

CHAPTER 13

Peacekeeping and Peacebuilding

Norrie MacQueen

Peacekeeping, and its younger close relative, humanitarian intervention, has become an increasingly important tool of conflict management in international relations. However, for reasons both legal and political, peacekeeping remains a notoriously difficult phenomenon to define with any precision. Although peacekeeping has long played a key role at the United Nations (UN) with more than sixty operations undertaken since the 1940s, the term does not appear in the UN Charter. Rather, peacekeeping developed as an ad hoc activity after the UN's much more ambitious schemes for military collective security proved unworkable. Once established as a regular activity of the UN, peacekeeping assumed a variety of guises in response to an equally diverse variety of conflicts and consequently, a hard definition of peacekeeping became impossibly elusive.

After peacekeeping activities migrated out of the confines of the UN and became a tool of other organizations and groups of states, the absence of a clear definition provided a useful ambiguity to cover a multitude of activities which might not traditionally be considered part of conflict resolution. Indeed, the word 'peacekeeping' has been used to sanitize a number of aggressive military activities. British military activity in Northern Ireland in the 1970s was often labelled 'peacekeeping', as has been Russian military activity in Chechnya in the 1990s. More recently, the US-led occupation forces in Iraq have also laid claim to the term. To different degrees, of course, the appropriateness of the term to these situations is contestable.

Loose use of the term 'peacekeeping' – or even its outright misuse – does not mean that definitions are impossible to arrive at. Indeed, traditional peacekeeping has three essential characteristics. First, peacekeeping can only be undertaken with the full

BOX 13.1 UN DEFINITIONS OF PEACEKEEPING

Peacekeeping is a technique that expands the possibilities for both the prevention of conflict and the making of peace.

Boutros Boutros-Ghali (UN Secretary-General), *An Agenda for Peace* (1992)

[Peacekeeping] has evolved rapidly in the past decade from a traditional, primarily military model of observing ceasefires and forcing separations after inter-State wars, to incorporate a complex model of many elements, military and civilian, working together to build peace in the dangerous aftermath of civil wars.

The Brahimi Report (2000)

UN peacekeepers – soldiers and military officers, civilian police officers and civilian personnel from many countries – monitor and observe peace processes that emerge in post-conflict situations and assist ex-combatants to implement the peace agreements they have signed. Such assistance comes in many forms, including confidence-building measures, power-sharing arrangements, electoral support, strengthening the rule of law, and economic and social development.

UN Department of Peacekeeping Operations

consent of the parties to the conflict. Second, the peacekeeping presence must be wholly neutral in respect of the conflict. Third, the peacekeepers may use force only in self-defence and as a last resort. The limits of traditional peacekeeping have come under increased scrutiny, and in the conflicts in Bosnia, Somalia, Rwanda and East Timor there remain very real questions as to the efficacy and intent of the peace-keepers. In all of these conflicts the consent of the local actors was at least question-able; the peacekeepers had – or were suspected of having – their own political agendas; and the use of force beyond the narrow definition of self-defence (or force security) proved to be unavoidable. This yawning gap between ideal and reality exists as a result of how the peacekeeping project has evolved over a number of decades. To unpick the problem of peacekeeping's identity it is necessary to examine how peace-keeping developed following the Second World War, and the subsequent underlying purposes and evolution of peacekeeping from the 1940s, through the Cold War and its contemporary applications in the modern era of global terrorism and failed states. Finally, it is important to consider – with due caution – the possible direction of peacekeeping and humanitarian military intervention in the twenty-first century.

THE ORIGINS OF PEACEKEEPING

The massive surge in peacekeeping activities that followed the end of the Cold War tends to distort the longer historical perspective. Peacekeeping certainly expanded after the superpowers withdrew from their spheres of influence (leaving the often unpopular and weak client regimes they had supported to fend for themselves) but these developments represented an intensification of an existing activity rather than the beginning of a new one.

As early as the 1920s and 1930s the UN's predecessor, the League of Nations, deployed international forces to troubled areas in Europe and in South America. Although not nearly of an operational capability similar to any contemporary notions of peacekeeping, the League's experience was absorbed into the 'institutional memory' of the UN and played a direct role in the development of its own peacekeeping efforts. The UN first established what was recognizably a peacekeeping operation in 1948. In that year international military observers were deployed on the borders of the new state of Israel as part of the Truce Supervision Organization (UNTSO), responsible for monitoring and reporting on the ceasefire agreed between Israel and its Arab neighbours following the war that had been triggered in the region by Israel's declaration of statehood. The following year a similar mission – the Military Observer Group in India and Pakistan (UNMOGIP) – was created to carry out the same role in the disputed region of Kashmir. (Both UNTSO and UNMOGIP are still operational to date.)

These first UN undertakings were not seen at the time as the beginnings of a major development in international security, but were regarded simply as cheap and sensible ad hoc responses to specific problems. The UN had much grander ambitions for international peace and security as envisaged in Chapter VII of the UN Charter (Articles 39–51) wherein a far-reaching and demanding system of collective security is established. Under the Charter, the five permanent members of the UN Security Council (the USA, the UK, the USSR, France and China) are afforded the power to deploy force wherever acts of aggression or threats to the peace might emerge across the world. The UN would thus succeed where the League of Nations had failed, by ensuring international security on a truly collective multilateral basis instead of leaving it to unilateral national efforts.

The Cold War conditions that quickly settled over the international system after 1945 rendered the UN chartered dream of multilateralism largely unattainable. In a world divided between two ideological poles, the Security Council was most often divided and at a stalemate, and whether a particular act amounted to aggression or not depended entirely on the political lenses through which the circumstances were viewed. The Korean War of 1950, where Communist North Korea attempted to force unification with pro-western South Korea, exemplifies the politicization of the Security Council. Although it was a supposed UN force that met this act of so-called aggression, its collective credentials were threadbare. Initially legitimized by the UN only because of the temporary absence of the USSR from the Security Council, the so-called Unified Command in Korea was in all important ways a coalition of the United States and its Cold War allies.

After the Korean War the UN faced something of an identity crisis, with critics suggesting that it was fast becoming merely an extension of the western alliance. A confluence of personalities and events in 1956 initiated a feasible way forward for the UN. In that year the Egyptian government's decision to nationalize the Suez Canal was met with hostility from the UK, France and Israel, who consequently made plans to invade and seize control of the Suez Canal from the Egyptians. The storm of international controversy that resulted from the UK, France and Israel's apparent act of neo-colonialist aggression cut across normal Cold War loyalties, with the US particularly angered by its allies' recklessness. In the absence of any US response, the UN found themselves in a position to participate, and Secretary General Dag Hammarskjöld and Canadian foreign minister Lester Pearson put together a plan for the creation of a multinational peacekeeping force – the United Nations Emergency Force (UNEF) – which would be made of contingents volunteered by UN members and which would interpose itself between the sides and oversee military disengagement. The operation was in many respects a larger-scale version of the military observer mission UNTSO and UNTMOGIP had established for Israel and Kashmir a few years previously. While it would comprise a substantial military force rather than just a monitoring mission, the underlying principles of neutral supervision and moral presence were identical to those of the observer missions. UNEF's neutrality guaranteed one of the key elements of successful peacekeeping: all parties could politically spin the operation in their preferred way. For Egypt, UNEF was there to punish Anglo-French aggression. By contrast, the UK and France could claim to be handing the Suez problem over to the UN after providing the essential first rapid reaction to Egypt's misbehaviour. There was never any likelihood that the UN force would find itself in a physical confrontation with any of the parties, all of whom were sovereign state members of the UN and anxious to be seen as responsible members of the larger international community.

BOX 13.2 UN PEACEKEEPING OPERATIONS IN THE MIDDLE EAST

1948–present	United Nations Truce Supervision Organization – Palestine (UNTSO)
1956–1967	First United Nations Emergency Force – Suez (UNEF I)
1958	United Nations Observation Group in Lebanon (UNOGIL)
1963–1964	United Nations Yemen Observation Mission (UNYOM)
1973–1979	Second United Nations Emergency Force – Sinai (UNEF II)
1974–present	United Nations Disengagement Observer Force – Golan Heights (UNDOF)
1978–present	United Nations Interim Force in Lebanon (UNIFIL)
1988–1991	United Nations Iran–Iraq Military Observer Group

Two years after the deployment of the UNEF Hammarskjöld drew on its lessons to produce a conceptualization of the new peacekeeping project wherein the trio of key principles of traditional peacekeeping – neutrality, consent and minimal defensive force – were laid out in detail.

Peacekeeping contrasted with the enforcement model of Chapter VII of the Charter in every key respect. While enforcement required the identification and punishment of an aggressor, peacekeeping need only identify a crisis. Chapter VII action was designed to secure a military outcome, while peacekeeping was about neutral interposition. Chapter VII action, in principle, was to be an obligatory commitment of UN membership, while peacekeeping forces were formed by voluntary contributors. The peacekeepers themselves would ideally come from small and mid-range powers, and finally the consent of all competing parties would be required before peacekeeping forces could be deployed.

The Suez Crisis, however, did little to clarify the legal basis of peacekeeping. Peace-keeping was clearly not the sort of military action envisaged by Chapter VII, and Chapter VI, concerned with the Pacific Settlement of Disputes, does not refer in any way to the use of military forces by the UN. Indeed, there was no obvious location for peacekeeping in the UN Charter. There emerged, instead, the informal notion of peace-keeping as the so-called 'chapter six-and-a-half' activity. But while peacekeeping as 'chapter six-and-a-half' encapsulated the general essence of peacekeeping, it did nothing to clarify its legal status. Neither did it provide a very clear explanation of its essential purposes in international politics.

WESTPHALIAN AND POST-WESTPHALIAN MODELS OF INTERVENTION

Dag Hammarskjöld established peacekeeping as a tool of high politics between sovereign states in order to serve international peace and security. Hammarskjöld's perspective on peacekeeping can be described as Westphalian because of his acknow-ledgement that there can be no focus of power, religious or other, above that of the territorial state.

The first phase of UN peacekeeping was plainly concerned with managing stresses and challenges within a state-centric Westphalian system. The creation of the state of Israel had brought a new and intensely contested state unit into being and the purpose of UNTSO was to help ease this adjustment to the system. Kashmir threatened the smooth extension of the Westphalian system which followed the decolonization of South Asia, and UNMOGIP was therefore put in place to help manage the tensions it provoked. In 1956 the Suez crisis posed new challenges to the stability of the state system in the form of an emergent Arab nationalism and European colonial nostalgia and UNEF was deployed to counter this multi-layered threat to the state system. Thus, peacekeeping could be quite comfortably located within the realist perspective on world politics: as a means of maintaining (or at least managing change within) the global structure of power.

More recently, however, a different perspective has been offered. In this, peacekeeping is – or should be – about the transmission and protection of universal norms and values rather than the regulation of inter-state relations. This post-Westphalian view of peace-keeping has developed rapidly since the end of the Cold War and a new peacekeeping (new in terms of both operational capability and fundamental purpose) has emerged out of the end of bipolarity.

Changes in the international system – notably the shift from traditional notions of sovereignty to that of a globalized, interdependent world – has likewise initiated a change to the principles of peacekeeping. Traditional power (or sovereignty) has been hollowed out by a global economic transformation. Additionally, the communi-cations revolution since the late twentieth century has lessened the significance of physical territoriality. In this new environment state sovereignty could theoretically be supplanted by global governance, and peacekeeping, rather than serving as a regulatory tool of Westphalianism, could become an arm of a fundamentally new type of inter-national relations.

Cosmopolitanism (meaning universal polity) assumes the existence of a set of basic values that are shared by all humanity, based on the physical security and human rights of the individual and not the territorial integrity of the state. Perhaps as a reflection of this shift in attitudes the term peacekeeping has increasingly been supplanted by the term humanitarian intervention. The traditional Westphalian view of a peacekeeping based on the essential troika of neutrality, consent and non-use of force has, it is argued, outlived its usefulness, and the failures of traditional peacekeeping to prevent ethnic cleansing in Bosnia, feed the starving in Somalia and to stop the genocide in Rwanda do little to counter such thinking.

But there is a counter-view that dominant values – which are usually those of the most powerful sections of any community, international or any other – are dangerously close to becoming universal values, and if military means are to be used to foster and extend them, does such action constitute peacekeeping, humanitarian intervention – or merely cultural imperialism? Indeed, it can be argued that the liberal view of humanitarian intervention is no different in principle from the prescriptions of American neo-conservatives for the extension of western values throughout the world. It is a difficult argument – amidst which the relative simplicity of the Westphalian model of peacekeeping, however modest – can seem attractive.

PEACEKEEPING IN COLD WAR AND DETENTE

Contemporary peacekeeping has evolved out of the original Westphalian concept and practice of easing the dual and interlinked pressures of the Cold War and decolonization. Traditional peacekeeping worked to immunize local conflicts (a large number of which derived from the withdrawal of European imperial control) from the larger infection of the Cold War. Following the Suez Crisis, traditional peacekeeping activities were successfully carried out under this mandate for over a decade. In 1958 UN military observers helped defuse major tension on the Lebanon–Syria border which had threatened to bring superpower involvement. Another undertaking in the Yemen–Saudi Arabia frontier area during 1963 and 1964 served a similar purpose. Meanwhile, a UN operation saw the transfer of the intensely contested territory of West New Guinea from Dutch to Indonesian control in 1962 and 1963 – a major undertaking that involved the creation of what amounted to a transitional UN state in the territory. West New Guinea constitutes a complex, multifunctional challenge for the UN that is often overlooked by those who see such ventures as 'new' peacekeeping of the post-Cold War era.

The success of these missions in fencing-off regional conflicts from the larger East–West division of the world at this time was, however, overshadowed by the problems that surrounded the UN's most ambitious peacekeeping project of the period: that in the former Belgian Congo. Far from sealing a local crisis off from the Cold War, UN involvement in the Congo became a cause of serious east–west confrontation and, at one point, threatened the future of the United Nations itself. The Congo operation also undermined the view of peacekeeping as an inter-state activity founded on the basic principles of consent, neutrality and force only in self-defence. Although the UN's involvement was a response to an international conflict (between the newly independent Congo and its former colonial ruler) it soon found itself amidst a disintegrating state

BOX 13.3 UN PEACEKEEPING OPERATIONS IN ASIA

1949–present	United Nations Military Observer Group in India and Pakistan (UNMOGIP)
1962–1963	United Nations Security Force in West New Guinea (UNSF)
1965–1966	United Nations India–Pakistan Observation Mission (UNIPOM)
1988–1990	United Nations Good Offices Mission in Afghanistan and Pakistan (UNGOMAP)
1991–1992	United Nations Advance Mission in Cambodia (UNAMIC)
1992–1993	United Nations Transitional Authority in Cambodia (UNTAC)
1994–2000	United Nations Mission of Observers in Tajikistan (UNMOT)
1999	United Nations Mission in East Timor (UNAMET)
1999–2002	The United Nations Transitional Administration in East Timor (UNTAET)
2002–2005	United Nations Mission of Support in East Timor (UNMISET)
2006–present	United Nations Integrated Mission in Timor–Leste (UNMIT)

where the principle of consent ceased to have any real meaning. Neutrality became an equally empty concept as there was no central ground to occupy, while demands mounted on the UN to use force as the only means of reuniting the Congo state. Accused by the eastern bloc of protecting neo-colonial interests and seeking the break-up of the Congo (specifically through the secession of the mineral-rich Katanga region), the UN force was equally criticized by sections in the west whose political interest in the region was challenged. The USSR exploited the UN's discomfort by demanding the root and branch restructuring of the organization along bloc lines. Although ultimately unsuccessful, Moscow was left profoundly disaffected by the whole peacekeeping project and what it regarded as its western bias. The Congo would also cost the life of Dag Hammarskjöld, who was killed in a plane crash in 1961 as he travelled to negotiate the end of one of the recurrent crises that punctuated the operation.

The experience delivered a sharp lesson to the UN on the shortcomings of over-simplified models of peacekeeping. More practically, the peacekeeping experience in the Congo triggered a long-term crisis for the financing and authorization of peacekeeping operations as a result of Soviet hostility. This particularly affected the next major undertaking, the UN force in Cyprus, which for years had to be conducted on the most precarious hand-to-mouth basis.

Peacekeeping was reinvigorated, at least for a time, by the growth of détente between the Cold War superpowers in the late 1960s and 1970s. Driven by the logic of nuclear mutually assured destruction, the superpowers sought to cooperate to defuse crises rather than jostling to score victories in them. For example, following the Arab–Israeli war of 1973 the United States enlisted the USSR to work together to deploy UN peacekeepers to conflict zones between Israel and Egypt (the Sinai) and Israel and Syria (the Golan Heights). The lead role assumed by the two superpowers guaranteed immediate UN acquiescence in the plan. However, questions remained concerning the superpower politicization of peacekeeping: Was it healthy for the UN to have its peacekeeping activities directed by the big powers, arguably for their own political purposes? Was the autonomy of the UN being subordinated to the interests of its strongest members? However, the superpower politicization of peacekeeping turned out to be a relatively short-lived dilemma. The 1978 UN interim force (UNIFIL) sent to southern Lebanon soon fell victim to the onset of the 'second' Cold War as Washington and Moscow failed to restrict the behaviour of their clients in the region (Israel and Syria respectively). The end of détente meant that no UN operation would be established until the end of the Cold War itself.

PEACEKEEPING SINCE THE COLD WAR

The end of the Cold War resulted in a huge surge in peacekeeping across the world as Cold War-era political and geographical barriers fell away. Peacekeeping is only operational in the space permitted by national interest and where states see their core interests at stake they will resist any external intervention, no matter how well intentioned. The 'permitted space' for peacekeeping expanded and contracted in correlation to the state of superpower relations – during the years of détente the space was relatively wide, but for most of the 1980s, when the Cold War was particularly intense, it narrowed to a point where, as we have seen, peacekeeping was virtually dormant. Therefore, the end of the Cold War resulted in a hugely expanded field of operability for peacekeeping. Regions untouchable during the Cold War – such as Central America, the Balkans, Afghanistan and Southeast Asia – were opened up to multilateral intervention.

BOX 13.4 UN PEACEKEEPING OPERATIONS IN THE AMERICAS

1965–1966	Mission of the Representative of the Secretary-General in the Dominican Republic (DOMREP)
1989–1992	United Nations Observer Group in Central America (ONUCA)
1991–1995	United Nations Observer Mission in El Salvador (ONUSAL)
1993–1996	United Nations Mission in Haiti (UNMIH)
1996–1997	United Nations Support Mission in Haiti (UNSMIH)
1997–present	United Nations Transition Mission in Haiti (UNTMIH)
1997	United Nations Verification Mission in Guatemala (MINUGUA)
1997–2000	United Nations Civilian Police Mission in Haiti (MIPONUH)
2004–present	United Nations Stabilization Mission in Haiti (MINUSTAH)

The end of the Cold War, however, also meant the end of superpower management of their foreign clients. States and regions previously stabilized by superpower control were now left to their own devices and the removal of this externally imposed order often led to conflict and chaos. For example, Somalia collapsed as a result of internal rivalries between the remaining American-sanctioned government and other Somali political groups, precipitating a massive humanitarian crisis that demanded a peacekeeping response. Similarly, the break-up of Yugoslavia and the resultant Balkan crisis would have been unlikely during the rigid bipolarity of the Cold War years. Indeed, the end of the Cold War resulted not only in increased areas of peacekeeping operability, but also in an increased number of conflicts requiring peacekeepers.

The end of the Cold War was but one factor in the increased range and pace of peacekeeping. Long-term political and ethnic tensions escalated into destructive civil wars in many parts of sub-Saharan Africa, such as Angola and Mozambique in the south to Liberia and Sierra Leone in the northwest.

BOX 13.5 UN PEACEKEEPING OPERATIONS IN AFRICA

1960–1964	United Nations Operation in the Congo (ONUC)
1988–1991	United Nations Angola Verification Mission I (UNAVEM I)
1989–1990	United Nations Transition Assistance Group – Namibia (UNTAG)
1991–present	United Nations Mission for the Referendum in Western Sahara (MINURSO)
1991–1995	United Nations Angola Verification Mission II (UNAVEM II)
1992–1993	United Nations Operation in Somalia I (UNOSOM I)
1992–1994	United Nations Operation in Mozambique (ONUMOZ)
1993–1994	United Nations Observer Mission Uganda–Rwanda (UNOMUR)
1993–1995	United Nations Operation in Somalia II (UNOSOM II)
1993–1996	United Nations Assistance Mission for Rwanda (UNAMIR)
1993–1997	United Nations Observer Mission in Liberia (UNOMIL)
1994	United Nations Aouzou Strip Observer Group – Chad–Libya (UNASOG)
1995–1997	United Nations Angola Verification Mission III (UNAVEM III)
1997–1999	United Nations Observer Mission in Angola (MONUA)
1998–1999	United Nations Observer Mission in Sierra Leone (UNOMSIL)
1998–2000	United Nations Mission in the Central African Republic (MINURCA)
1999–present	United Nations Organization Mission in the Democratic Republic of the Congo (MONUC)
1999–2005	United Nations Mission in Sierra Leone (UNAMSIL)
2000–present	United Nations Mission in Ethiopia and Eritrea (UNMEE)
2003–present	United Nations Mission in Liberia (UNMIL)
2004–present	United Nations Operation in Côte d'Ivoire (UNOCI)
2004–2006	United Nations Operation in Burundi (ONUB)
2005–present	United Nations Mission in the Sudan (UNMIS)

Clearly, the political and operational requirements of peacekeeping – including the level of demand for operations – had changed significantly since Suez. In 1992 the then UN Secretary General Boutros Boutros-Ghali produced *An Agenda for Peace*, the first high-level analysis of the state of peacekeeping since the Summary Study in 1958. Boutros-Ghali called for a fundamental reform of peacekeeping in response to changing demand and operational conditions. Formal contributors' agreements were proposed which would tie UN members into commitments and a large reserve fund was also called for, to remove the financial uncertainty in which peacekeeping had to operate.

Essentially, however, Boutros-Ghali's reforms did not alter the voluntary basis of peacekeeping and did not attempt to reinvigorate Chapter VII-type enforcement. Boutros-Ghali proposed the establishment of what he called Peace Enforcement Units to supervise peace settlements between previously conflicting parties. Often one or other of the parties in such a settlement would renege on the terms of the agreement (as happened in Angola) and Boutros-Ghali proposed that UN forces should, in such circumstances, be empowered to enforce compliance. Finally, Boutros-Ghali called for investigation into how regional and other non-UN organizations could participate in peacekeeping to relieve the mounting pressure on the UN's resources created by post-Cold War demand.

An Agenda for Peace was written at a time of relative optimism about the future of peacekeeping, and few of its recommendations have been properly adopted. The UN still struggles to recruit suitable peacekeeping contingents and states have proved resistant to making any extensive prior commitments to peacekeeping, preferring to preserve as much discretion from situation to situation as possible. Nor did the idea of peace enforcement get off the ground – the Rwandan genocide of 1994 proving that even with world opinion fully engaged, UN members are reluctant to commit their troops to the violence and uncertainty of a conflict which few feel to be central to their own national interests.

The idea of peacekeeping by non-UN bodies did not fare much better. Historically, peacekeeping has been undertaken by a range of other actors such as the 1979 NATO operation in Sinai following the extraction of UNEF-II (whose mandate the USSR refused to renew) and the western multinational forces deployed to Beirut during the early 1980s. However, non-UN peacekeeping was, and remains, politically and operationally fraught. Positively, intervention by regional forces often means that peacekeepers have greater awareness of local political and social circumstances and are consequently more attuned than UN international forces. Also, regional neighbours often have a more pressing interest in the resolution of local conflicts than multinational forces (literally) from the other side of the word. Negatively, however, regional forces are more likely to be under-equipped and under-trained for peacekeeping duties, as has proven to be the case for African Union forces in Sudan. Beyond these material issues, if local forces have greater reasons to resolve local conflicts, they may also have national interests involved in these conflicts and an interest in achieving particular outcomes. The Economic Community of West African States through its (rather misnamed) Military Observer Group (ECOMOG) has been involved in conflicts in various parts of the region since the 1990s. These interventions, however, have often seemed to take particular sides and have had the character of enforcement operations designed to achieve the objectives of dominant regional states. Operations where the UN has a monitoring role over local interventions – such as over ECO-MOG in Liberia, and the Commonwealth of Independent States (CIS) in Georgia – have not been particularly successful.

Greater success has come from United Nations legitimization of so-called 'coalitions of the willing' led by dominant regional states. The Australian-led intervention in East Timor to abate the violence following the referendum for independence from Indonesia in 1999 is one such example of successful regional intervention. However, regional intervention, too, has limitations. Following the organization's failure to act robustly in the face of genocide in Rwanda in 1994, the UN instead legitimized a French-dominated intervention (Operation Turquoise) that was fiercely criticized as a French attempt to maintain influence in the region and to shield its allies in the Hutu regime.

The twentieth century ended with mixed prospects for peacekeeping. Employed to a degree which would have been unimaginable half a century earlier, peacekeeping was coming under mounting pressure to meet the increasing demands placed upon it. Additionally, questions remained over the methods, effectiveness and long-term viability of peacekeeping. The fundamental purpose of peacekeeping in a supposedly post-Westphalian world had also yet to be effectively addressed.

PEACEKEEPING IN THE NEW MILLENNIUM: THE BRAHIMI REPORT

The new century began with another inquiry into the nature and future of peace-keeping with then Secretary General Kofi Annan (previously head of UN Peacekeeping) forming a high-level panel of diplomats and senior military figures under the chair of former Algerian foreign minister Lakhdar Brahimi. The Brahimi Report took as its starting point a self-evident truth; that the term peacekeeping is more often than not a misnomer. Frequently, peacekeeping operations 'do not deploy into post-conflict situations so much as they deploy to create such situations', which obviously has a profound influence on how operations are pursued and the outcomes that they seek. Consequently, Brahimi proposed significant qualifications to the trad-itional peacekeeping principles of consent, neutrality and force. Brahimi argued that consent (whether by the host states to an operation or the parties involved in the conflict) remains important but cannot constitute an absolute veto on the operation. Consent is open to manipulation by competing parties for their own purposes and should consequently not deter peacekeepers from carrying out their mandate. Once in place, a peacekeeping operation has a responsibility to a larger constituency than the immediate participants in a conflict. Brahimi's report seems to imply that owner-ship of peacekeeping lies with the international system – or even the international community if the post-Westphalian perspective is adopted – and it is to this larger constituency that peacekeepers are ultimately answerable. In other words, neither African warlords, nor Balkan dictators should be in a position to set the terms of the peacekeeping presence or the manner in which multilateral interventions are conducted.

On the related issue of the avoidance of bias in peacekeeping, Brahimi makes an important distinction between impartiality and neutrality. Impartiality must mean respect for 'the principles of the Charter and the objectives of a mandate', but this is not the same as 'neutrality or equal treatment of all parties in all cases for all time, which can amount to a policy of appeasement'. The experience in Bosnia, where pro-Serbian forces killed civilians while neutral UN forces stood by, was an obvious case in question. Local parties, Brahimi observed, often 'consist not of moral equals, but of obvious aggressors and victims, and peacekeepers may not only be operationally justified in using force but morally compelled to do so'. To set aside misguided notions of neutral-ity, as Brahimi urges, would have had obvious implications not only in the former

◼ BOX 13.6 UN PEACEKEEPING OPERATIONS IN EUROPE

1964–present	United Nations Peacekeeping Force in Cyprus (UNFICYP)
1992–1995	United Nations Protection Force – Croatia/Bosnia/Macedonia (UNPROFOR)
1993–present	United Nations Observer Mission in Georgia (UNOMIG)
1994–1996	United Nations Confidence Restoration Operation – Croatia (UNCRO)
1995–1999	United Nations Preventive Deployment Force – Macedonia (UNPREDEP)
1995–2002	United Nations Mission in Bosnia and Herzegovina (UNMIBH)
1996–1998	United Nations Transitional Authority in Eastern Slavonia, Baranja and Western Sirmium – former Yugoslavia (UNTAES)
1996–2002	United Nations Mission of Observers in Prevlaka – former Yugoslavia (UNMOP)
1999–present	United Nations Interim Administration Mission in Kosovo (UNMIK)

Yugoslavia but in Rwanda during the genocide and many other situations in which peacekeeping forces have appeared supine in the face of aggression.

It remains to be seen how far Brahimi's recommendations – and the realities they reflect – will have an impact on the practice of peacekeeping and humanitarian intervention in the twenty-first century, but there exists some ground for optimism. The intensity of demand for peacekeeping seems to have eased somewhat, even if only temporarily. Demand for interventions in Africa has lessened since the 1990s (though major problems remain to be resolved in Sudan, the Democratic Republic of Congo and Côte d'Ivoire) and it is unlikely that a crisis on the scale of that precipitated by the break-up of Yugoslavia will appear on the European horizon in the foreseeable future. The relative calm after the storms of the 1990s provides a useful environment for experiences to be analysed and lessons learned and these will surely focus on the unrealized potential of the peacekeeping project, but also – and at least as important – its inescapable limitations. But one thing can be predicted with some confidence – until world politics is transformed to a degree which would make feasible the utopian security scheme envisaged by the architects of the United Nations – peacekeeping with all its shortcomings will remain a fundamentally important tool for the management of international conflict.

◼ REFERENCES AND FURTHER READING

Bellamy, A.J., Williams, P. and Griffin, S. (2004), *Understanding Peacekeeping*, Cambridge: Polity.

Boutros Boutros-Ghali (UN Secretary-General) (1992), *An Agenda for Peace: Preventive Diplomacy, Peace-making and Peacekeeping*, New York: United Nations.

Brahimi Report (2000), 'Report of the Panel on United Nations Peace Operations', issued as United Nations Documents A/55/305 (General Assembly); S/2000/809 (Security Council), 21 August.

MacQueen, N. (2006) *Peacekeeping and the International System*, London: Routledge.

Pugh, M. (ed.) (1997) *The UN, Peace and Force*, London: Frank Cass.

Richmond, O. (2005) *The Transformation of Peace*, Houndmills: Palgrave.

UN Department of Peacekeeping Operations, http://www.un.org/Depts/dpko/dpko/faq/q1.htm

Weiss, T. (2007) *Humanitarian Intervention: Ideas in Action*, Cambridge: Polity.

Wheeler, N. (2003) *Saving Strangers: Humanitarian Intervention in International Society*, London: Oxford University Press.

White, N.D. (1997) *Keeping the Peace: The United Nations and the Maintenance of International Peace and Security*, Manchester: Manchester University Press.

Woodhouse, T. and Ramsbotham, O. (eds) (2000) *Peacekeeping and Conflict Resolution*, London: Frank Cass.

CHAPTER 14

Gender and Other 'Others'
Alison Watson

Gender was first recognized as an issue in international relations (IR) in the early 1970s with the publication of Berenice Carroll's 'Peace Research: The Cult of Power' in the *Journal of Conflict Resolution* (Murphy 1996: 513). However, it was the publication of a special issue of *Millennium: Journal of International Studies* in 1988 that effectively legitimated the study of gender in IR. In the introduction to the *Millennium* special issue Fred Halliday highlighted that, unlike other social sciences, IR had failed to recognize the significance of the study of gender – either in terms of its role or its consequences – with regard to how the international system operates. Instead, the consideration of gender, and the knowledge that international relations could potentially derive from it, had remained hidden. Halliday suggested that gender could have significant consequences for the study of IR:

> [O]ne aspect is a study of how gender issues and values do and could play a role within international relations; the second aspect is analysis of the gender-specific consequences of international processes, be these military, economic, political or ideological. The latter modification has, of course, broader implications for the whole study of international relations, since it rests upon the argument that international relations should study the consequences of international processes within societies, and the resulting impact of these internal changes on international relations, as well as analysing the sphere of international relations *tout court*.
>
> (Halliday 1988: 420)

This chapter will consider the meaning of gender in the social sciences and outline how feminist literatures feed into its study. The place of gender in some of the major areas of IR – most notably in conflict and post-conflict literatures and in the work done in international political economy – will also be considered. Work on gender, which has been so critical of traditional IR models, may itself also now be the subject of critique but has paved the way for other critical analyses of actors and identities that have been marginalized from mainstream literatures.

GENDER IN (AND) THE SOCIAL SCIENCES

Gender can be a confusing term. On the one hand, gender explains the fundamental biological differences between the sexes: such as females bear children and are generally physically weaker than males. However, gender can also describe how such differences may be translated into socially constructed conditions and hierarchies between the sexes. For example, women are perceived to be more pacific and men are assumed to be more militaristic; women are assumed to be more emotional and men are assumed to be more rational. Thus it is often assumed that men are better decision-makers because they think with their heads, as opposed to women who are often assumed to think with their hearts. Such constructions significantly impact the position of the different sexes in society and have led directly to the persistent stereotyping of specific gender roles.

Thus, gender has multiple meanings in that it used to describe both the biological differences between men and women and the inequalities that have resulted from them; inequalities that also resonate more widely within the study of issues relating to sexual orientation and gender identity and are fundamental to issues of human rights as a whole. In a recent Human Rights Watch report, for example, Scott Long notes that:

> [M]ovements for the rights of lesbian, gay, bisexual, or transgender people, along with movements that assert sexual rights more generally, are arguably the most vulnerable edge of the human rights movement. In country after country they are easy to defame and discredit. But the attack on them also opens space for attacking human rights principles themselves – as not universal but 'foreign,' as not protectors of diversity but threats to sovereignty, and as carriers of cultural perversion.
>
> (Long 2005: 2)

The significance of the debate concerning gender meanings is illustrated in the period preceding the Fourth World Women's Conference in Beijing in 1995 when there was considerable discussion around the issue of reproductive and sexual rights, and consequently the debate spread to references to the word 'gender'. The assumption put forward by a number of women's groups was that gender should be considered as a social construct (as opposed to a biological given) and as such, gender could be altered, or there could be multiple genders. Whilst such thinking was acceptable to groups seeking any number of gender and sexual identity rights, it was not something that was seen as acceptable to religious groups who wanted 'sex' rather than 'gender' to be the official conference terminology (Petchesky 2001: 122). Issues of gender, and of its construction are additionally cross-cut by issues of religion, class, culture, race and generation. Each of these taken together has a bearing on how any one individual's identity is constructed and perceived:

> [W]hile biological sex varies very little, gender varies enormously. What it means to possess the anatomical configuration of male or female means very different things depending on where you are, who you are and when you are living.
>
> (Kimmel 2004: 3)

It is perhaps for this reason that so many writers on gender preface their work by outlining how they perceive their own identities – and in particular their feminist identities – to have been constructed. Susan Muller Okin found that her 'direct experience of the difficulties of being a fully participating parent while being a member of the workplace' had precipitated her writing of *Justice, Gender and the Family* (Okin 1989: vii); bell hooks 'came to feminist consciousness in the patriarchal household of . . . [her] upbringing' (hooks: 2000, xi); whilst Cynthia Enloe in *The Curious Feminist* discusses how she became interested in becoming a feminist and how this in turn means that no woman's life should be beyond the scope of her interest.

It is pertinent to note that much of the social science work on gender concentrates upon how women's identity is constructed as opposed to emphasizing the significance of constructions of masculinity to the male persona. Moreover, the majority of this work has been conducted by women, leading to questions regarding how male scholars are able to give attention to the 'woman problem':

> [W]hat are the mechanisms, linguistic and otherwise, whereby these men are able to evacuate questions of their sexuality, their subjectivity, their relationship to language from their sympathetic texts on 'feminism', on 'woman', on 'feminine identity?
>
> (Jardine 1987: 56)

Kimmel has argued that the lack of male writing on gender is a feature of the hierarchies that gender constructions themselves produce (Kimmel 2004: 7). Male writers recognize gender less, it is argued, because they themselves occupy the privileged gendered position in society and are consequently far less able to consider the impact that gender has upon society in general. For the most part, it has been left to feminist scholars to outline and describe the significance of gender as a social construct.

◼ BOX 14.1 INTRODUCTORY OUTLINES

- 'Gender' can be used to describe both biological differences and the resultant societal constructions that result from them
- Gender has different meanings depending on age, history, race and identity
- These meanings also impact upon the way in which analysts write about them

GENDER AND FEMINIST SCHOLARSHIP

According to Simone de Beauvoir's well known dictum '[o]ne is not born, but rather becomes a woman' (de Beauvoir 1997: 301), and it has been the *raison d'être* of feminist writers to describe how such a 'becoming' takes place. It is fair to say, however, that the writing on gender and feminist thought has fundamentally changed since the feminist movement's high point during the 1970s. At that time the confusion over the nature of gender identity was evident, and crucial, with works such as Ann Oakley's *Sex, Gender and Society* viewing gender as sometimes an identity and sometimes a construction. By the 1990s such questions had become less significant as the result of a growing body of literature in a diverse set of areas – including post-modernist thought, queer theory and activism, and transgendered politics – that had theorized a relationship between bodies, sexes, sexualities and genders that was far more complex and contingent than earlier feminist writing had previously accounted for. Sexual rights had become a significant issue, opening up new spaces within the human rights literature for acknowledging diverse sexualities and their legitimate need for expression as well as establishing a kind of code that (like writings on reproductive rights before it) meant different things to different speakers (Petchesky: 2001, 118).

The result of this has been an increasing diversity in feminist writings. At one end of the spectrum radical feminists such as Mary Daly and Andrea Dworkin write of the oppression of women as being fundamental and prevailing, and consequently advocating the rejection of a variety of roles – including that of being a mother – and sometimes even rejecting men themselves. In *Gyn/Ecology*, Daly asserts that women 'do not begin life in innocence [but] in patriarchy' (Daly 1979: 413) which they must overcome. The roots of such patriarchy, she argues, lie in the damage that has been done to the bonds between women – the fragmentation of the sisterhood – such that women themselves may be coerced into patriarchy. For example, Daly asserts that female gynaecologists educated in mainstream American medical schools are 'token torturers' of women and thus complicit in patriarchy.

At the other end of the spectrum, liberal feminists, such as Betty Friedan, Gloria Steinem and Naomi Wolf argue for equality of rights between women and men. In doing so they enter into the long tradition of liberal feminism – typified in Mary Wollstonecroft's 1792 *A Vindication of the Rights of Women* – that exists within liberal political thought. Although often gone unheard, liberal feminists have consistently argued that liberal ideas applied just as much to women as they did to men, whether in terms of the natural rights of women discussed in the eighteenth century, the utilitarian arguments in favour of equal legal rights for women in the nineteenth century, or the twentieth-century development of the liberal theory of the welfare state. It is argued that throughout these movements, liberal feminists have demanded that the state actively pursue a policy of social reforms in order to ensure equal opportunities for women.

Liberalism emphasizes individualism and critics of liberal feminism have argued that this makes it difficult to see which underlying social structures disadvantage the women within them. Black and postcolonial feminists have asserted that mainstream liberal feminism has largely reflected only the values of middle-class white women. However, radical feminists have been subject to similar criticism – Audre Lorde noted in 'An Open Letter to Mary Daly' that:

[W]hat you excluded from *Gyn/Ecology* dismissed my heritage and the heritage of all other noneuropean women, and denied the real connections that exist between all of us.

(Lorde 1979)

Such criticism led to the development of strands of feminist thought to take these differences into account. Socialist feminists, for example, believe that there is a direct link between class structure and the oppression of women and seek to challenge both the capitalist system and the patriarchal system as a result. Alison Jaggar in *Feminist Politics and Human Nature* argued that women hold a special status in society, but through a combination of class and sexual subordination have historically been oppressed. Jaggar thus rejects the notion that biology predetermines destiny, whilst also rejecting liberal feminism's emphasis on the individual. Capitalist and patriarchal systems are seen to reinforce each other in the oppression of women: capitalism used poor women as a source of cheap labour in the factories whilst isolating middle-class women and forcing unmarried women into employment. At the same time capitalism brought working-class women into a more public role as they took part in growing large-scale popular movements both at work and in the community. In the course of such activism, some demanded their rights as women whilst at the same time resisting class oppression. It was out of such action, coupled with the reaction of middle-class wives and daughters to patriarchal control within the home, that the first feminist movement was instigated.

In a similar vein to socialist feminism, ecofeminists believe in an oppressive (and reinforcing) agenda in the oppression of women. For social feminists, such an agenda is capitalism; for ecofeminists the agenda is the degradation of nature, a phenomenon that is explored in terms of the inter-relationships between sexism, racism, ecology and capitalism. Vandana Shiva argues that women's special connection to the environment has been ignored:

[W]omen in subsistence economies, producing and reproducing wealth in partnership with nature, have been experts in their own right of holistic and ecological knowledge of nature's processes. But these alternative modes of knowing, which are oriented to the social benefits and sustenance needs are not recognised by the reductionist paradigm, because it fails to perceive the interconnectedness of nature, or the connection of women's lives, work and knowledge with the creation of wealth.

(Shiva 1989: 24)

Furthermore, cultural feminists believe that the fundamental biological differences between women and men is less of a political stance than a desire to focus on change at an individual level. Carol Gilligan's work argues that women have a different moral voice and that the origins of aggression may be different for women compared to men. Judith Butler, however, rejects the binary view of sexuality – the division of gender into male and female – preferring instead:

those historical and anthropological positions that understand gender as a relation among socially constituted subjects in specifiable contexts.

(Butler 1999: xxiii)

The diverse range of views concerning feminist thought in turn feed into a diverse range of views concerning how international relations is impacted by gender issues, and the variety of ways that international processes can result in gender specific consequences.

BOX 14.2 INCARNATIONS OF 'GENDER'

- Radical feminists regard the oppression of women as the most significant form of oppression
- Liberal feminism argues for equality between the sexes
- Both radical and liberal feminists have been criticized for being too class/race-centric
- Socialist feminists seek to address gender inequality through 'class'
- Eco-feminists believe that the degradation of nature goes hand-in-hand with the oppression of women
- Cultural feminists focus on change at the individual level

GENDER IN (AND) INTERNATIONAL RELATIONS

In line with Halliday's work, gender in IR has concentrated both upon how gender issues and values play a role within international relations, as well as upon the gender-specific consequences of international processes (be they military, economic, political or ideological). However, the results of such studies are very much shaded by previous feminist authorship. For example, a radical feminists' view of how the patriarchal system impacts upon IR and how women are thus affected will be different from that of a liberal feminist, as will their prescriptions for solution. Nevertheless, there are a number of recurring themes in IR/gender literature. Perhaps the most obvious of these has been the challenge to frameworks that reinforce patriarchy in the international system, and how that system has been described. Realist analyses were perhaps the first to come under the spotlight for their view that international politics was dependent upon the pursuit of power. Where liberal theorists had criticised realists' inability to recognize the activities of other actors, such as international organizations and financial institutions, those seeking to introduce gender into the IR mainstream criticized realism's commitment to the role of the state, and to states*men* within it. J. Ann Tickner asserted that the work of Hans Morgenthau – so crucial to the development of realist theory – provided only a partial description of international relations because it was based on assumptions regarding human nature that privilege masculinity and are thus only partial. (Tickner, 1988: 431) Crucial also was the historical representation of the Athenian *polis* in realist thought which represented how states were assumed to operate. V. Spike Peterson specifically argued that:

[I]t was in the Athenian context that specifically Western constructions of the state, security, representation, sovereignty, and the 'sovereign subject', public and private, and 'what constitutes the political' were established; these constructions – and the metaphysics they presuppose – profoundly shaped modern state formation, and they continue to 'discipline' IR.

(Runyan and Peterson 1991)

Discussion of the 'sovereign subject' and of the distinction between the public and the private roles of men and women remain significant themes, continuing to have implications to the present day. For example, the right to be a true sovereign citizen of the state is historically conferred only upon those who bear arms in defence of that state, and if women have not traditionally borne such arms, then it follows that women cannot be classed as full citizens with all of the benefits from society that this entails. Thus, if citizenship confers upon those who own it the right to vote for political leaders, or indeed to stand as political leaders, then women's lack of citizenship historically precluded them from taking on a significant role in public political life. Thus the initial decision not to have women bear arms – either because women are seen as less aggressive, or because women have to stay home in order to look after their families, or because they are seen as more emotional and less rational – has constructed women into a second-class non-decision-making role.

These ideas are echoed in the conflict and post-conflict literatures. Jean Bethke Elshtain's characterization of how the 'beautiful soul' – the caring, innocent, peaceful and private woman – contrasts with that of the 'just warrior' who assumes the public military role of the defence of the state, is a case in point. In *Women and War*, Elshtain asserts that such characterizations prevents any true examination of men's and women's wartime roles. The characterization of women as peace-loving and men as having more militant tendencies is simplistic, but it is readily accepted by society. In fact, women play a variety of roles in wartime. Women may fight less than men, but they do fight, and have done so throughout history. They also support war efforts in other ways, from the women who worked in munitions factories during the Second World War, to those who provide logistical support as nurses, cooks and technicians, to those women who support men (fathers, husbands, boyfriends and sons) in their participation. These are issues that have been developed by Cynthia Enloe who in *Bananas, Beaches and Bases* asked the simple question: Where are the women? Enloe argues that strategies undertaken by women in their roles as wives, mothers and workers may be personal ones, but they are also political strategies. Based on the notion that the personal can be political, Enloe reveals that private choices can impact the global political system in significant ways and to ignore them means also to ignore a fundamental element of the international system. Indeed, factoring private choices may change how international politics is examined, and may also alter perceptions regarding what are considered 'valid' subjects of study within the discipline of IR.

In addition to the role of women in war, there is also significant literature on the impact that war has upon women. With the advent of so-called 'new wars' in which civilians are the overwhelming casualties, women (and their children) are more than ever the victims of war. Women are also most likely to become refugees and more likely to experience sexual violence (such as forced prostitution) as a result. Consequently, conflict and post-conflict literatures on the incidence and impact of sexual violence in wartime go straight to the heart of feminist discourses surrounding the patriarchal society. Susan Brownmiller argues that the crime of rape flowed from a patriarchal society where '[c]oncepts of hierarchy, slavery and private property flowed from, and could only be predicated upon, the initial subjugation of woman' (Brownmiller 1993: 8). Although sexual violence in wartime has probably existed as long as war itself it is only recently that it has been recognized as a crime under international humanitarian law. Central to such recognition was the establishment of the International Criminal Tribunal for the former Yugoslavia (ICTY) in 1993, and the International Criminal Tribunal for Rwanda (ICTR) in 1994, both of which have served to highlight crimes of sexual violence during wartime (in a way that is distinct from previous international war crimes tribunals).

The fact that such recognition has come so late and remains so minimal is indicative of an ongoing problem wherein emphasis in IR scholarship is focused on the perpetrators of violence, rather than on the victims of it. The same is true of post-conflict scholarship. IR is more interested in war than in peace, and given that women play – and have done so historically – a major role in attempts to secure and maintain peace, women's efforts in this regard are doubly ignored. However, the involvement of women in peace activism has been one way in which women have been able to assume a public political role. By advocating causes that had a social (caring) currency (such as Eglantyne Jebb's founding of the Save the Children Fund, or Anne Knight's work in the anti-slavery movement), women were able to assume public political roles that would otherwise have been difficult for them to achieve. This does not mean, of course, that such women took on such causes merely to aid their own fight for equality but, rather, that their voices were heard and listened to in their struggle for social justice in a way that they were not within mainstream political discourse. Anti-slavery campaigner Elizabeth Heyrick wrote that 'a woman . . . was especially qualif[ied] . . . to plead for the oppressed' (Hochschild 2005: 325). Indeed, some women drew parallels between the positions of women and the position of slaves. Women also assumed a public political role as part of the workers' rights movements, an acknowledgement of the economic role within society that women have historically played. Women's roles in workers' rights movements remain a significant theme in IR scholarship, and work done within the sub-field of international political economy (IPE) now recognizes that acknowledging gender may challenge the ways in which the global political economy has traditionally been examined. In particular, a number of writers have examined the place of women in the global economy in terms of economic class and development and the gender specific consequences of the international system as it stands. However, women's work often goes unrecognized because of assumptions surrounding the traditional roles of women. Indeed, despite the fact that women constitute a significant percentage of the public workforce in developing countries, policy-makers still tend to assume that women are instead largely involved in domestic household tasks, and thus the significance of their contribution goes unrecognized. The result is that women are then overlooked when policies are made, and their needs remain unaddressed. Early work such as that done by Esther Boserup concentrates on outlining the extent of the economic contribution that women make. More recently, work by writers such as Chandra Mohanty has been crucial in highlighting the concerns of 'Third World feminists', whilst once again Cynthia Enloe's work has proved significant in its examination of the effect of globalization on women's labour and wage ratios. Nevertheless, as a recent review article by Penny Griffin highlights:

> [I]t remains the case that, in spite of the consistently high quality *and* quantity of gender analysis in International Relations (IR) and International Political Economy (IPE), gender has not been able to achieve more than a marginal status therein. Increasingly visible as a category of analysis, gender remains also rather trivialized in the minds of the mainstream, as a category pertaining only to the lives of women, women's labour rights and women's social movements.
>
> (Griffin 2007: 720)

BOX 14.3 RECURRING THEMES IN IR/GENDER LITERATURE

- Challenges to IR frameworks, such as realism and its apparent reinforcement of patriarchy in the international system
- Challenging the significance of bearing arms in defence of one's country, and the public and private roles of women
- Examination of the roles women play during wartime and peacetime as soldiers, as peace activists and as employees

THE GENDER CRITIQUE AND SOME OTHER 'OTHERS'

Writings on gender, so keen to challenge prevailing stereotypes, have themselves become the subject of critique. Arguably, such critiques began early – at least for the feminist movement in general – with the so-called feminist backlash identified by Susan Faludi in her book *Backlash: The Undeclared War Against Women*. Faludi examined what she saw as the myth of the improvement in women's economic and social lives, arguing that rather than there being more opportunities for women, women who had taken such opportunities were now victims of a counter-assault on their ambitions and values.

Similarly, Adam Jones argued the need for gender theorists to be aware of 'ideological blind-spots' in his work: 'Does Gender make the World Go Round?' Jones also raised concerns about gender reductionism (such that there appears to be at times in the work of gender theorists a denial of the biological realities that in actual fact exist). Nowhere is this more clearly apparent than in the stratification of views within the feminist litera-ture on the role of mothers. For some feminist authors, the sanctity placed on the role of the mother is one way in which a society dominated by patriarchal values colludes in its subjugation of women. For feminists writing in the 1970s, the notion of motherhood itself was one that was allied with that of the patriarchal society, the very act of mother-hood providing a potential obstacle in women's search for equal rights. A decade later the voice of the mother was increasingly heard but there remained concern that this was the result of a movement back towards the emphasis that women's role within society was largely a private one. For others, however, motherhood was a lever to be used against patriarchal values and an authorization of activism. Sara Ruddick typified such thinking by portraying motherhood as a distinctive discourse not necessarily confined to women, but that itself may lead to the development of an active agenda for peace, typified by both the symbolic elevated moral status that mothers may hold and the reality of the role of those mothers that mobilize in resisting war.

Although the gender critique has itself been roundly criticized by gender theorists, there are times when the work on gender does not itself seem to recognize how significant it could be to the discipline as a whole. Thus, work on gender has itself opened up a larger discourse regarding other marginalized groups. For example, race remains little discussed within mainstream IR, and issues of generation have only recently begun to be examined.

Moreover, a significant amount of work now examines the emotionality versus rationality argument within the context of international relations. Carol Pateman probes the Hobbesian social contract, and in doing so questions the myth that emotion belongs to women and rationality to men. Jean Bethke Elshtain talks about the good soldier being like the good mother in terms of the emotions each feels in the line of duty. Such concern with emotionality arguably leads in to some of the newer critical work that is being conducted on the role of alternative representations of international relations, surrounding issues such as grief, pain, mourning and the politics of care.

BOX 14.4 BEYOND GENDER

- Feminism and work on gender has itself been the subject of critique
- Such work has opened up other fields of research, including work on race, on generation and on emotions in IR

CONCLUSION

Work on gender as an issue of international relations has contributed widely to changing the way in which international relations can most fruitfully be examined. It remains important to examine the place of women in international society and the impact that the international system has upon women. It is also important to examine how looking at gender can open up other fundamental questions of what the study of IR should entail. Crucially, gender allows an examination of the international system with a different lens, and a consideration of people as fundamental to IR as opposed to marginal to it – and this is perhaps the greatest lesson of all.

REFERENCES AND FURTHER READING

Boserup, E. (1970) *Women's Role in Economic Development*, London: George Allen and Unwin.

Brownmiller, S. (1993) *Against Our Will: Men, Women and Rape*, New York: Fawcett Books.

Butler, J. (1999) *Gender Trouble: Feminism and the Subversion of Identity*, London: Routledge.

Daly, M. (1979) *Gyn/Ecology: Metaethics of Radical Feminism*, London: Women's Press Ltd.

de Beauvoir, S. (1997) *The Second Sex*, New York: Vintage.

Elshtain, J.B. (1988) *Women and War*, Basic Books.

Enloe, C. (2001) *Bananas, Beaches and Bases: Making Feminist Sense of International Politics*, Berkeley: University of California Press.

Enloe, C. (2004) *The Curious Feminist: Searching for Women in a New Age of Empire*, Berkeley: University of California Press.

Faludi, S. (1993) *Backlash: The Undeclared War Against Women*, New York: Vintage.

Gilligan, C. (1982) *In a Different Voice: Psychological Theory and Women's Development*, Cambridge, MA: Harvard University Press.

Griffin, P. (2007) 'Refashioning IPE: What and How Gender Analysis Teaches International (Global) Political Economy', *Review of International Political Economy*, 14: 719–736.

Halliday, F. (1988) 'Hidden from International Relations: Women and the International Arena', *Millennium: Journal of International Studies*, 17: 419–428.

Hochschild, A. (2005) *Bury the Chains: The British Struggle to Abolish Slavery*, Houndmills: Macmillan.

hooks, b. (2000) *Feminist Theory: From Margin to Center*, Boston: South End Press.

Jaggar, A.M. (1983) *Feminist Politics and Human Nature*, London: Rowman and Littlefield.

Jardine, A. (1985) 'Men in Feminism: Odor di Uomo or Compagnons de Route?', *Critical Exchange*, 18.

Jardine, A. (1987) 'Men in Feminism', in A. Jardine and P. Smith (eds), *Men in Feminism*, London: Methuen, 54–61.

Jones, A. (1989) 'Engendering Debate', *Review of International Studies*, 24: 299–303.

Jones, A. (1996) 'Does "Gender" Make the World Go Around?: Feminist Critiques of International Relations', *Review of International Studies*, 22 (4): 405–429.

Kaldor, M. (1999), *New and Old Wars: Organized Violence in a Global Era*, Cambridge: Polity Press.

Kimmel, M.S. (2004) *The Gendered Society*, Oxford: Oxford University Press.

Long, S. (2005) 'Anatomy of a Backlash: Sexuality and the Cultural War on Human Rights', *Human Rights Watch*, January.

Lorde, A. (1984) 'An Open Letter to Mary Daly', in *Sister Outsider, Essays and Speeches by Audre Lorde*, Berkeley: The Crossing Press, 66–71.

Mohanty, C.T. (2003) *Feminism without Borders: Decolonizing Theory, Practising Solidarity*, Durham, NC: Duke University Press.

Murphy, C.N. (1996) 'Seeing Women, Recognizing Gender, Recasting International Relations', *International Organization*, 50 (3) 513–538.

Oakley, A. (1972) *Sex, Gender and Society (Towards a New Society)*, London: M.T. Smith.

Okin, S.M. (1989) *Justice, Gender and the Family*, New York: Basic Books.

Pateman, C. (1988) *The Sexual Contract*, Stanford: Stanford University Press.

Petchesky, R.P. (2001) 'Sexual Rights: Inventing a Concept, Mapping an International Practice', in Blasius, M. (ed.), *Sexual Identities and Queer Politics*, Princeton: Princeton University Press, 118–139.

Ruddick, S. (1995) *Maternal Thinking: Towards a Politics of Peace*, Boston: Beacon Press.

Runyan, A.S. and Peterson, V.S. (1991) 'The Radical Future of Realism: Feminist Subversions of IR Theory', *Alternatives*, 16, 1: 67–106, p. 91.

Shiva, V. (1989) *Staying Alive: Women, Ecology and Development*, London: Zed Books.

Tickner, J.A. (1988) 'Hans Morgenthau's Principles of Political Realism: A Feminist Reformulation', *Millennium: Journal of International Studies*, 17: 429–440.

Watson, A.M.S. (2007) 'Children Born of Wartime Rape: Rights and Representations', *International Feminist Journal of Politics*, 9: 20–34.

USEFUL WEBSITES

Human Rights Watch: www.hrw.org
United Nations Development Programme: www.undp.org/women
Women's Environment and Development Organization: www.wedo.org
Women's human rights: www.whrnet.org

CHAPTER 15

Religion and International Relations
John Anderson

The demise of religion, or religion's relegation to the private sphere, has been a recurrent theme for over two centuries. However, recent decades have witnessed a global resurgence of politicized religion, with religious motivation being claimed by various actors who seek to change societies, to bring down authoritarian regimes, to promote both conflict and reconciliation. Religious motivation has also played a strong role in modern global terrorism. This chapter will examine this phenomenon through an examination of the relationship between religion and international politics. The first section will explore and explain the alleged absence of religion from the study of international politics. Second, the development of a global resurgence of political religion will be analysed. Finally, several case studies will be used to demonstrate how religion has entered the international political arena.

INTERNATIONAL POLITICS AND THE ABSENCE OF RELIGION

Despite the apparent resurgence of political religion since the 1970s, scholars of international relations only recently took the phenomenon seriously, often preferring to argue that religion was merely a façade behind which could be found more traditional considerations of power and interest. The reasons for such thinking can be outlined as follows.

Secularization theory

Thinkers such as Karl Marx and Sigmund Freud proffered the idea that religious belief would decline as society became more modern. Secularization theory, however, suggests that the social and political *significance* of religion would decline as the world became more secular, leading to a process of social fragmentation and differentiation wherein the state would assume responsibility for many of the welfare services hitherto supplied by the churches. Secularization theory was also a response to scientific rationality and the growth of rationality, though this does not necessarily suggest that science and religion are incompatible. The roots of secularization theory can be traced back to the Protestant Reformation of the sixteenth century when Reformers undermined the notion of a single truth by emphasizing the right of all believers to interpret scripture for themselves. In doing so, the Reformers undermined the efforts of states to promote a single religious vision, the long-term consequence of which is still felt in the exclusion of much of religion from the public sphere and the legal exclusion of religion from public life in states such as France and the USA.

Westphalian assumptions

The absence of religion from politics can also be traced back to the Westphalian assumptions that inform much of the study of international relations. The Peace of Westphalia (1648) brought to an end the religious conflicts of the Thirty Years War and consequently based much of its principles on the further privatization of religion and an exclusion of religion from the public sphere. The treaties of Westphalia allowed the ruler of each state to control religion within his own borders without interference or hindrance from other states, a series of principles that angered the Catholic Church and Pope Innocent X who denounced the treaty as 'damnable, reprobate, inane and devoid of meaning for all time'. Whilst the treaties established the role of states and the essentially secular principles that have come to be associated with political realism – sovereignty and non-intervention – they also established the principle that religion was best kept out of international politics. Underlying this principle was the assumption that if allowed into the public sphere, religion always led to division, intolerance, chaos and destruction.

Traditional theoretical perspectives

Traditional theoretical perspectives such as realism, liberalism and Marxism failed to consider religion as an important or significant factor in international relations. Early realist thinkers such as Hans Morgenthau and Reinhold Niebuhr may be rooted in an Augustinian view of human nature as fundamentally flawed and prone to evil, but traditional realism focuses on states, power and interests, and consequently marginalizes the importance of ideas, values, culture and religion. In a world of powerful state actors there remained little room for non-state religious actors, though Machiavelli pointed out in the sixteenth century that religion could be a useful tool for legitimating or justifying political action. Interestingly, Marxist approaches to international relations tend to share the view that religion is secondary to other factors such as economic forces and interests. Liberalism, by way of contrast, allotted great significance to transnational actors but failed to recognize religion as a significant transnational actor, save for a few studies of the Vatican and other such groups.

For all of these reasons – and inevitably the descriptions given here represent a considerable simplification of much more complex arguments – the discipline of international relations has been rather slow to respond to the re-appearance of politicized religion.

THE GLOBAL RESURGENCE OF POLITICAL RELIGION

By the 1980s secularization theory was under serious challenge from a global resurgence of religion. Nietzsche's proclamation that God is Dead came under increasing scrutiny as people in many parts of the world re-embraced religion and reinvigorated religious ideals. However, many scholars suggested that such events were less a religious revival – after all, most of the peoples concerned had always been religious – but a de-privatization of religion with religious actors returning to the public sphere. In other words this was a resurgence of *politicized* religion, and one that was affecting many parts of the world, such as the Iranian Revolution of 1978–9 where the Western regime of the Shah was overthrown by a religious coalition led by Ayatollah Khomeini, or in the 1978 election of an activist Pope, John Paul II, who used his frequent travels to promote his faith-based ideas about human rights. More recently, there has emerged the American Christian Right, a group of conservative Protestant organizations seeking to bring American public life into conformity with their understanding of Christian teaching. There has also been a gradual replacement of nationalism by Islam as the key mobilizing ideology in the struggles of the people of the Middle East and wider Muslim world, and religion has played a role in motivating terrorist activity, as was evident in the Islamist terrorism of 9/11. Additionally, there has been the use of religion by nationalist politicians in India, Yugoslavia and elsewhere who want to mobilize their people in pursuit of specific goals and as a means of identifying the enemy. The significance of religious organizations in political action and debate is also increasing (as in the contributions made by the Roman Catholic and other churches to undermining authoritarian regimes and promoting human rights observance) and the role of religious actors in promoting reconciliation after times of conflict (as in South Africa).

Despite the better efforts of religious organizations, media focus typically distorts religious political activity as extremist or fundamentalist. Indeed, much of the modern religious political agenda stems from a conservative perspective and promotes religious observance and traditional values, but this should not be confused with the promotion of political violence or extremism. In the case of religiously inspired political violence, religious scriptures are often used selectively and the groups often utilize very modern communications and weaponry.

BOX 15.1 WHY A RELIGIOUS RESURGENCE?

- An alternative to the failure of post-colonial, nationalist regimes to deliver either prosperity or justice
- A reaction to the social and psychological dislocation of modernization
- A reaction to social and economic deprivation
- A moral response to the brutality of authoritarianism and its undermining of human dignity
- As an effort to revive traditional values in a globalized world
- A consequence of modern communication allowing greater interfaith exchange

RELIGIOUS ENGAGEMENT WITH POLITICS

This section will consider case studies of religious engagement with international politics focusing on issues relating to revolution, nationalism, political change, conflict and terrorism. The case study selections do not represent a comprehensive study of the topic, but, rather provide a cross-selection of topical issues that provide a basis for assessing the relative roles played by religion in international politics.

The Iranian Revolution and the Islamic revival

Populist views of religious engagement with politics are often coloured by extremist events such as 9/11, and likewise, the roots of Islamic radicalism are often traced back to the Iranian Revolution of 1979. However, political Islam's intellectual roots lie much earlier in the twentieth century when thinkers such as Hassan al-Banna (1906–1949) in Egypt and Maulana Abdul A'la Maududi (1903–1979) in Pakistan began to explore the political implications of Islam. Typically described as fundamentalists, al-Banna and A'la Maududi argued that a truly just society should be based on religious values and laws, but such movements made relatively little headway as a result of authoritarian suppression of religious activism. However, the Iranian Revolution of 1979 provided the opportunity for the spread of political Islamicist ideas that inspired further Muslim movements to challenge both domestic tyranny and foreign domination.

The 1970s saw the Shah of Iran, Muhammed Reza Pahlavi (1919–1980) embark on a rapid modernization programme based on the country's extensive oil revenues. However, in addition to bringing wealth to Iran, the Shah's modernization programme also brought extensive disruption that resulted in a potent alliance between the urban poor, the merchant class whose influence had been undermined, and sections of the clergy who rejected many of the innovations (such as secular education programmes and breaking up of large estates upon which religious institutions depended). Following a period of repression, the Shah's army proved increasingly unwilling to suppress the rising protest movement and in January 1979 the Shah fled the country leaving a coalition government dominated by the Ayotollah Khomeini. Two months later a referendum led to the replacement of the monarchy by an Islamic Republic and in subsequent months a new constitution was drafted that gave extensive power to the clergy; simultaneously, all those not loyal to Khomeini were gradually removed from office in a context of extreme brutality against opponents.

BOX 15.2 AYATOLLAH RUHOLLAH MUSAVI KHOMEINI (1902–1989)

- Until the 1960s Khomeini was a cleric devoted to study and writing
- In 1961 Khomeini emerged as leader of the clerical opposition to the Shah's Westernizing reforms
- Khomeini was exiled to Iraq after participating in a rebellion that was brutally put down by the army
- In Iraq, Khomeini continued to develop his ideas about Islamic governance
- In 1978 Khomeini was expelled from Iraq and travelled to France where he maintained growing support
- In February 1979 Khomeini returned to Iran where he controlled a successful Islamic-led revolution

Khomeini came to power advocating the need for substantial clerical oversight concerning public life, and in the years prior to his death argued that the supreme spiritual guide (himself and his successors) could contradict Islamic precepts in the interests of the state. Following Khomeini's death in 1989 the total dominance of the clerics was reduced and there emerged a degree of pluralism within the political system, albeit within certain religious inspired constraints. In terms of a religious/political context, the Iranian revolution is important for two reasons. First, it created considerable international insecurity as traditional Muslim regimes feared contagion and powerful states such as the USA opposed the spread of Islamic revolution by supporting radical movements in Lebanon, Palestine and elsewhere. Second, it provided both Sunni and Shiite Muslim activists with the belief that political Islam could triumph over domestic tyrants or international oppressors.

Prior to the Iranian Revolution broader developments in the Islamic world had begun to presage change and rethinking. Contributing factors, such as Israel's defeat of the Arab armies in the 1967, the failure of Arab nationalism to deliver either prosperity or justice, the oil boom which strengthened Muslim self-confidence, and the Iranian Revolution itself all led to a rediscovery of Islam as a source of identity and political mobilization. Throughout the Middle East and in the wider Muslim world there occurred a revitalization of religious practice and an organizational revolution as wide varieties of groups sought to provide welfare and social services, as well as promote political change. The goals and methods of such organizational groups often differed – ranging from social support, propaganda and electoral campaigning to political violence and terrorism – but all proclaimed the need to create a society based upon the principles of Islam. Whether Islam has a single political message was less clear and often these groups differed violently about what an Islamic society would look like – the Taliban's Afghan version was not to the taste of most – but they all agreed that in some sense Islam was the answer to the problems facing their societies.

Religion and nationalism in India and Yugoslavia

The populist view of the relationship between religion and national identity often assumes that conflict is the inevitable result. Historically, there occurred a natural and obvious relationship between religion and national identity – each usually contributing towards and informing the other. Ancient Israel provides an example of such an explicit link between a single group of people and a single religion. More recently such a relationship occurs by the role of clergymen in creating national languages and of churches in providing national myths of victory and defeat. In contexts where there are no immediate distinctions between peoples, religious difference can serve as a means of identifying the community and establishing alternative groups based on religious difference. Such distinctions, in turn, can lead to conflict and violence when religious and/or secular leaders use the rhetoric of sacred causes or holy wars. However, the ease with which religious difference can be manipulated by political entrepreneurs means that it is often difficult to disentangle religious motivations from more politically motivated considerations relating to power or interests.

Developing a Hindu fundamentalist movement is problematic given the absence of a core scripture or distinctive religio-legal tradition within the Hindu faith. Consequently, Hindu activists in India (where 80 per cent of the population are Hindu) have developed a variant in the shape of religious nationalism based on the notion of *Hindutva* or Hinduness. Based on the rejection of Islamic and Christian influences, *Hindutva* can be traced to the post-Second World War creation of India as a secular and religiously neutral state. The notion of *Hindutva* became an established political reality with the 1980s creation of the Indian People's Party (BJP) and their consequent parliamentary representation and participation in coalition governments throughout the 1990s. The BJP has sought to reduce what it sees as privileges granted to minority communities, to approve so-called cow-protection laws, and to promote Indian nuclear development as a counter to the perceived Muslim threats coming from Pakistan. Most controversially, the BJP presided over the demolition of the Ayodha mosque in 1992 following a centuries-old religious dispute between Muslim and Hindu communities concerning the site of the Mosque's construction in the early 1500s. During the 1980s, the Hindu nationalist movement organized a campaign in which communities throughout the country consecrated bricks to be used for construction of an alternative Hindu temple and in 1992 Hindu demonstrators broke into the compound and tore the mosque down (despite a Supreme Court injunction to the contrary). During the 1990s the BJP committed itself to building a grand Hindu temple on the site. Though the role of religion can be disputed in the creation of Hindu nationalism, there is little doubt that the rise of Hindu nationalism has contributed significantly to the inter-communal tensions that have beset India since independence.

In Yugoslavia the role of religion as an ethnic identifier contributed to ethnic cleansing and mass murder on a scale not seen in Europe since 1945. Previously held together by President Josip Broz Tito's commitment to a common Yugoslav nationality, the federal system gradually fell apart after his death in 1980. Religion may not have been the primary cause of violence, but became a tool used by politicians to sharpen the conflict following the dislocations of the communist collapse: Serbian spokesmen revived memories of Catholic treachery and past Muslim occupations, and Catholics and Muslims often reciprocated in kind. The Serbian religious press in particular played a role in demonizing opposing nationalities. During the war that followed religious sites were often targeted for destruction. Although not a religious war in that the objectives had more to do with power, territorial gain and interest, the language of difference was often infused with a religious rhetoric that sometimes contributed to brutal atrocities by all sides in the conflict.

Religion and democratization in Latin America and Eastern Europe

The first two case studies have focused on contexts where the religious contribution to politics has often involved conflict or violence, but of equal (though less newsworthy) importance are the roles played by religious organizations and ideas in achieving peaceful political transformations and conflict resolution, or the so-called third wave of democratization. Since the mid-1970s a series of countries in Southern Europe, Latin America, Africa, Asia and Eastern Europe have overthrown authoritarian regimes and adopted more democratic forms of governance. In many such circumstances the Christian churches, and in particular the Roman Catholic Church, have made a significant contribution to political change. Though the Protestant tradition had contributed to, or at least accepted, the development of democratic politics, the Roman Catholic Church had vigorously opposed notions of popular sovereignty and human rights through much of the nineteenth and early twentieth centuries. Catholic hierarchies in Latin America, Southern Europe and elsewhere had tended to support authoritarian political regimes – sometimes this was because they shared a vision of the good society as hierarchical, disciplined and ordered, but it was also often the result of shared interests as many of these regimes privileged the church by providing financial support or allowing them to control the education system. However, the experience of communism and fascism, and the horrors of the Second World War encouraged the church to rethink certain political issues under the assurances from leading American churchmen that democratic governance could benefit Catholics in many countries. Consequently, at the Second Vatican Council (1962–5) the Catholic Church adopted a series of ecclesiastical reforms that gave the Catholic Church's qualified approval to democracy, human rights and freedom of conscience. In turn, this led to a growth of Catholic activism in criticizing human rights abuses and speaking up for the victims of repression, promoting and defending civil society organizations and offering support services as mediators or negotiators in the process of political change.

In part, the critique of authoritarian regimes focused on social injustice, with bishops and priests speaking out against economic policies that deprived the poor of land or income, and against landlords whose abuses were supported by the forces of the state. The most radical form of this critique was to be found in *liberation theology* which combined traditional Christian concerns for social justice with Marxist analysis of economic exploitation and, sometimes, a willingness to countenance violence as a legitimate response to the violence of the oppressors. More common, however, was an emphasis on human dignity and human rights, with bishops in Chile, Brazil, South Africa and Poland challenging the idea that restoring order required the disappearance, torture or murder of alleged subversives. In practical terms this critique led to a growing involvement with civil society including the creation of organizations to defend human rights in practical ways such as providing legal aid, carrying out meticulous investigation of abuses, or publicizing issues abroad. A typical example of such an organization was the *Vicaria de Solidaridad* (Vicariate of Solidarity) in Chile which was fully backed by the Catholic hierarchy despite the complaints of military dictator General Pinochet. On other occasions it meant providing actual and symbolic spaces where those critical of the regime could gather, as in Spain where the Monastery of Montserrat provided a meeting place for banned oppositionists or the Polish pilgrimage to the Black Madonna at Jasna Gora which attracted tens of thousands of Poles to proclaim their religion and to make evident their opposition to a regime ostensibly committed to an atheist view of the world. In Poland, Catholic churches frequently provided meeting places, hosted unofficial discussions, used their newspapers to defend human rights, and used their contacts with the government to seek redress of grievances. The Catholic Church's campaign for change was further strengthened with the election of a Pole as Pope John Paul II in 1978, who used his position to promote human rights around the world and to criticize those who adopted more radical political positions.

While the role of the Catholic Church should not be exaggerated – indeed, there was a host of factors contributing to political change and in some countries the churches were not involved at all – the fact remains that religious activism has played a key role in de-legitimizing authoritarianism and promoting the idea of human rights and democracy. Furthermore, after the ending of apartheid in South Africa, Protestant and Catholic clergymen played a key role in developing the Truth and Reconciliation Commission.

The impact of the Christian Right on domestic politics and foreign policy

The United States is an exceptional country in religious terms. As a modern, secular state whose constitutional jurisprudence provides for a radical separation of religion and state, the United States – according to secularization theory – should have experienced a religious decline. However, the United States remains one of the most religious Western states where religious issues continue to shape the political agenda. Religion in general and Protestantism in particular have been part of the American landscape since the first settlers arrived in the seventeenth century, but for much of the mid-twentieth century the predominant conservative Christian community tended to turn inward, focusing on personal salvation, church growth and mission to the wider world. Encouraged by conservative Republican leaders who saw in the evangelical movement a potential political constituency, the 1970s saw fundamentalist church leaders, both evangelical and Pentecostal, begin to explore the possibility of political engagement.

Christian leaders were encouraged into politics by the process of cultural change taking place in the USA from the 1960s onwards – developments that the conservative Christian church saw as both objectively undesirable and as threatening to their influence and ability to hold their communities together. Controversial developments such as Supreme Court judgements to further raise the wall of separation between church and state, a perceived growth in sexual permissiveness, the 1973 legalization of abortion, and the questioning of traditional Christian familial and societal values contributed to the creation of a series of Christian Right organizations such as the Moral Majority (1980s) and the Christian Coalition (1990s). Such organizations became active in the Republican Party, seeking to take over local branches and played a key role in selecting candidates for electoral contests. Concurrently, they became involved in local politics, seeking to use local courts, legislatures and school boards to promote their agendas which were based on traditional Christian values, and advocated issues such as denying rights to homosexual couples, censoring school textbooks or promoting the teaching of Biblical creationism as a scientific truth.

However, it is arguable that the Christian Right's influence on policy outcomes was far more limited than their ability to shape agendas. President Reagan promised much but failed to deliver the restrictions on abortion hoped for by the Christian Right, whilst President Clinton in the 1990s was steadfastly unsympathetic to the Christian Right agenda. Moreover, Christian Right campaigns were undermined by a series of scandals involving religious leaders and further hindered by the fragmented nature of the American political system wherein a victory won in one court or legislature can easily be overturned by the decisions of another body or a change in electoral fortunes.

In 2000 George W. Bush became the first US President to advocate a Christian agenda from the White House. In consequence members of the Bush administration have been far more willing to use religious language and to promote faith-based initiatives. Of course, many American presidents have made use of religious rhetoric, with George Washington and Abraham Lincoln as obvious examples, but President Bush was rare in his explicit commitment to linking political and religious conservatism. While Bush supporters consider that his agenda merely offers a place at the table to the religious part of the American population, Bush critics believe he is undermining the separation of church and state that underpins American democracy. Liberal concerns that the United States is waging a religious crusade may be exaggerated, but the fact remains that the Bush administration has created a foreign policy that it is at least partially shaped by Biblical teachings.

Religion and terrorism

The events of 9/11 brought renewed focus to the connection between religion and terrorism, though the roots of this relationship date back to the campaign of the Jewish Zealots to remove the Roman occupiers from Palestine. From the late nineteenth to the late twentieth century terrorism was largely the preserve of nationalist movements but the last few decades have seen religious inspired terrorism once again become a prominent feature of the international system. Religious inspired terrorism can take many forms, and has been conducted in the name of multitudes of different religions or religious sects, including the Japanese Aum Shinrikyo group (who released Sarin gas into the Tokyo subway system in 1995) and the American based Christian Patriots (who bombed a federal building in Oklahoma City in 1995). Mark Jurgensmeyer has noted that religious terror often has certain key features (see Box 15.3).

BOX 15.3 JURGENSMEYER'S KEY FEATURES OF RELIGIOUS TERRORISM

- Aimed to make a symbolic point rather than achieve an instant victory
- Has a performance dimension drawing on notions of ritual central to religious systems
- Often linked to a significant date
- Comprises a theological dimension rooted in sacrifice and martyrdom for the greater good
- Often tied to wider notions of cosmic warfare between the forces of good and evil

Indeed, Jewish assassin Yigal Amir spoke of a 'mystical urge' to carry out the assassination of Israeli Prime Minister Yitzak Rabin in 1995, and was found to be heavily influenced by radical Jewish thinking concerning the need to remove Arabs from Jewish God-given territory. Amir attempted to justified his crime using religious rhetoric and in terms of the necessity of killing those who might betray Israel to the Arab enemy.

Additionally, the Palestinian organization Hamas (Zeal) is renowned for the use of suicide bombers who are often filmed prior to the event using religious rhetoric to justify their actions, and speaking of their imminent encounter with God and of martyrdom as a sacred duty. Hamas bombers frequently describe their acts as defensive sacrifices for the greater cause of destroying the Israeli state and simultaneously defend attacks on civilians by suggesting that there are no innocent Israeli victims.

The 9/11 bombers also adopted the rhetoric of their crimes being conducted in the name of a greater religious good, with footage of Al Qaeda leader Osama Bin Laden showing him to frequently adopt a moralistic religious rhetoric as justification for the use of terrorism.

PUTTING RELIGION BACK INTO INTERNATIONAL RELATIONS

This chapter has highlighted some of the ways in which religion has impacted upon international politics in recent years. Though still neglected to a certain degree, the religious/political nexus is increasingly discussed within the academy and there have been a number of significant attempts to engage with religion.

Samuel Huntington's controversial 1996 book *The Clash of Civilizations* suggested that the ideological conflict of the Cold War was likely to be replaced by cultural conflict between civilizations. In Huntington's view civilizations were shaped above all by their religious traditions, and he saw the immediate and most likely source of tension being that emerging between the West and Islam – and Islam as a whole, not just fundamentalist Islam. Critics quite rightly responded that Huntington's notion of civilization was rather unsatisfactory and his assumption that states of the same religion would necessarily cooperate was simply wrong. Yet what was more important was that Huntington sought to engage with the role of religious and cultural factors in politics and sparked a debate that brought religion to centre stage in debates about international relations.

Others scholars have remained more sceptical, suggesting that even those conflicts that appeared to be religious in nature were essentially about something else. In contexts where injustice or social and economic inequality were rife, skilled political entrepreneurs could utilize religious slogans to mobilize populations or justify particular policies. Thus in Yugoslavia, where religion was one of the only differences between communities, persons like President Slobodan Milosevic could appeal to ancient religious memories that went back to the time of the Ottoman occupation and promote past injustices as if they had happened yesterday. Here religion was used instrumentally to explain, persuade and justify both current grievances and future remedies.

A third approach is rooted in what is loosely described as the constructivist take on international relations, and stresses that social conflicts are not just about obvious grievances but are rooted in cognitive structures associated with religion, ideology and ethnicity. Rather like sociologists of religion, constructivists suggest that we should take seriously what people say when they claim their political actions are motivated by religion. The 9/11 bombers may have had more worldly concerns and may have been manipulated by others, but they also claimed to be serving Allah through their actions.

In any case it is hard to avoid the conclusion that religion is back on the public agenda, even in secular Europe where the growth of immigrant communities has added a new dimension to traditional church–state politics. At the time of writing there is little sign that religion will go away. Muslim groups claiming to be operating within the *jihadi* tradition associated with Osama Bin Laden continue to cause havoc in Iraq, Afghanistan, the Middle East and elsewhere; periodic outbursts of communal violence persist in the Indian sub-continent; and some within the Bush administration continue to use the language of conservative Christianity in their public pronouncements, whilst the Democrats search for a way to embrace religion more fully. Additionally, there has been a global expansion of Pentecostalism, the political implications of which remain to be seen. The obituary of God, gods and religion may have been frequently written, but reports of their political death are distinctly premature.

FURTHER READING

Appleby, S. (2000) *The Ambivalence of the Sacred*, Oxford: Rowman and Littlefield.

Bruce, S. (2003) *Religion and Politics*, Cambridge: Polity Press.

Casanova, J. (1994) *Public Religion in the Modern World*, Chicago: Chicago University Press.

Fox, J. and Sandler, S. (2006) *Bringing Religion back into International Relations*, New York: Palgrave.

Huntington, S. (1996) *The Clash of Civilizations and the Remaking of World Order*, New York: Simon and Schuster.

Jelen, T. and Wilcox, C. (eds) (2002) *Religion and Politics in Comparative Perspective*, Cambridge: Cambridge University Press.

Jurgensmeyer, M. (2000) *Terror in the Mind of God*, Berkeley: University of California Press.

Norris, P. and Ingelhart, R. (2004) *Sacred and Secular: Religion and Politics Worldwide*, Cambridge: Cambridge University Press.

Thomas, S. (2005) *The Global Resurgence of Religion and the Transformation of International Relations*, New York: Palgrave.

CHAPTER 16

Political Islam

Andrea Teti

One of the most repeated slogans of the 1979 Iranian revolution was 'neither East nor West, [only] an Islamic Republic.' For others, the adoption of religious symbols such as veiling (*hijab, niqab*) was an alternative and highly visible statement of protest against the US-backed Iranian Shah (king). The revolution's rejection of Western models in favour of an Islamic republic – led by Ruhollah Mustafavi Khomeini who would later dominate the post-revolutionary government and hold the position of Iranian Grand Ayatollah – led to Western fears of a Green Peril rising in the East. Unlike Arab nationalists who sought simply to redraw existing state borders, the Islamic Republic and its Muslim sympathizers were considered to represent a dangerous and unprecedented pan-Islamic political movement.

The use of religion as a banner for political opposition is an age-old phenomenon that has its contemporary roots in European imperialism, specifically the Ottoman empire and the fierce debates about whether or not shared religion could provide the necessary solution to the empire's cross-border weaknesses. In the twentieth century religion has provided a similar banner and rallied opposition to authoritarian monarchies and secular nationalist regimes. The Iranian revolution served simply to thrust the politicization of Islam into the West's political attention. Consequently, the notion of Islam as an inherently political and perhaps violent movement has been central to Western debates regarding Middle Eastern politics.

However, the history of Islam as a religion and the history of governments and movements that would employ Islamic rhetoric to serve their own political agendas are two very separate and distinct areas of study. This chapter will illustrate the key features of the relationship between Islam and politics.

PRINCIPLES OF ISLAM

Islam considers itself to be the third and final of the three revealed religions, following Judaism and Christianity. For Muslims, the Prophet Muhammad is the Seal of a line of prophets starting with Adam and including most of the prophets of Judaism and Christianity, such as Abraham, Moses and Jesus. Islam's beliefs and rules of worship are based on three sources: a holy scripture (*Qur'an*), stories about the Prophet's life (*hadith*), and Islamic legal scholarship (*shari'a*).

BOX 16.1 FIVE PILLARS OF ISLAM

1 *Shahada*: The recognition of the oneness of God, and that Muhammad is His Prophet
2 *Salat*: Prayer five times a day
3 *Zakat*: A 'social responsibility' tax to care for the poor
4 *Hajj*: Pilgrimage to Mecca once in one's lifetime, if possible
5 *Ramadan*: Observing daytime fasting and undertaking spiritual reflection during the month of Ramadan

However, similar to other world religions, Islam's principles and practices have been interpreted widely and evolved differently in different geographic locations and between different cultural groups. Indeed, shortly after the Prophet's death in 632 CE a schism occurred between two Islamic groups, Sunni and Shi'a, concerning who should be the Prophet's rightful successor: Abu Bakr (Muhammad's uncle) or 'Ali (his son-in-law).

Within Sunni Islam there are four major theological and legal schools: Hanafi, Hanbali, Maliki, Shafii. Sufism (mysticism) has also played a major role in the religion's history and is epitomized by the writings of the Sufi mystic poet Rumi, and recently Wahhabism (ultra-conservativism) which has influenced the creation and government of Saudi Arabia.

One of the many poorly understood aspects of Islam is its jurisprudence. Shari'a is a body of legal scholarship on the basis of which individual legal codes can be drawn up. Shari'a is not a specific legal code or Islamic law but rather a field of legal scholarship based on the principles contained in the Qur'an and the hadith. For most Sunnis, shari'a is based on the Qur'an and the hadith: through *qiyas* (analogy) and *ijma* (consensus) the body of scholars arrive at principles of law. *Ijtihad* (interpretation) is the exercise of judgement in applying principles and precedents in jurisprudence to new cases. After the rule of the Prophet's Companions, known as the Rightly Guided Caliphs, the door of ijtihad was closed, at least in theory, preventing innovation in Islamic jurisprudence.

Debates over nineteenth-century reforms throughout the Ottoman empire focused on a number of concepts, including a possible reinvigoration of the Caliphate which would supposedly aid the empire in regaining a position of power in Europe. The question of whether features of European Christian or secular institutions should be adapted or even introduced wholesale in the Ottoman context drew considerable debate and centred particularly around Islamic concepts such as *dhimma, shura* and *ijtihad.*

BOX 16.2 LEGAL AND THEOLOGICAL INTERPRETATIONS

The Five Pillars of Islam have remained constant, but legal and theological interpretations, and particularly practices have varied across regions and over time:

- *Purdah* (modesty): The notion that women must dress modestly in public has found various expressions: loose scarves of the Sudan; *chador* in Iran; *burqa* under the Taliban; non-provocative dress but no *hijab* in Turkey. There is no Qur'anic injunction specifying how women should dress. What 'modesty' entails has been interpreted differently over time and in different places (e.g. urban/rural, Gulf/Levant/Maghreb)

- *Marriage*: Technically, men can take up to four wives. This was a provision related to a specific historical context, with great paucity of men, and given women's weak social and economic position at the time it was useful for them to be protected in this way. Most Muslims today see this as arcane. Moreover, legal opinion holds this right subject to men being able to look after all wives *equally* – but, as the Qur'an itself points out, this equality is impossible to achieve in practice

Dhimma is a formulation allowing non-Muslims (especially *ahl al-kitab* or People of the Book, Jews, Christians, Sabeans and Zoroastrians) to live freely in Muslim states in their own communities and governed by their own laws, as long as they pay a small tax. This system of communities, known as *millet* under the Ottomans, allowed the peaceful coexistence of different faiths within the same territories.

Shura (consultation) is an important principle for the selection of a community's leader and dictates that the entire community should be capable of agreeing on a leader. In the Ottoman context, Shura was particularly emphasized in response to the need, felt by some, to lessen the absolutist character of the Ottoman empire.

Finally, *ijtihad* occupied a particular place in the Ottoman reform debate. It was argued that the problems of the era were unprecedented and thus requiring the elaboration of new principles and rules. This required re-opening of the door of ijtihad generated understandable controversy.

EARLY ISLAM AND ITS RELATION TO THE STATE

Islam was born in 610 CE when the Prophet Muhammad received his first revelation. Muhammad began preaching in 622 CE and, gradually Muslims became a political force. After encountering opposition within Mecca the first Muslims undertook the *hijra* ('emigration') to Medina in 627–8 CE where they achieved political influence through an alliance with the local Jewish majority. The subsequent Constitution of Medina to regulate relations between communities is Islam's first written historical document and remains central to several contemporary debates (such as whether Muslims can live under non-Muslim authority). The fact that the Constitution of Medina did not give rise to an Islamic state but to a religiously pluralist state is very significant.

There are very few specific religious provisions on types of government in either the

Qur'an or the hadith, aside from the principle of consultation and the place of the People of the Book (*ahl al-kitab*). Although the Sultan (temporal leadership) and the Caliph (leader of the faithful) were originally separate figures, they were united under Muhammad's example. The historic forms of Islamic government and the legal justifications invoked were related instead to the specific situations of the era.

The early expansion of the empire and subsequent contact with numerous other societies resulted in the development of a distinctive Islamic culture inspired significantly by the Helapostic tradition, which in turn regarded itself as a highly developed and sophisticated culture (e.g. Moorish Spain). Since this classical period, Islam has been used by temporal powers to legitimize its actions such as the effect of *jihad* (Ayubi, 1991) on contemporary theology and jurisprudence. However, Arabo-Islamic empires and their successors also provide key examples of ethno-religious pluralism, matched in Europe perhaps only by Frederick II's Sicily (itself based on his Muslim predecessor's model). Such examples serve to demonstrate the influence of political priorities in the societies in question: having expanded so rapidly, they could not expect to uniformly impose their cultural, religious and political identity, but needed some form of accommodation with the cultures they had absorbed and served as a development of the Median principle of coexistence with the People of the Book.

BOX 16.3 PRE-NINETEENTH-CENTURY ISLAM

- Constitution of Medina 622 CE:
  - first written historical document of Islam
  - did not give rise to an Islamic state
  - Muslims could live in a pluralist society
- Few provisions on types of government
- Islamic governments were related to specific circumstances
- Islam used by 'temporal powers'

ISLAM IN POLITICAL DEBATE: THE LATE NINETEENTH AND EARLY TWENTIETH CENTURY

Throughout the nineteenth century the Ottoman empire's economic and military weakness (comparable to that of Europe) became increasingly clear and heavily influenced political debate of the era and elicited two specific responses. First, there were those who argued that the Islamic community had weakened because of an abandonment of the early spirit and purity of Islam. Second, there were those who argued that the empire faced an unprecedented threat and should attempt to adapt technical knowledge and institutions from Europe. Such debates eventually led to the *tanzimat* laws and other such local reforms within the empire (notably in Egypt). Jamal al-Din al-Afghani, Muhammad 'Abduh, and Rashid Rida are the three central figures of the late ninteenth-century Islamic reform debates and are considered to be the Fathers of Islam to whom both moderates and radicals today trace their intellectual roots.

Afghani dreamt of a reinvigorated Caliphate unifying the Muslim world under one political and spiritual leadership. Despite limited political success, Afghani is important for three reasons: first, his influence on later figures like Rida and Hasan al-Banna; second, he was the first major intellectual to react against European influence by formulating a programme of political opposition based on innovative religious grounds; and, third, he reinvigorated attitudes towards the supposed Golden Age of early Islam – a creative move that has characterized virtually all attempts to shape contemporary attitudes towards burning issues such as the relationship between Muslims and secular states.

Born to a wealthy family, Muhammad 'Abduh represents mainstream intellectualism and elitism. A teacher at Cairo's prestigious al-Azhar University, 'Abduh was a gradualist who advocated the adaptation of various European institutions to the Egyptian/Ottoman/Islamic context. In particular 'Abduh stressed the need for consultative government, and argued that rather than importing institutional structures from Europe, Muslims should rediscover the early Islamic institution of shura and should re-open the door of *ijtihad* in order to meet the unprecedented challenges of European imperialism by elaborating new principles of jurisprudence.

The work of Rashid Rida marks a turning point in Islamist thought and in the attitudes of Islamic intellectuals towards Europe. A student of 'Abduh and co-editor of *al-Liwa al-Islami* (with Afghani), Rida was heavily influenced by the experience of living under the British military occupation of Egypt. Consequently, Rida emphasized the need for active resistance and argued that (defensive) jihad should be widened to include defence against political, as well as religious, oppression.

BOX 16.4 ISLAMIC THINKERS

- *Afghani*: Reinvigorated Caliphate; one leader; had great influence; looks back to 'Golden Age'
- *'Abduh*: Gradualist; adaptation; consultitive government; new principles of jurisprudence
- *Rida*: Turning point; active resistance

To understand such developments it is important to contextualize events with Egypt's independence from Britain. In 1875 Egypt declared bankruptcy and Viceroy Ismail was deposed. In his place a system of Dual Control – a sort of *ante diem* IMF – was established. After Ismail, Egyptian rulers were mostly pliant to UK interests and, under threat of nationalist opposition, shared the UK's interest in curtailing nationalist access to power. Following a coup in 1880 by the nationalist Colonel 'Arabi, the British invaded Egypt and began over seventy years of military and political dominance in the country. British policies, such as distinct courts for Egyptians and for foreigners, gradually established a system of discrimination that contributed to a radicalization of both nationalist and religious opposition.

FROM PEACEFUL REFORM TO ARMED RESISTANCE

Three events epitomize the impact of British imperialism in Egypt. First, the UK's declaration of a protectorate during the First World War that effectively formalized the British occupation. Second, the refusal to admit an Egyptian delegation to the Versailles negotiations. Third, the establishment of a Mandate following the war which flew in the face of Wilson's Fourteen Points and the supposed spirit of the Versailles settlements. In 1922, after three years of unrest, the British unilaterally recognized Egyptian independence but retained the right to a military presence and to intervene in foreign policy and local politics – effectively emptying independence of meaning.

In the 1920s and 1930s, Europe saw the emergence of extremist politics across the ideological spectrum, and likewise Egypt experienced the advent of radical Egyptian nationalism. Although the Egyptian nationalist Wafd party was regularly voted into power, the king and the British collaborated in an increasingly authoritarian repression of popular protest to undermine the Wafd's influence. In practice, this helped discredit Egyptian nationalism, but it also created the context for alternative ideologies – Islamist, Arabist, and socialist – to challenge the Wafd's 'liberal nationalism'.

Hassan al-Banna

In 1928 schoolmaster Hassan al-Banna established the *Ikhwan al-Muslimun* (Muslim Brotherhood) as an organization for providing welfare services, and aiming to encourage and defend morality. The Ikhwan – and groups such as the Young Men's Muslim Association (YMMA) – aimed to reform society's morals, rather than imposing a vision of Islam through force of arms.

The Ikhwan was soon drawn into politics and developed explicit political aims. The political context favoured the radicalization of both the Ikhwan's political philosophy and its tactics – just as it did those of its secular counterparts – and developed an armed wing to achieve political goals through the use of force. However, its main tools remained peaceful and focused on grassroots-level education and infiltration of the power structure. The combination of the Ikhwan's welfare services and religious credentials, alongside the king's increasing authoritarianism and the discrediting of the Wafd, soon led the Ikhwan to become the largest political organization in Egypt.

It is important to understand that the Ikhwan, despite its own rhetoric, is not a manifestation of *traditional* Islamism: on the contrary, it is a prime example of a reformist view of Islam and a *modern* political organization: mass-based, drawing support mainly from middle and lower classes and using a cell-based structure. Finally, and significantly, the Ikhwan prioritizes Egypt: it struggled first and foremost for *Egyptian* independence from foreign oppression, and only secondarily for the revival of the Islamic community as a whole.

Sayyid Abu-'l A'la al-Mawdudi

Pakistani author and journalist Sayyid al-Mawdudi (1903–1979) elaborates his most radical theories during the political turmoil preceding the separation of Hindu-majority India, and Muslim-majority Pakistan. He is perhaps most important for his emphasis on

Islam as inseparably faith and state (*din wa dawla*), arguing that sovereignty cannot rest with the people but only with God, and that a religious state cannot simply be Muslim-majority, it must be governed according to what he saw as true Islam, and only by true Muslims. Both radical Islamist and conservative Western values often assert that Islam is *din wa dawla*, but as with radical interpretations of the idea of jihad this is a recent and thoroughly modern idea. However, it does not represent mainstream Islamic legal theory, much less the mythical past of a golden age, nor even the opinion of most Muslims – its growing popularity, particularly among Islamists and a radicalized portion of diasporic communities is the result of political and socio-economic marginalization.

Sayyid Qutb

With Qutb (1906–1966), the Ikhwan takes a more radical turn. After having helped Nasser come to power and consolidate his rule, the Ikhwan was heavily repressed. Politically, Nasser's early triumphs helped isolate Islamists as his popularity rode the rising tide of Arab nationalism. Moreover, Nasser's newly established single party co-opted, marginalized or repressed his main rivals, such as large landowners, the Communists, and the Ikhwan. This radicalized sectors of the Ikhwan, and the impact of Nasser's repression on Brotherhood ideology is clearest with Sayyid Qutb. Qutb joined in 1951 after two years in the USA, and took over leadership after al-Banna's death. Arrested in 1954 and executed in 1966, Qutb experienced first-hand the harshness of Nasser's repression. In his most important tract, *Milestones*, Qutb embraces the idea of *hakimiyya* and argues for a new definition of jihad as:

> destroying the kingdom of man in order to bring about the kingdom of God [*hakimiyya*]. . . Those who understand the true nature of this religion will realise the absolute necessity for the Islamic movement, as well as and effort by preaching, [of including] armed struggle, and that this should not be understood as purely defensive.

The reference to conventional defensive interpretations of the theory of jihad is unmistakable. The depth of contemporary corruption was, for Qutb, such that society should be regarded as being in a state of *jahiliyya* (pre-Islamic ignorance), and therefore to be rejected in its entirety and requiring a radical overhaul.

Thus, in al-Banna, al-Mawdudi and Qutb, radicalization in religious discourse and political practices is clearly a response to an immediate political context: the combination of internal repression and external interference.

BOX 16.5 RADICAL THINKERS

- *Hassan al-Banna*: Muslim brotherhood; welfare and unity; transformation from below; radical and modern political organisation; armed wing (though mostly peaceful)
- *Al-Mawdudi*: Islam inseparably involves faith and state; Muslim majority should govern as 'true believers' in 'true Islam'
- *Qutb*: Radicalized; necessity for armed struggle

The question of jihad

Jihad has become central not only to the political theory of radical religious groups but also to Western (mis)representations of Islam's relation to politics. Such portrayals influence judgement on Middle Eastern politics, but also issues such as immigration. This section looks at the classical notion of jihad and its evolution during the late nineteenth and early twentieth centuries, outlining the influence of the experience of European imperialism in its radicalization.

Conventional interpretations of jihad are distinctly different from most common – but erroneous – translation as holy war. Jihad translates as struggle or striving, but the dominant conventional theorization does not embrace the idea of jihad as holy war. Nor is jihad central to classical Islamic political theory, as is often claimed. In the Qur'an, organized violence is referred to as *ghazwa* (raid), *harb* and *qital* (war) and uses terms with roots *qtl* or *hrb*, not *jhd* – the text's linguistic symbolism distinguishing the former from the latter. Indeed, verses in which the root *jhd* appears are seldom directly and exclusively linked to armed conflict, but always linked to personal effort or struggle. Jihad and war are thus two distinct concepts. Substituting the word jihad with any of the different meanings presents a clear example of how meaning is subsequently lost in translation. Consider the verse 'Fear God and attempt to move closer to Him and His religion, and fight on His path' (Qur'an V, 35). The text uses the root *jhd*, not *hrb* or *qtl*, and using the two interchangeably entirely changes the verse's meaning.

So what is jihad? Conventional interpretations distinguish between at least two kinds of jihad. The greater (and most important) jihad is to strive against negative inclinations, or to refrain from speaking or behaving piously. The lesser jihad (which includes the jihad of the sword) permits the use of force only when Muslims are actively being prevented from practising their faith.

In developing early theories of jihad, legal scholars close to the empire provided an interpretation allowing political leaderships to justify expansion into richer lands outside the Arabian peninsula. Subsequently, the empire's preoccupation became its internal stability and classical jurisprudence emphasized – particularly on the question of insurrection against an emperor – that jihad be undertaken only when Muslims are actively prevented from practising their religion (and only when there has been a fatwa by legitimate authorities). Such theorizations had little to do with a supposed essence of Islam and much more to do with leaders' political priorities.

Modern radicals' interpretation of the term jihad is very different. Where the classical interpretation of the lesser jihad is defensive of faith and remained tolerant of diversity within the empire and even non-Muslim rule, its modern extremist counterpart is exclusive, aggressive, and uses the language of defending the faith towards an Islamization of state and society. Indeed, for some this new jihad of the sword as become the neglected duty or sixth pillar of Islam.

The stark difference between notions of jihad as a spiritual tool and as a duty of revolution begs an explanation. The gradual shift can be clearly paralleled to the approximate 150 years of European (neo)imperial pressure. Similarly, in twentieth-century Egypt historically specific experiences led directly to political radicalization: the Ikhwan was initially a peaceful organization, but in the context of the wider political radicalization of the 1920s and 1930s developed an armed wing which carried out

BOX 16.6 JIHAD

- Struggle or striving
- Often misinterpreted
- 'Greater jihad' against negative inclinations
- 'Lesser jihad' permits jihad of the sword and the use of force to defend the faith
- Modern radicals are exclusive, aggressive and believe in Islamization

targeted uses of violence. Under Nasser, Sadat and Mubarak's repression, violence became an increasingly important tool for Qutb's Ikhwan with several groups – albeit relatively small – splintering from the Ikhwan to form revolutionary parties, challenging the strong religious prohibition on innocent/civilian casualties and defining their violence as a response to oppression and imperialism. However, it is important to note that today's Brotherhood is a peaceful organization that has long ceased any association with violence.

Islam and revolution?

Particularly since the Iranian revolution, the potential causal link between Islam and revolution has become a hot topic. However, the Iranian revolution does not serve to support this supposition and was not an Islamic revolution, but an uprising by a wide range of forces across Iranian society – including the communist party – in reaction to an authoritarian monarchy which was perceived as being too close to the US, was brutal in its repression of political dissent, and whose modernization project had underestimated the great strain it placed on society. Only afterwards did Islamists gain primacy among other factions. The role of Islam in the revolution was that of a symbol of opposition to an arbitrary modernization, which felt too much like Westernization or the wholesale abdication of a proud millennia-long identity in favour of a narrow materialism, consumerism and abdication to foreign interests. Slogans like Westoxification and Neither East nor West signify the political rather than religious causes of the revolution.

Religious principles, therefore, do not in themselves bring about revolutions. Causes and agents in the Iranian case were multiple. Great differences between rich and poor, political oppression, human rights abuses, an uncomfortable discourse of development, opportunity and democracy were the motors of the revolution – Islam was simply its most visible banner. So much so that the significance of the revolution was felt across historically impervious Sunni–Shi'a and Arab–Persian divides. The Iranian case was a model for Islamists, not for doctrinal reasons, but because for the first time it demonstrated the feasibility of a revolution, and of a culturally authentic political system. It promised the possibility of throwing off the yoke of oppression, and the end of political and cultural imperialism.

Islamist nationalist movements such as Hizballah (Lebanon) and Hamas (Palestine) are further cases in point. For Hizballah and Hamas, independence of a national community is more important than Islamization, the latter being necessary to achieve the former. Ironically, both are reactions to the Israeli presence in south Lebanon and in the occupied territories. Furthermore, Hizballah and Hamas were only able to rise to prominence after earlier secular counterparts – Arab nationalism and the PLO – were perceived to be failing.

FROM ARMED STRUGGLE TO ELECTIONS

It should not, however, be assumed that violence is the singular or dominant translation of Islam into politics. Indeed, there have been several cases of Islamist groups emerging to political prominence, even power, without being violent or particularly radical. Turkey, Jordan, Morocco, and Egypt all provide cases in point. In Jordan and Morocco, Islamists have been co-opted into a political process dominated by an authoritarian monarchy, in Turkey an Islamist party was voted into power, while in Egypt Islamists provide the only credible, mass-based opposition to an authoritarian regime. This trajectory signals a range of connections between Islam and politics beyond the extremist imagery that characterizes most media and political debates.

The emergence of this complex range of Islamist politics is rooted in external political influences in the Middle East, the failure of anti-imperial nationalism and the regional dominant authoritarian regimes. Arab nationalism was severely damaged by defeat in the Six-Day War of 1967, but it was the negotiation of the Camp David Accords following the October War of 1973 which finally broke its back. Subsequently, Islam has increasingly been used to justify government policy, and as a language of opposition and to hold governments accountable for failed promises and corruption. The Six-Day War was not only a military debacle, but also a considerable ideological blow that destabilized the reputation of both Arab nationalism and its most high-profile supporter, Nasser himself. (Nasser resigned over the Six Day War, and, although he was immediately brought back by popular acclaim, died barely two years later.)

Nasser was succeeded by Sadat in the Egyptian presidency and despite low expectations the supposedly innocuous vice-president oversaw a momentous shift in Egyptian politics. Firstly, in order to secure his position against Nasser's single party, the Arab Socialist Union (ASU), Sadat established his Arabist credentials and severed the ASU's Soviet powerbase. Sadat also set about organizing what would become the 1973 October War (or 'Ramadan' or 'Yom Kippur' war), which brought the US and Israel to the negotiating table. Secondly, Sadat needed a domestic counterweight to the ASU's power, which he found in the Muslim Brotherhood.

Sadat outflanked the ASU by allying himself with the USA and by liberalizing domestic politics and economics just enough to provide a political and economic counterweight to the ASU. This tactical choice had far-reaching strategic implications. The Ikhwan leadership had been radicalized by prison, some extreme sections splintering into groups like *Gamaat al-Islamiyya* or *al-Jihad*. The price of Sadat's international realignment was a peace with Israel which left his Arab counterparts badly weakened, and a personal trip to Israeli-occupied Jerusalem and a speech to the Knesset for which he would never be forgiven. Also, economic liberalization (*infitah*) badly hit the poorest sectors of society causing extensive riots. In addition to Sadat's periodic crackdowns on opposition, his political and economic reforms proved his political undoing and it eventually became clear that he could not control the forces that he had unleashed to secure his position. Sadat was assassinated in October 1981.

Sadat's successor, Hosni Mubarak, continued the alternating cycles of liberalization and repression used by his predecessor to manipulate domestic politics. Mubarak also declared a state of emergency that has been continually renewed to this day. Mubarak guaranteed his own presidency by allowing elections to make sure the National Democratic Party (NDP) stayed in power. Mubarak also maintained the ban on the Ikhwan, preventing their participation in electoral politics, and met armed resistance with an iron fist. The Ikhwan, however, engaged in innovative political strategies: they entered into electoral alliance with weakened secular parties that allowed Brothers to run for office. By the late 1990s, armed groups had been eradicated, but political pressure on Mubarak remained. Brotherhood candidates were standing as independent political candidates, and they rapidly became the largest opposition in parliament. Moreover, migrant labour returning from the Gulf brought back more conservative social attitudes, and Brotherhood supporters rose through the ranks of professional associations. The state's continued weakness as a welfare provider contrasted starkly with the array of the Brotherhood's services.

Political Islam: a failure?

This pattern provides important indications regarding developments throughout the Middle East. Since the 1970s, the economic and political crisis of postcolonial development projects stimulated the growth of a diverse political opposition. The oil-related economic slump of the mid-1980s increased pressure on already struggling economies of cash-strapped non-oil-producing states, highlighting both their economic and political difficulties. The 1990s only saw an increase in such pressures as the end of the Cold War undermined the need for limited liberalization to combat Soviet influence, and America's triumph made democratic discourse unassailably central to international politics. The second Gulf War – which breached another Arab nationalist taboo, the invasion of one Arab state (Kuwait) by another (Iraq) – also stoked the embers of anti-Americanism. Such actions served only to weaken Washington's allies' domestic position and provided opposition movements with ammunition to accuse them – with more than some justification – of not only being in Washington and Riyadh's pockets, but of not living up to the democratic standards they publicly proclaimed.

Some have argued that the absence of Islamic revolutions such as Iran's demonstrates the failure of political Islam (Roy, 1994). However, such arguments underestimate the influence exerted – either directly in governments or indirectly in opposition – by popular Islamist movements. Some Islamist parties have been allowed to contest elections and have won the vote democratically (as in Turkey or Palestine). In other cases, governments have tried to pre-empt and hamper Islamist electoral success through a combination of police harassment, legislative obstacles, and superficial pandering to a conservative Islamic agenda (as in Egypt or Algeria).

BOX 16.7 SUMMARY OF POLITICAL ISLAM

A failure?
- Egypt
- Economic difficulties
- Repression
- Failure to accept pluralism
- Rising radical influences

Islam(ism) and democracy

Samuel Huntington's (1993) argument that Islam constitutes a civilization inherently different and more violent than any other is used to explain the supposedly general failure of political Islam and also to explain why the Middle East did not democratize after the end of the Cold War (as did its Eastern European counterparts). This argument, however tempting, ignores the relationship between political oppression and radical politics generally and risks obfuscating the real nature of Islamist politics, or the causes of the emergence of radical ideologies and violent practices. In the Middle East, it is clear that it is the inability and/or unwillingness of local regimes and their international counterparts to accept the consequences of genuine pluralism, and consequent authoritarian practices, that has radicalized the opposition.

In Western debates, questions about the relationship between Islam and violence are virtually symbiotic with doubts about Islam's compatibility with democracy. The argument is often made that while democracy requires secularism, openness and acceptance of non-religious authority, Islam as a religion – and therefore any 'Islamist' politics – demands a theocratic state in which there can be no debate about appropriate social order. It should be clear by now that such arguments are historically and jurisprudentially inaccurate.

Nonetheless, there has been considerable debate about the scope for liberalizing Middle Eastern politics. Ghassan Salamé (1994) suggests that aside from a few notable examples, democratization in the Middle East has been largely cosmetic, with institutions having their democratic potential undermined or curtailed (e.g. skewing electoral law in favour of ruling parties, or rigging the results).

Laura Guazzone (1995) points to an Islamist dilemma: Islamist groups may use the democratic process to win power, only to then use their democratically won political power to cancel elections. However, given the nexus between radicalism, local authoritarianism and external interference, allowing real pluralism may give more moderate voices a chance to meet popular political demands, thus preventing wider socio-political marginalization and radicalization.

Such debates about the relationship between Islam and violence or Islam and democracy are significant not so much for their intellectual depth, but because they illustrate a particularly Western way of thinking about Islam. As Said (1995) and others point out, much Western public discourse about the Orient suggests a Manichean representation of the West as advanced, progressive, democratic, egalitarian, secular, rational, and peaceful, and of the East as backward, stagnant, authoritarian, discriminatory, religiously dogmatic, fanatical and violent. This representation is not supported by the histories of Western or Middle Eastern states, but has enabled policies such as colonialism, or the mandate system, which would have been difficult to justify had non-Western cultures been accorded equal dignity to those of the West.

ISLAMISM IN THEORY AND IN PRACTICE

It is clear that Islamist movements are a primarily political phenomenon and cannot be said to stem from some essence of Islam. The supposedly intrinsic nature of Islam may be a historical myth, but it is a myth that both supporters and opponents use for political purposes. Islam is not Islamism. Moreover, the historical varieties of political Islam clearly demonstrate that a wide range of phenomena fall under this label – within which violent extremism is but a minority position. Islamism is simply a set of political and social movements aiming to return Islam to politics and society. In contemporary political contexts, this translates into demands for changes in the law, changes in political leadership and changes in foreign policy. In social terms, this means demands for more conservative morality and changes in education. However, there is little agreement between different Islamist movements as to the degree or type of Islamization that is necessary or desired.

Moreover, in some countries Islamists have come to power in more or less violent revolutions (Iran, Sudan), while in others they have been allowed to run for election. In Turkey Islamists were able to achieve political power through the democratic process, but in Algeria elections were cancelled by a military coup – plunging the country into an infamously bloody civil war – in order to stop an Islamist political victory. In most Middle Eastern countries mainstream Islamist parties aim to participate in the political process and achieve power – or at least influence policy – peacefully. Some groups, often much smaller splinter organizations, engage in violent tactics, as was evident with some Egyptian and Algerian groups in the 1990s, and Hamas in Palestine or Hizballah in Lebanon today.

What is most important, however, is how Islamist groups have adapted to state pressure by innovating their political tactics. Larger groups with greater popular support have been able to achieve a variety of goals, such as pushing for changes in the law to meet their interpretation of Shari'a. Since the 1980s, these tactics have allowed their influence – whether in power or in opposition – to grow throughout the region.

BOX 16.8 ISLAMIST MOVEMENTS

Islamist movements are primarily political phenomena – but with very varied and different interpretations of Shari'a

In several cases shari'a is acknowledged as one of, or even the principal source of, law. Also, religious courts have been allowed to rule on personal status issues (e.g. marriage/

divorce or inheritance). Moreover, the restrictions on participation in electoral politics have often led Islamist groups on the one hand to promote precisely the democratic and pluralist discourse they are accused of wanting to undermine, and on the other hand to attempt to gain control of various professional associations which act both as access to, and channels of patronage (e.g. lawyers' and judges' guilds, medical associations, etc.). They have also attempted, with various degrees of success, to gain support in the army and bureaucracy.

Perhaps Islamist groups' most important function, however, is as charitable organizations, providing welfare services which states are incapable of supplying. This role, for both principled and pragmatic purposes, has given Islamist groups considerable political weight (e.g. Egypt's Ikhwan) and has provided a vital bedrock of support for those organizations which also have paramilitary wings (e.g. Hamas or Hizballah). Moreover, Middle Eastern states' welfare weakness will always allow opposition to score easy points – and something which economic liberalization tends to increase.

Slogans – such as the Ikhwan's 'Islam is the solution' – are indicative not of some supposed link between the essence of Islam and politics, but of Islam's populist roots. The rhetoric of Islamist politics since the late nineteenth century has emphasized lack of corruption, culturally and religiously authentic values, individual political empowerment, fairer distribution of national income, and resistance to foreign meddling. Despite currently waning popularity, it is important to note that this emphasis precisely mirrors that of nationalist and socialist groups and it is no coincidence that all such movements, despite their ideological differences, set themselves the goal of opposing both domestic authoritarian regimes and international great power interference.

The impact of Islamism as a way of articulating political demands is clear not only from Islamist movements, but also from states' reaction. Several among these, notably Morocco, Jordan and Egypt under Sadat, have attempted to appropriate religious symbolism to legitimize their own rule. Sadat wished to be portrayed as the Believer President, Moroccan and Jordanian kings have used their lineage – which they trace back to the Prophet Muhammad's family – to legitimize their rule, and the Saudis and other ruling Gulf families use combinations of traditional and religious symbols to legitimize their rules.

How important is Islam?

Does Islam set the Middle East apart from other regions? If so, is this difference purely one of degree, or is Islam unique and utterly different? The answers to such questions are vital: answering in the affirmative raises the spectre of Huntington's clash of civilizations between Islam and the West, while a negative answer sweeps away the very foundations upon which such arguments stand.

Islam is seen as more political than other religions. Yet, other religions are also highly political, as even cursory overviews of the history of Buddhism, Hinduism, Christianity, or Judaism show. Moreover, like others, Islam leaves room for interpretation concerning the relationship between religion and politics.

Islam has been used as a vehicle for conferring political legitimacy, and has been made to serve authoritarianism, monarchy and democracy. As such, Islam is in no way dissimilar to its counterparts, as clearly in most countries – Western as well as non-Western – religion plays an important and influential role. Not all Western states have a strict separation of Church and politics (UK, Japan), and even in those that do – such as Spain, Germany, France or Italy – Christianity, its churches, and the parties which subscribe to their values play a considerable role in society. Additionally, it is worth considering that most US Presidents have been active Christians and Israel is an explicitly Jewish state.

Given the connection between authoritarianism and radical politics, it seems more plausible to explain the manifestation of extremism in relation to local authoritarian contexts. Moreover, while media images conjured by violent extremism may paint a very specific picture of Islam, most Muslims and most Islamist politics remain non-violent and desirous of more, not less, democracy.

CONCLUSION: IS ISLAM THE SOLUTION?

First, there is the connection between Islam and politics: Islamism must be understood as a thoroughly modern phenomenon utilizing mass appeal, organization, and tactics as political tools. Second, the full diversity of Islam's doctrinal positions and political practices should be acknowledged. Third, Islamist political roots as a manifestation of frustrated ideals, authoritarian governments and international interference should be recognized.

Post-9/11 politics often falls victim to the idea of Islam as an inescapably radical and violent political force. However, the history of the development of Islamism reveals a very different picture – that of a set of ideological positions and political practices that are directly respondent to contemporary issues such as corruption or foreign interference. Indeed, the radicalization of these religious political ideologies is intertwined with a history of oppressive domestic regimes and of global intervention. In this sense, the similarities between the political origins and trajectories of these movements and their nationalist counterparts are more significant than their differences.

Moreover, as Halliday (2003) and Esposito (1999) demonstrate, the idea that Muslim societies – let alone Islam *per se* – must necessarily have a confrontational relationship with other cultures is a myth. Indeed, notions of a Green Peril date back at least to the late 1970s, particularly to the aftermath of the Iranian revolution, and were then revived in the early 1990s purportedly as a response to the search for a new enemy after the end of the Cold War. The idea that Islam *per se* presents a threat is therefore not only historically wrong, but also far from new: the heat generated by the tragic events of 9/11 is but the latest version of this idea. The fact remains that violent Islamists are a small fringe and that the wider anti-Western centre of gravity in Middle Eastern politics has nothing to do with religion, and everything to do with the corrupt and socially ineffective regimes which are eager to receive Western support in the name of democracy but all too reticent to translate it into practice.

BOX 16.9 THE MYTH OF ISLAM

The idea that Muslim societies must necessarily have a confrontational relationship with other cultures, societies or systems is a myth

The real challenge, therefore, is to deal with the underlying issues of political representation, accountability, and social welfare which give rise to Islamist movements. The political fact of the matter is that Islamism remains the most potent opposition to authoritarian regimes and cannot be eradicated. The presence of Islamists in power in Turkey also debunks the myth that Islam is necessarily anti-democratic, or even anti-Western. In this context, external and internal policies can help bring such groups into the political fold, or radicalize them. Consequently, it is also important to examine the measures taken under the aegis of the so-called War on Terror and whether such measures are the most effective way of tackling Islamist movements, particularly those which are not radical, or violent.

This chapter has covered considerable territory, necessarily ignoring much that falls under the rubric of 'Islam and Politics'. There has been no in-depth discussion of 9/11 and its aftermath, and little attention to important phenomena such as the relationship between Muslim immigrants and their European host societies, their impact on the debate on asylum and on immigration, or the development of a European Islam.

Perhaps most important is an implicit over-simplification which runs throughout this chapter. Muslims, in their engagement with politics, are essentially represented as either middle-of-the-road democrats, secular and absorbed into mainstream Western societies, or as radical and possibly violent extremists, probably bearded and dressed in *galabiyyas*. This is a gross over-simplification at best, but one which is unfortunately common to much supposedly expert opinion. The reality is that Muslims' understanding of the relationship between their religious beliefs and their political engagements is as highly diverse as anyone else's. One needs just to look on the Internet to get a taste of this diversity: consider Middle Eastern rap artists whose YouTube videos incite the destruction of Israel; or the thoroughly non-political Western-style Urdu pop videos of second- and third-generation European Muslims from the Indian subcontinent; European and North American Muslims who use punk, metal and experimental electronica to express their uncompromising positions on Palestine, or who find no contradiction between being a radical bra-burning feminist and a committed Muslim. Similar ranges of expression can be found in other e-contexts such as MySpace or Facebook, or indeed the Middle Eastern bloggers who have become central to the new media in the region. In all these contexts, geographically, culturally and politically hybrid expressions of what it means to be Muslim continuously find new expressions, and are all equally valid ways of articulating the relationship between Islam and Politics in precisely the same way that one finds similar expressions of the relationship between other religions and politics.

This diversity of Muslims' contemporary politics is at least as important as the historical, theological and jurisprudential diversity of the movements outlined above. In conclusion, the key to understanding political Islam is not that it is Muslim, but that it is political.

▮ FURTHER READING

Abdel-Malek, A. (ed.) (1983) *Contemporary Arab Political Thought*, London: Zed Press.
Ahmad, A. (1984) *Islam in the Era of Postmodernity*, London: Palgrave Macmillan.
Ayubi, N, N. (1997) *Political Islam*, London: Routledge.
Beinin, J. and Stork, J. (eds) (1997) *Political Islam: Essays from Middle East Report*, Berkeley: University of California Press.
Choueiri, Y. (1990) *Islamic Fundamentalism*, London: Continuum.
Eickelman, D. and Piscatori, J. (1996) *Muslim Politics*, Princeton: Princeton University Press.
Esposito, J.L. (1999) *Islamic Threat: Myth or Reality?*, New York: Oxford University Press.
Esposito, J.L. and Voll, J. (1996) *Islam and Democracy*, Oxford: Oxford University Press.
Guazzone, L. (ed.) (1995) *The Islamist Dilemma: The Political Role of Islamist Movements in the Contemporary Arab World*, Reading: Ithaca Press.
Halliday, F. (2003) *Islam and the Myth of Confrontation*, London: I.B. Tauris.
Hourani, A. (1983) *Arabic Thought in the Liberal Age*, Cambridge: Cambridge University Press.
Hourani, A., Khoury, P. and Wilson, M. (eds) (1993) *The Modern Middle East*, Berkeley: University of California Press.
Huntington, S.P. (1993) 'The Clash of Civilizations?', *Foreign Affairs*, 71: 222–49.
Roy, O. (1994) *The Failure of Political Islam*, London: I.B. Tauris.
Sadowski, Y. (1997) 'The New Orientalism and the Democracy Debate', in J. Benin and J. Stork (eds), *Political Islam: Essays from Middle East Report*, London: I.B. Tauris.
Said, E. [1978] (1995) *Orientalism: Western Conceptions of the Orient*, London: Penguin.
Said, E. (1997) *Covering Islam: How the Media and the Experts Determine How We See the Rest of the World*, London: Vintage.
Salamé, G. (ed.) (1994) *Democracy without Democrats?*, London: I.B. Tauris.
Salvatore, A. (1999) *Islam and the Political Discourse of Modernity*, Ithaca, NY: Ithaca Press.

CHAPTER 17

Conclusions
Mark F. Imber

It is hoped that this account has served to introduce the keen student to the complexity and variety of issues that are fundamental to the discipline of international relations. The first-year university student encounters three particular obstacles to engaging with and progressing in international relations. First, the subject is not generally taught at secondary or high-school level, although elements may appear in the A-level and S-level modern studies. Second, neither is the parent discipline of politics widely encountered in the school curriculum; and many students already trained in history, geography, economics or philosophy are sometimes inclined to view IR as a branch of one of these disciplines. Third, as a branch of politics, international relations is characterized by deep divisions of approaches, broadly similar to those that characterize all political debates: the conservative view which favours arguments that support an enduring status quo, the liberal position which favours reform within some framework of rules, and the revolutionary approach which seeks to overthrow and change the basis of any given political system. Students often find that after overcoming the first two obstacles to working out what the IR question actually is, there are usually at least three answers to that question.

This text is designed to encourage questions and does not presume to impose any of the many possible answers and for this reason the first section of this book expressly addresses definitions, IR theory and fundamental questions of sovereignty, states and nations. The role of theory is to provide the tools with which to understand and explain the workings of the international political system. Students still reluctant to engage with theory need to consider how else so-called common sense is acquired and how vulnerable their studies remain if they rely on web-masters, editors and the media moguls' selection of daily headlines to determine their choice of issues and the means to analyse them. No one is born with an innate capacity to ask intelligent questions about international relations – it is an acquired skill. The well-read theorist is better able to choose and select the awkward issues and awkward questions, which advance humane learning most effectively.

The study of international relations is neither a simple nor an innocent profession and the complexity and breadth of the field has been revealed in the issues selected for this volume. A student concluding their first year of study should have become aware that international relations is similar to all humane discourse in that it represents a dialogue between optimism and pessimism concerning the human condition and human potential. The evidence for pessimism is very rapidly identified. The evidence for optimism has always been harder to assemble. The two twentieth-century world wars were the most destructive in the course of human history in terms of battle-deaths, the bombing of cities, genocide and the first use of nuclear weapons. Additionally, twentieth-century warfare deliberately involved and targeted civilians in total warfare. Despite a current fall in the numbers of wars between states, the threat to international peace and security is much more frequent in the form of civil wars and transnational forms of violence such as terrorism.

On several occasions in the twentieth century progressive opinion believed that the rational case for war had been replaced by the rational case for peace. One of the best-selling texts on the subject published in 1912, Norman Angell's *The Great Illusion*, argued that the European nations were so reliant on open communication and trade between them that no reasonable ground for war existed. As late as 1933 the devout optimist Leonard Woolf was able to commission and to publish a collection of essays, *The Intelligent Man's Way to Prevent War*. Alas, there has not yet proven to be any such intelligent means of prevention.

It is no accident that the formal creation of international relations in 1919 was driven by the experience of the First World War, and that the maintenance of international peace and stability has remained at the core of the subject since then. As a branch of political inquiry, conflict of interests between different actors is fundamental to the study and practice of international relations. Sovereignty, state and nation have continued to survive and indeed thrive in our post-Cold War world and now, as in 1919 and in 1945, predictions of the end of war as an instrument of politics have proven premature.

The chapters in this volume concerning power, force and security, intervention and terrorism have provided ample justification and illustration of the security dilemma in which all sovereign states exist. International relations are predicated on the absence of any rule-making authority superior to each of the 192 states that comprise the international system: in short, sovereignty creates a system in which states being free are also alone, and at the last resort responsible for their own security. All states are capable of using violence, although on every possible statistical measure very few states actually practise the use of force in the twenty-first century. The advocates of democratic peace theories, widespread economic interdependence and globalization, universal human rights and cosmopolitan compassion all attest to the inherent limitations on the use of force as an instrument.

So it is perhaps surprising, especially for UK students who read this text, that between 1997 and 2003 the British government took the decision to deploy force as an instrument of policy on four separate occasions. First, the UK deployed troops to Sierra Leone in support of the legal government, and second, against Serbia in Kosovo in concert with other NATO powers. Third, the UK deployed to Afghanistan under a UN mandate, and fourth, UK troops were deployed without UN endorsement in Iraq. For a state such as the UK (considered to be an open, modern, democratic, middle ranking power) to four times practise use of force demonstrates that the question of if and when to use force is never far away, and whether or not we approve of these actions, the democratic system means that all such decisions are made in the name of the populations that they seek to serve. The vocabulary of contemporary conflict seeks to both justify and ameliorate the use of force as intervention, enforcement, or even as humanitarian intervention. Indeed, the revival of the Just War debate has been one of the most fundamental debates in post-1989 international relations. As has been shown, decisions on intervention are far more complex than a moral debate over 'right' or 'wrong'. Intervention nearly always has unintended and unforeseen effects and nearly always involves a commitment of longer duration than that originally foreseen. The decision to intervene is frankly comparatively easy compared to the decision when to withdraw. Every government since 1914 has hoped the 'boys will be home before Christmas'. Neither they, nor the girls that now fight alongside them in Afghanistan or Iraq, or who keep the peace in Kosovo, many of them the same age as most readers of this book, now expect to be home any time soon.

Other long-term, hard security issues confront electorates with decisions that have consequences over prolonged periods. As a student-citizen it is hoped that you are better placed to consider such issues as whether or not to renew the Trident nuclear weapons force, or whether the UK should commission two new aircraft carriers to replace existing capacity. Trident is a weapons systems whose very existence is predicated on a deterrence theory and the sincerest desire to never use it. Every government, Labour and Conservative since 1951, has nonetheless opted to renew rather than abandon the nuclear weapons option, when faced with each system's obsolescence, however attenuated the case for its use might appear. The carrier question signals the British desire to maintain air-power capacity on the global stage. Presumably this is operationally essential to maintain the option of humanitarian intervention in remote locations, however selective and often criticized such initiatives might be. Those of a pacifist persuasion that would argue the threat or use of force is never justified might consider that in its turn neutrality is never neutral in its effects. Conventional wisdom still attributes a great moral burden to those who advocated non-intervention against the rise of German and Italian expansionism after 1934. The point for the student to consider is that arguments over the utility and legality of the use and non-use of force remain crucial to the discipline, and the consequences of any such decision will continue to be felt for years to come.

However, international relations also thrives on the creation of rules between states in the dense network of cooperative behaviour that is also a characteristic of the international political system. The optimistic and creative project to explain and understand the means to control the threat and use of force provides the optimistic counter to what remains for the most part a branch of human inquiry dominated by a pessimistic view of human potential.

The third section of the text has sought to emphasize and to explain this potential for cooperation. The role of international regimes and organizations, the promotion of environmental sustainability, the governance of the global commons, the enlargement of global trade, and the creative and constructive use of peacekeeping to limit violence and assist re-construction in post-conflict situations all serve to illustrate the capacity of the international system to act beyond the limits of the security dilemma. This text has also considered the role of two great social movements; gender and the role of religion.

Central to all of these issues is the expansion of multilateral diplomacy and its effects on trade, aid, human rights protection and the environment. Almost continuous rounds of truly global diplomacy, conducted in organizations such as the WTO, the UN, and WHO are a permanent feature of international relations. These global agencies and negotiations were previously conducted under the banner of Cold War politics wherein liberals were pitched against neo-Marxist analyses. The Cold War era divisions of the UN system have been superseded since 1990, but questions about mass poverty, debt, the role of women, the vulnerability of children, and the revival of world religions have created a plural field of ideas in which simple notions of secular modernization and the ubiquitous end-of-history (the liberal end-state if you like), are facing renewed challenges.

On a regional scale, the emergence of wider and deeper attempts to construct regional organizations, such as the EU, NAFTA, ASEAN and the African Union each represent the emergence of new agendas and attitudes to solving them that emphasize legality, reciprocal advantage, and the irrelevance of the threat or use of force to resolve the issue under discussion.

This trend in post-Cold War international relations has been greatly assisted by the accompanying transformations of democratization and the social and technical dimensions of globalization. The wave of democratization has converted dictatorships and one-party-state rule which were previously dominant across Latin America, Eastern and Central Europe, Africa and South and East Asia, into a numerical majority of states. In 2006, according to the American NGO, Freedom House, elected governments represented 126 of the 192 states that comprise the UN membership: 90 states were classified as 'free' comprising 43 per cent of world population, and 58 governments ranked as 'partly-free' comprising 30 per cent of the world population.

Not only does democratization create powerful incentives for governments to negotiate for change on issues such as trade, aid, human rights, women and children's status, environmental protection and plight of the commons, this same democratization has sustained the rise of the non-governmental organizations, many funded by the subscriptions of millions of individuals by the click of a mouse across borders and continents. In these ways the formerly rigid demarcation between governments and citizens, domestic and international, local and global, is further eroded.

This twenty-first-century version of Enlightenment idealism is not universally welcomed. In China, in many Arab and Central Asian countries and the remaining dictatorships of Africa, democratization, understood as free and fair elections contested between freely organized parties, is not tolerated. Nor is the NGO culture of highly publicized scrutiny and the promotion of human rights and environmental standards welcomed. These governments, which simultaneously crave the economic gains of globalization, whilst they try to control its technology and social implications, will struggle to overcome the contradiction in their position. A fundamental future issue for international relations is whether large, increasingly powerful regional states such as China, can choose selectivity from the menu of both globalization and democratization. The so-called 'great fire-wall of China', and the constraints under which Internet service providers operate in that country, is a good illustration of this dilemma. The extraordinary mobile-phone and blog-derived accounts of the Burmese government's suppression of democracy protests in September 2007, show how the new technologies can provide the oxygen of publicity to democrats.

An introductory textbook must equip the student to continue to ask the most insightful questions as your study of IR deepens and becomes more specialized in later years. That specialization typically proceeds along two empirical lines of inquiry. Some degree programmes, staff and students continue to emphasize the global level of analysis whilst others develop their insight and knowledge of particular regions and indeed some single-country's conduct of their international relations. The distinctions are not watertight. In an age of near uni-polarity and continuing US domination of the diplomatic field, how can any student of IR avoid making the study of US foreign policy some part of their studies? A second way to continue your studies involves a greater or lesser concentration upon what have been termed the hard-security or soft-security issues. Politics, and therefore international relations, rest upon a complex mixture of cooperative and conflicting interests in the resolution of great public issues. Even those issues as far removed from the relevance of military force as can be imagined – say negotiations on climate change – can be held hostage to the 'irruptions from below'. For example incidents such as 9/11 diverted and changed US attitudes to the UN, to allies, to friends and neutrals. Budget priorities and federal spending patterns changed. The 'war on terror' has profoundly affected the negotiation of numerous other issues. The maintenance of international peace and security remains the utmost challenge, but also presents the greatest opportunity to enrich the lives of all the world's peoples.

Appendix I

Human Development Index

The Human Development Index (HDI) is a summary measure of human development published by the United Nations Development Programme (UNDP). The HDI provides an alternative to the common practice of evaluating a state's progress in development based on per capita Gross Domestic Product (GDP). The HDI is the signature trademark of the Human Development Report (HDR), an independent report commissioned by the UNDP. The HDI measures the average achievements in a country in three basic dimensions of human development:

- A long and healthy life, as measured by life expectancy at birth.
- Knowledge, as measured by the adult literacy rate (with two-thirds weight) and the combined primary, secondary and tertiary gross enrollment ratio (with one-third weight).
- A decent standard of living, as measured by GDP per capita in purchasing power parity (PPP) terms in US dollars.

Before the HDI itself is calculated, an index is created for each of these dimensions. To calculate these indices – the life expectancy, education and GDP indices – minimum and maximum values (goalposts) are chosen for each underlying indicator. For example, in 2004 the maximum and minimum values for life expectancy were 85 and 25 years, respectively. Performance in each dimension is expressed as a value between 0 and 1. The HDI is then calculated as a simple average of the dimension indices:

HDI = 1/3 (life expectancy index) + 1/3 (education index) + 1/3 (GDP index)

The Appendix I table shows the HDI value for 2004. A higher value indicates a higher level of development as indicated by the HDI.

HDI rank	Country	2004	HDI rank	Country	2004
1	Norway	0.965	8	United States	0.948
2	Iceland	0.960	9	Switzerland	0.947
3	Australia	0.957	10	Netherlands	0.947
4	Ireland	0.956	11	Finland	0.947
5	Sweden	0.951	12	Luxembourg	0.945
6	Canada	0.950	13	Belgium	0.945
7	Japan	0.949	14	Austria	0.944

HDI rank	Country	2004	HDI rank	Country	2004
15	Denmark	0.943	62	Bosnia and Herzegovina	0.800
16	France	0.942	63	Mauritius	0.800
17	Italy	0.940	64	Libyan Arab Jamahiriya	0.798
18	United Kingdom	0.940	65	Russian Federation	0.797
19	Spain	0.938	66	Macedonia, TFYR	0.796
20	New Zealand	0.936	67	Belarus	0.794
21	Germany	0.932	68	Dominica	0.793
22	Hong Kong, China (SAR)	0.927	69	Brazil	0.792
23	Israel	0.927	70	Colombia	0.790
24	Greece	0.921	71	Saint Lucia	0.790
25	Singapore	0.916	72	Venezuela, RB	0.784
26	Korea, Rep. of	0.912	73	Albania	0.784
27	Slovenia	0.910	74	Thailand	0.784
28	Portugal	0.904	75	Samoa (Western)	0.778
29	Cyprus	0.903	76	Saudi Arabia	0.777
30	Czech Republic	0.885	77	Ukraine	0.774
31	Barbados	0.879	78	Lebanon	0.774
32	Malta	0.875	79	Kazakhstan	0.774
33	Kuwait	0.871	80	Armenia	0.768
34	Brunei Darussalam	0.871	81	China	0.768
35	Hungary	0.869	82	Peru	0.767
36	Argentina	0.863	83	Ecuador	0.765
37	Poland	0.862	84	Philippines	0.763
38	Chile	0.859	85	Grenada	0.762
39	Bahrain	0.859	86	Jordan	0.760
40	Estonia	0.858	87	Tunisia	0.760
41	Lithuania	0.857	88	Saint Vincent and the Grenadines	0.759
42	Slovakia	0.856			
43	Uruguay	0.851	89	Suriname	0.759
44	Croatia	0.846	90	Fiji	0.758
45	Latvia	0.845	91	Paraguay	0.757
46	Qatar	0.844	92	Turkey	0.757
47	Seychelles	0.842	93	Sri Lanka	0.755
48	Costa Rica	0.841	94	Dominican Republic	0.751
49	United Arab Emirates	0.839	95	Belize	0.751
50	Cuba	0.826	96	Iran, Islamic Rep. of	0.746
51	Saint Kitts and Nevis	0.825	97	Georgia	0.743
52	Bahamas	0.825	98	Maldives	0.739
53	Mexico	0.821	99	Azerbaijan	0.736
54	Bulgaria	0.816	100	Occupied Palestinian Territories	0.736
55	Tonga	0.815			
56	Oman	0.810	101	El Salvador	0.729
57	Trinidad and Tobago	0.809	102	Algeria	0.728
58	Panama	0.809	103	Guyana	0.725
59	Antigua and Barbuda	0.808	104	Jamaica	0.724
60	Romania	0.805	105	Turkmenistan	0.724
61	Malaysia	0.805	106	Cape Verde	0.722

HDI rank	Country	2004	HDI rank	Country	2004
107	Syrian Arab Republic	0.716	143	Madagascar	0.509
108	Indonesia	0.711	144	Cameroon	0.506
109	Viet Nam	0.709	145	Uganda	0.502
110	Kyrgyzstan	0.705	146	Swaziland	0.500
111	Egypt	0.702	147	Togo	0.495
112	Nicaragua	0.698	148	Djibouti	0.494
113	Uzbekistan	0.696	149	Lesotho	0.494
114	Moldova, Rep. of	0.694	150	Yemen	0.492
115	Bolivia	0.692	151	Zimbabwe	0.491
116	Mongolia	0.691	152	Kenya	0.491
117	Honduras	0.683	153	Mauritania	0.486
118	Guatemala	0.673	154	Haiti	0.482
119	Vanuatu	0.670	155	Gambia	0.479
120	Equatorial Guinea	0.653	156	Senegal	0.460
121	South Africa	0.653	157	Eritrea	0.454
122	Tajikistan	0.652	158	Rwanda	0.450
123	Morocco	0.640	159	Nigeria	0.448
124	Gabon	0.633	160	Guinea	0.445
125	Namibia	0.626	161	Angola	0.439
126	India	0.611	162	Tanzania, U. Rep. of	0.430
127	São Tomé and Principe	0.607	163	Benin	0.428
128	Solomon Islands	0.592	164	Côte d'Ivoire	0.421
129	Cambodia	0.583	165	Zambia	0.407
130	Myanmar	0.581	166	Malawi	0.400
131	Botswana	0.570	167	Congo, Dem. Rep. of the	0.391
132	Comoros	0.556			
133	Lao People's Dem. Rep.	0.553	168	Mozambique	0.390
134	Pakistan	0.539	169	Burundi	0.384
135	Bhutan	0.538	170	Ethiopia	0.371
136	Ghana	0.532	171	Chad	0.368
137	Bangladesh	0.530	172	Central African Republic	0.353
138	Nepal	0.527	173	Guinea-Bissau	0.349
139	Papua New Guinea	0.523	174	Burkina Faso	0.342
140	Congo	0.520	175	Mali	0.338
141	Sudan	0.516	176	Sierra Leone	0.335
142	Timor-Leste	0.512	177	Niger	0.311

Source: United Nations Development Programme: Human Development Report, http://hdr.undp.org/en/statistics/

Appendix II

World military expenditure: percentage of Gross National Product, 2005–6

Rank	Country	Military expend-itures (% of GDP)	Rank	Country	Military expend-itures (% of GDP)
1	Oman	11.40	29	Tajikistan	3.90
2	Qatar	10.00	30	China	3.80
3	Saudi Arabia	10.00	31	Zimbabwe	3.80
4	Iraq	8.60	32	Cuba	3.80
5	Jordan	8.60	33	Djibouti	3.80
6	Israel	7.30	34	Cyprus	3.80
7	Yemen	6.60	35	Namibia	3.70
8	Armenia	6.50	36	Colombia	3.40
9	Eritrea	6.30	37	Gabon	3.40
10	Macedonia	6.00	38	Turkmenistan	3.40
11	Burundi	5.90	39	Egypt	3.40
12	Syria	5.90	40	Algeria	3.30
13	Angola	5.70	41	Botswana	3.30
14	Mauritania	5.50	42	Pakistan	3.20
15	Maldives	5.50	43	United Arab Emirates	3.10
16	Kuwait	5.30	44	Guinea-Bissau	3.10
17	Turkey	5.30	45	Lebanon	3.10
18	El Salvador	5.00	46	Congo, Republic of the	3.10
19	Morocco	5.00	47	Solomon Islands	3.00
20	Singapore	4.90	48	Cambodia	3.00
21	Swaziland	4.70	49	Ethiopia	3.00
22	Bahrain	4.50	50	Indonesia	3.00
23	Bosnia and Herzegovina	4.50	51	Sudan	3.00
			52	Rwanda	2.90
24	Brunei	4.50	53	Comoros	2.80
25	Greece	4.30	54	Ecuador	2.80
26	Chad	4.20	55	Kenya	2.80
27	United States	4.06	56	Chile	2.70
28	Libya	3.90	57	Korea, South	2.70

Rank	Country	Military expenditures (% of GDP)	Rank	Country	Military expenditures (% of GDP)
58	Azerbaijan	2.60	101	Cote d'Ivoire	1.60
59	Lesotho	2.60	102	Uruguay	1.60
60	France	2.60	103	Togo	1.60
61	Brazil	2.60	104	Nepal	1.60
62	Sri Lanka	2.60	105	Netherlands	1.60
63	Bulgaria	2.60	106	Bangladesh	1.50
64	Congo, Democratic Republic of the	2.50	107	Denmark	1.50
			108	Sweden	1.50
65	India	2.50	109	Nigeria	1.50
66	Iran	2.50	110	Germany	1.50
67	Vietnam	2.50	111	Peru	1.50
68	Romania	2.47	112	Albania	1.49
69	Australia	2.40	113	Belize	1.40
70	United Kingdom	2.40	114	Belarus	1.40
71	Croatia	2.39	115	Kyrgyzstan	1.40
72	Portugal	2.30	116	Senegal	1.40
73	Sierra Leone	2.30	117	Ukraine	1.40
74	Fiji	2.20	118	Tunisia	1.40
75	Uganda	2.20	119	Papua New Guinea	1.40
76	Taiwan	2.20	120	Mongolia	1.40
77	Burma	2.10	121	Argentina	1.30
78	Malaysia	2.03	122	Cameroon	1.30
79	Estonia	2.00	123	Niger	1.30
80	World	2.00	124	Malawi	1.30
81	Seychelles	2.00	125	Liberia	1.30
82	Uzbekistan	2.00	126	Belgium	1.30
83	Finland	2.00	127	Latvia	1.20
84	Afghanistan	1.90	128	Venezuela	1.20
85	Norway	1.90	129	Burkina Faso	1.20
86	Mali	1.90	130	Spain	1.20
87	Lithuania	1.90	131	Canada	1.10
88	Bolivia	1.90	132	Central African Republic	1.10
89	Slovakia	1.87			
90	Czech Republic	1.81	133	Bhutan	1.00
91	Guyana	1.80	134	Madagascar	1.00
92	Thailand	1.80	135	Switzerland	1.00
93	Zambia	1.80	136	Panama	1.00
94	Italy	1.80	137	Paraguay	1.00
95	Hungary	1.75	138	New Zealand	1.00
96	Poland	1.71	139	Austria	0.90
97	Benin	1.70	140	Kazakhstan	0.90
98	Slovenia	1.70	141	Luxembourg	0.90
99	Guinea	1.70	142	Tonga	0.90
100	South Africa	1.70	143	Somalia	0.90

Rank	Country	Military expenditures (% of GDP)	Rank	Country	Military expenditures (% of GDP)
144	Philippines	0.90	159	Gambia, The	0.50
145	Ireland	0.90	160	Bahamas, The	0.50
146	Dominican Republic	0.80	161	Mexico	0.50
147	São Tomé and Principe	0.80	162	Laos	0.50
148	Japan	0.80	163	Costa Rica	0.40
149	Mozambique	0.80	164	Guatemala	0.40
150	Ghana	0.80	165	Moldova	0.40
151	Cape Verde	0.70	166	Haiti	0.40
152	Malta	0.70	167	Mauritius	0.30
153	Honduras	0.60	168	Trinidad and Tobago	0.30
154	Nicaragua	0.60	169	Tanzania	0.20
155	Suriname	0.60	170	Bermuda	0.11
156	Jamaica	0.60	171	Equatorial Guinea	0.10
157	Georgia	0.59	172	Iceland	0.00
158	Barbados	0.50			

Source: *Central Intelligence Agency: The World Factbook: Rank Order, Military Expenditure, Percent of GDP*, http://www.cia.gov/library/publications/the-world-factbook/rankorder/2043rank.html
Note: This page was last updated on 19 July 2007.

Appendix III

States in European organizations, 2007

States	Council of Europe[1]	OECD[3]	NATO[4]	OSCE[5]	European Union[6]
Albania	✓ 13.07.1995		PfP 23.02.94	✓ 19.06.1991	
Andorra	✓ 10.11.1994			✓ 25.04.1996	
Armenia	✓ 25.01.2001		PfP 05.10.94	✓ 30.01.1992	
Austria	✓ 16.04.1956	✓ 1961	PfP 10.02.95	✓ 25.06.1973	✓ 01.01.1995
Azerbaijan	✓ 25.01.2001		PfP 04.05.94	✓ 30.01.1992	
Belarus			PfP 11.01.95	✓ 30.01.1992	
Belgium	✓ 05.05.1949	✓ 1961	✓ 04.04.1949	✓ 25.06.1973	✓ 23.07.1952
Bosnia and Herzegovina	✓ 24.04.2002		PfP 14.12.06	✓ 30.04.1992	
Bulgaria	✓ 07.05.1992		✓ 29.03.2004	✓ 25.06.1973	✓ 01.01.2007
Canada		✓ 1961	✓ 04.04.1949	✓ 25.06.1973	
Croatia	✓ 06.11.1996		PfP 25.05.00	✓ 24.03.1992	
Cyprus	✓ 24.05.1961			✓ 25.06.1973	✓ 01.05.2004
Czech Republic	✓ 30.06.1993	✓ 1995	✓ 12.03.1999	✓ 01.01.1993	✓ 01.05.2004
Denmark	✓ 05.05.1949	✓ 1961	✓ 04.04.1949	✓ 25.06.1973	✓ 01.01.1973
Estonia	✓ 14.05.1993		✓ 29.03.2004	✓ 10.09.1991	✓ 01.05.2004
Finland	✓ 05.05.1989	✓ 1969	PfP 09.05.94	✓ 25.06.1973	✓ 01.01.1995
France	✓ 05.05.1949	✓ 1961	✓ 04.04.1949	✓ 25.06.1973	✓ 23.07.1952
Georgia	✓ 27.04.1999		PfP 23.03.94	✓ 24.03.1992	
Germany	✓ 13.07.1950	✓ 1961	✓ 09.05.1955	✓ 25.06.1973	✓ 23.07.1952
Greece	✓ 09.08.1950	✓ 1961	✓ 18.02.1952	✓ 25.06.1973	✓ 01.01.1981
Holy See				✓ 25.06.1973	
Hungary	✓ 06.11.1990	✓ 1996	✓ 12.03.1999	✓ 25.06.1973	✓ 01.05.2004
Iceland	✓ 07.03.1950	✓ 1961	✓ 04.04.1949	✓ 25.06.1973	
Ireland	✓ 05.05.1949	✓ 1961	PfP 01.12.99	✓ 25.06.1973	✓ 01.01.1973
Italy	✓ 05.05.1949	✓ 1961	✓ 04.04.1949	✓ 25.06.1973	✓ 23.07.1952
Kazakhstan			PfP 27.05.94	✓ 30.01.1992	
Kyrgyzstan			PfP 01.06.94	✓ 30.01.1992	
Latvia	✓ 10.02.1995		✓ 29.03.2004	✓ 10.09.1991	✓ 01.05.2004
Liechtenstein	✓ 23.11.1978			✓ 25.06.1973	
Lithuania	✓ 14.05.1993		✓ 29.03.2004	✓ 10.09.1991	✓ 01.05.2004
Luxembourg	✓ 05.05.1949	✓ 1961	✓ 04.04.1949	✓ 25.06.1973	✓ 23.07.1952
The former Yugoslav Republic of Macedonia	✓ 09.11.1995		PfP 15.11.95	✓ 12.10.1995	
Malta	✓ 29.04.1965			✓ 25.06.1973	
Moldova	✓ 13.07.1995		PfP 16.03.94	✓ 30.01.1992	
Monaco	✓ 05.10.2004			✓ 25.06.1973	

Montenegro	✓ 11.05.2007		PfP 14.12.06	✓ 22.06.2006	
Netherlands	✓ 05.05.1949	✓ 1961	✓ 04.04.1949	✓ 25.06.1973	✓ 23.07.1952
Norway	✓ 05.05.1949	✓ 1961	✓ 04.04.1949	✓ 25.06.1973	
Poland	✓ 26.11.1991	✓ 1996	✓ 12.03.1999	✓ 25.06.1973	✓ 01.05.2004
Portugal	✓ 22.09.1976	✓ 1961	✓ 04.04.1949	✓ 25.06.1973	✓ 01.01.1986
Romania	✓ 07.10.1993		✓ 29.03.2004	✓ 25.06.1973	✓ 01.01.2007
Russian Federation	✓ 28.02.1996		PfP 22.06.94	✓ 25.06.1973	
San Marino	✓ 16.11.1988			✓ 25.06.1973	
Serbia	✓ 03.04.2003[2]		PfP 14.12.06	✓ 10.11.2000	
Slovak Republic	✓ 30.06.1993	✓ 2000	✓ 29.03.2004	✓ 01.01.1993	✓ 01.05.2004
Slovenia	✓ 14.05.1993		✓ 29.03.2004	✓ 24.03.1992	✓ 01.05.2004
Spain	✓ 24.11.1977	✓ 1961	✓ 30.05.1982	✓ 25.06.1973	✓ 01.01.1986
Sweden	✓ 05.05.1949	✓ 1961	PfP 09.05.94	✓ 25.06.1973	✓ 01.01.1995
Switzerland	✓ 06.05.1963	✓ 1961	PfP 11.12.96	✓ 25.06.1973	
Tajikstan			PfP 20.02.02	✓ 30.01.1992	
Turkey	✓ 09.08.1949	✓ 1961	✓ 18.02.1952	✓ 25.06.1973	
Turkmenistan			PfP 10.05.94	✓ 30.01.1992	
Ukraine	✓ 09.11.1995		PfP 08.02.94	✓ 30.01.1992	
United Kingdom	✓ 05.05.1949	✓ 1961	✓ 04.04.1949	✓ 25.06.1973	✓ 01.01.1973
United States of America		✓ 1961	✓ 04.04.1949	✓ 25.06.1973	
Uzbekistan			PfP 13.07.94	✓ 30.01.1992	

Notes

✓ = membership and date of entry.

1, 2 With effect from 3 June 2006, the Republic of Serbia is continuing the membership of the Council of Europe previously exercised by the Union of States of Serbia and Montenegro. Candidate for membership: Belarus. Observers to the Committee of Ministers: Canada, Holy See, Japan, Mexico, United States of America.

3 Australia (1971), Japan (1964), Korea (1996), Mexico (1994) and New Zealand (1973) are also members.

4 PfP = Partnership for Peace: Signatures of Partnership for Peace Framework Document.

5 Pre-1995 the CSCE. OSCE – Mediterranean Partners for Cooperation: Algeria, Egypt, Israel, Jordan, Morocco, Tunisia. OSCE – Asian Partners for Cooperation: Japan, Republic of Korea, Thailand, Afghanistan, Mongolia.

6 Dates also apply to pre-European Union Communities. Treaty of Paris signed on 18 March 1951 and into force 23 July 1952. Treaty (ies) of Rome signed on 23 March 1957 and into force 1 January 1958. Treaty of Maastricht signed on 7 Febuary 1992 and into force 1 November 1993. Official candidates for admission: Croatia (2004), FRYOM (2005) and Turkey (1999). Official potential candidates for admission: Albania, Bosnia and Herzegovina, Montenegro, and Serbia.

Source: Trevor C. Salmon

Appendix IV

Selected international economic organizations

World Bank	International Monetary Fund	World Trade Organization
Its mission evolved from the International Bank for Reconstruction and Development (IBRD) as facilitator of post-war reconstruction and development to the present day mandate of worldwide poverty alleviation in conjunction with its affiliate, the International Development Association.

Reconstruction remains an important focus of its work, given the natural disasters and post conflict rehabilitation needs that affect developing and transition economies. It has, however, broadened its portfolio's focus to include social sector lending projects, poverty alleviation, debt relief and good governance.

It has sharpened its focus on poverty reduction as the overarching goal of all its work. | The IMF is an international organization. It was established to promote international monetary cooperation, exchange stability, and orderly exchange arrangements; to foster economic growth and high levels of employment; and to provide temporary financial assistance to countries to help ease balance of payments adjustment. (See *Purposes of the IMF* in the Articles of Agreement.)

Since the IMF was established its purposes have remained unchanged but its operations – which involve *surveillance, financial assistance*, and *technical assistance* – have developed to meet the changing needs of its member countries in an evolving world economy. | Is an international organization designed to supervise and liberalize international trade. The WTO came into being on 1 January 1995, and is the successor to the General Agreement on Tariffs and Trade (GATT), which was created in 1947, and continued to operate for almost five decades as a *de facto* international organization.

The World Trade Organization deals with the rules of trade between nations at a near-global level; it is responsible for negotiating and implementing new trade agreements, and is in charge of policing member countries' adherence to all the WTO agreements, signed by the bulk of the world's trading nations and ratified in their parliaments. Most of the WTO's current work comes from the 1986–94 negotiations called the Uruguay Round, and earlier negotiations under the GATT. |
| 185 states as members | 185 states as members | 151 states as members |

Source: Trevor C. Salmon

INDEX